Until the early twentieth century wells and springs were the only water supply most people had, and therefore these natural water sources once had a far greater importance for people than they do now. Over time some of them developed a deeper significance than simply being a water supply: they became known as holy wells, and were also sometimes part of a wider sacred landscape. Legends told how they had been miraculously formed by saints, and many became the focus of pilgrimage. A large number were famed for their ability to cure illness; while others were used for divination, or for cursing.

Over the last hundred years the local lore associated with these sacred wells and springs has largely been forgotten. The publication of Janet and Colin Bord's book *Sacred Waters* in 1985 created a revival of interest in holy wells, and in recent years research has gathered pace. Janet has now collected together some of the more intriguing aspects of the lore of holy wells, including their links to pre-Christian practices, and here presents her findings in topic-by-topic descriptions. Among the 75 topics covered are: Baptism – Bells – Blood – Creation of Wells – Cursing – Divination – Dragons – Eye Wells – Fairies – Fertility – Ghosts – Goddesses – Guardians – Heads – Healing – Love Magic – Offerings – Pilgrimage – Pins – Rags – Relics – Rituals – Saints and Wells – Shrines – Skulls – Treasure – Visions – Warts – Well Cults – Wishing Wells – Witches. There is also a list of recommended wells to visit.

The book has 135 illustrations, including photographs of wells and items found there, as well as old illustrations and modern artist's depictions of the history, folklore and practices associated with holy wells.

Janet Bord lives in North Wales, where she and her husband Colin run the Fortean Picture Library. They have written more than twenty books on folklore and mysteries since their first successful joint venture, *Mysterious Britain* (1972).

By the same author

Footprints in Stone

Mazes and Labyrinths of the World

Fairies: Real Encounters with Little People

The Traveller's Guide to Fairy Sites

With Colin Bord

Mysterious Britain

The Secret Country

A Guide to Ancient Sites in Britain

Earth Rites

Sacred Waters

Ancient Mysteries of Britain

Atlas of Magical Britain

The Enchanted Land

Dictionary of Earth Mysteries

Cures and Curses

Ritual and cult at holy wells

Janet Bord

Heart of Albion

Cures and Curses
Ritual and cult at holy wells

Janet Bord

Cover illustration by Janet Bord shows
Ffynnon Galchog at Llanfwrog, Denbighshire.

ISBN 1 872883 95 8
EAN 978 1872 883 953

© Text copyright Janet Bord 2006

© Illustrations copyright Janet Bord except where indicated otherwise 2006

The moral rights of the author and illustrators have been asserted.
All rights reserved. No part of this book may be reproduced
in any form or by any means without prior written
permission from Heart of Albion Press, except for
brief passages quoted in reviews.

Published by

Heart of Albion Press
2 Cross Hill Close, Wymeswold
Loughborough, LE12 6UJ

albion@indigogroup.co.uk

Visit our Web site: www.hoap.co.uk

Printed in England by Booksprint

Contents

Introduction and acknowledgements   1

What is a 'holy well'?   3

An alphabetical introduction to the holy well lore of the British Isles and Ireland

Ampullae	5
Animals	8
Baptism	8
Bath	10
Bells	12
Blood	14
Bowssening	15
Bullauns	16
Celtic influence	18
Circumambulation	19
Cloutie wells	21
Coins	22
Coventina's Well	23
Creation of wells	25
Cursing	27
Deposition	32
Desecration and destruction	34
Divination	36
Dragons	37
Drumming wells	39
Ebbing and flowing wells	40
Eye wells	41
Fairies	43
Fertility	46
Fishes and frogs	47
Flower of the well	49
Folklore	50
Footprints	52
Fortune-telling	53
Ghosts	53
Goddesses	56
Guardians	59
Heads	61

Healing	64
Holy water	70
Holywell	71
Immersion	74
Incubation	75
Llyn Cerrig Bach	76
Love magic	79
Miraculous powers	82
Modern use of holy wells	83
Mosses and other plants	85
Names	86
Offerings	88
Overflowing	90
Petrifying wells	92
Pilgrimage	92
Pins	95
Prehistory	96
Prophecy	99
Rags	101
Rejuvenation	102
Relics	103
Revelry	105
Reverence	109
Rituals	110
Roman water shrines	111
Saints and wells	113
Saints' deaths	116
Saints in the landscape	119
Shrines	121
Skulls	123
Stones	126
Treasure	127
Trees	129
Visions	131
Visiting	134
Votive offerings	135
Walsingham	138
Warts	139
Well buildings	141
Well cults	143
Well-dressing	145
Wells inside and close to churches	147
Wishing wells	148
Witches	150

Some holy wells to visit: 25 favourite wells in England and Wales	154
Bibliography	169
Index	178

St Edith's Well at Stoke Edith (Herefordshire), in a bank below the church. It began to flow, according to legend, when St Edith was in a state of exhaustion and knelt to pray. She was mixing mortar to build the original church and was having to fetch water from a brook some distance away. In later years the water was renowned for its healing properties.

Introduction and acknowledgements

Water seems always to have exercised a fascination over people, traceable way back in prehistory and through medieval times to the present day, as exemplified by customs, traditions and rituals connected with water sources in general and holy wells in particular. Twenty years ago, I wrote (with my husband Colin) a book on holy wells and water lore, *Sacred Waters*, and in the ensuing years I have continued to visit and learn about holy wells, especially in Wales where I live, so that I now feel the urge to write about them again. As my interest is primarily in the folklore, ritual and tradition relating to holy wells, I have decided to write a sequence of short essays on assorted topics that especially interest me, rather than attempt a full-scale study of holy wells and their history, which would take even the most knowledgeable of well devotees many years to research and write. Presented alphabetically, these 75 essays provide a mixed bag of well lore and legend, covering such diverse topics as baptism, circumambulation, cursing, dragons, fertility, ghosts, goddesses, immersion, overflowing, pilgrimage, revelry, saints, skulls, votive offerings, warts and witches. For those who wish to investigate further, sources are given where known – but it has to be remembered that much of folklore consists of local beliefs that are impossible to source, and as such are based almost entirely on hearsay. I have also added brief details of some wells in England and Wales that are worth visiting – but any reader whose main interest is visiting holy wells will have to look out for my next book, a guidebook to the holy wells of England, Wales, and Scotland, which I hope will be published in 2008.

Anyone wishing to read more about other aspects of holy wells will find a rich harvest of publications in the Bibliography. There is also much information to be found on the Internet. Two issues of the online holy wells journal *Living Spring* were issued, and these can be read on the website www.bath.ac.uk/lispring. The printed magazine *Source,* a goldmine of high quality research, is sadly no longer published, but many of the articles originally published in *Source* can now be found online through the same web address.

I wish to acknowledge the work of all those researchers whose publications I have consulted; and I especially wish to acknowledge the help received from Grace Moloney of Clogher Historical Society, Co. Monaghan. I owe a deep and sincere debt of gratitude to my long-time friend and colleague Tristan Gray Hulse whose knowledge of holy wells is second to none, and who has tried his hardest to instil some semblance of intellectual rigour into these pages. However, any failings on that and any other score are my responsibility alone.

Many of the photographs are my own, but I wish to thank the other photographers whose pictures I have used – they are all credited in the relevant captions – and the organisations from which I have sourced pictures, again all credited in the appropriate places. Thanks also go to the artist Anthony Wallis, whose atmospheric drawings can be found throughout the book. Most of the illustrations, including the drawings, are held in the archives of the Fortean Picture Library (www.forteanpix.co.uk).

Janet Bord

North Wales
June 2006

What is a 'holy well'?

Defining the holy well is not a straightforward matter. One thing is clear: a holy well is not always a well! That is, it is not always a stone-lined tank, sometimes with a structure built above it, which is what the word 'well' means to most people. A holy well is almost never a deep draw-well: in fact it is almost invariably a surface spring, which on occasion may degenerate into a muddy hole in the ground. Sometimes it may be a pond, a pool, or even a small lake. Sometimes it may be water that has collected inside a tree stump (see **Trees**); or inside a **bullaun** (basin stone). Unusual locations include seashore wells which are periodically covered by the tide, or coastal wells high on the cliffs, or in sea-caves; wells close to rivers or streams which are inundated during flooding; wells in bogs and on mountain-tops; and wells inside churches (see **Wells inside and close to churches**). Holy wells are by no means always easy of access, and pilgrims would sometimes have to be daring and/or persistent to actually reach the well which was their goal. One near Lacken in Co. Wicklow was covered by the water of Poulaphuca Lakes and thereafter no one could get to it – until the summer of 1978 when the water level was lowered and people flocked to the well in their thousands.

It is straightforward enough to list where 'holy wells' can be found and what they look like, but much less easy to define what a 'holy well' actually is, that is, why is it holy? What differentiates a holy well from an ordinary village well where people would draw water for domestic use? There are several aspects to defining a holy well, including its possible location within a sacred landscape, the involvement of saints or other holy persons in its history and folklore, and possibly also the well's healing reputation. The simplest definition of a holy well might be that if people thought of it as such, and treated it as such, then it *was* a holy well. This definition sees a holy well as a water source which may be one element in a sacred landscape, which may have gained a healing reputation over many generations, and around which folklore has grown up, and which has become a focal point in the life of the community; so much so, that it becomes revered and venerated, and is known as a holy well. Some wells may have acquired their holy reputation through being used as a source of water for church **baptism** – and see **Holy water** for an exploration of how water becomes holy.

The term 'holy well' cannot predate the Anglo-Saxon period, as 'holy' comes from the Anglo-Saxon word *halig,* and this appears to substantiate the view that there is a conceptual break between the sacred water sources of pre-Christian antiquity and those that came into being following the conversion to Christianity. The term 'holy well' is also essentially an English-language formation – for example, there is no equivalent in Welsh, *ffynnon* meaning simply 'well' or 'spring'.

Sources: Positions of Irish wells: Logan 1980: Ch.5. **Poulaphuca Lakes:** Logan 1980: 61. *Halig*: Harte 2000.

An alphabetical introduction to the holy well lore of the British Isles and Ireland

Words in **bold** refer to other entries in this Introduction; names in *italics* refer to wells that are included in 'Some Holy Wells to Visit'; names in ***bold italics*** refer to entries in both the Introduction and 'Some Holy Wells to Visit'.

A

Ampullae

In the present context, an ampulla is a miniature flask used in the Christian world in late classical, early medieval and medieval times to carry away holy oil or water from sacred places, such as shrines and holy wells. They were only large enough to hold a small amount of liquid, and were essentially sacred relics, though they might be worn round the pilgrim's neck, or otherwise displayed, as proof of a pilgrimage successfully completed, as well as being the pilgrim's own personal healing source, bearing as they did the miraculous powers of the shrine or well he or she had visited. Numerous ampullae from ***Walsingham*** (Norfolk) have been found buried at field boundaries in other parts of England, suggesting that they were intentionally placed there to protect or encourage the growing crops (see **Deposition**).

Ampullae were usually made of pewter or terracotta, and once the water was placed inside, the opening of the pewter ones would have been sealed by pressing or beating the 'lips' together. The ampulla would have to be cut open to get the water out again. Their use in England may have begun towards the end of the twelfth century (no earlier examples have been found), and they were in use throughout the medieval Christian world. Numerous interesting examples have been found, such as the one from close to the foot of Old London Bridge which has a scallop-shell on one side (originally the emblem of the pilgrimage to Mont S. Michel in northern France, then of that to Compostela in Spain, but it later became the emblem of all pilgrimage in Europe) and the scene of St Thomas Becket's martyrdom on the other. This showed that it came from Canterbury, where Becket was murdered in the cathedral on 29 December 1170; his **blood** and brains were said to have been put into the well in the north choir aisle, making the water from that well in effect a 'relic' of the saint. Reputedly the well water ran red afterwards for some time, and the water was known as St Thomas's Blood, or the Water of St Thomas. Many ampullae have been found

The ampulla bearing a depiction of St Menas, found at Meols. Photo: Grosvenor Museum/ Chester City Council.

in rivers and estuaries, and they were probably thrown there as thank-offerings for a pilgrimage safely completed – and of course some may have been deposited beforehand by much-travelled pilgrims in order to ensure a safe journey.

The evidence therefore suggests multiple uses of ampullae, including: as relic (for personal use, or for presentation to one's local church); as pilgrim token (to prove that the pilgrimage was undertaken) or souvenir (as the 'present-from-Blackpool' variety); use of the contents for healing; as thank-offering for safe return home; as blessing on the fields; and probable other uses also, including perhaps the consecration of 'new' holy sites, by, for example, adding the water from the ampulla to a well in order to make it holy (see, for example, the story of St Cadog in **Healing**).

Pilgrims also brought ampullae of healing water home from pilgrimages abroad, such as the earthenware example found at Meols on the Wirral (Cheshire). It bears the figure of St Menas, which shows it came from Abu Mina in Egypt, as St Menas was a fourth-century Christian martyr beheaded by the Roman occupiers of Egypt, and his grave at Abu Mina became a great pilgrimage centre of early Christianity. It was sacked by the Moslems in about 640, and so any Menas ampullae found in archaeological excavations cannot have been deposited any later than the middle of the seventh century. At that time, Meols was a crossing-place into North Wales and so the Menas ampulla may have been deliberately deposited, along with other later pilgrims' tokens found there, in order to ensure a safe river crossing. (See also **Well cults**)

The two bottles on the right are from St Winefride's Well, Holywell; the others come from Fatima (centre) and Lourdes (left).

Today, rather than ampullae, pilgrims take home bottles of water from those holy wells which cater for large numbers of visitors, notably *St Winefride's Well* (Flint) (see **Holywell**) and **Walsingham** (Norfolk). The first recorded instance of a quantity of water being taken away in a container larger than an ampulla dates back to the early twelfth century when in the earliest *Life* of St Winefride there was an account of a priest filling a flagon or amphora with water from the well, which was then 'transmitted everywhere to the sick, and drunk'. An account of *circa* 1620 refers to 'a little bottle' – and in the 1890s the priest who oversaw the rebirth of the Holywell pilgrimage, Fr Beauclerk S.J., had special glass bottles made that were moulded with an image of St Winefride and the words 'St Winefrides Well Holywell' on them. Today's bottles are made of plastic, and on payment of a small charge bottles of well water are sent out by mail; or an empty bottle can be bought at the well shop and filled by the purchaser. No charge is made for the water.

Sources: Description: Spencer 1971: 59–66. **Walsingham:** Spencer 1980: 16–17. **Early use:** Leclerq 1924. **Canterbury:** Sumption 2002: 83. **Abu Mina:** Leclerq 1933; 'Pilgrim's Flask from Meols', *Journal of the Chester and North Wales Architectural, Archaeological and Historic Society,* vol.43 (Chester: G.R. Griffith Ltd, 1956): 48–9. **Bottles:** Hulse 1995: 8–10.

There is a bucket inside Giggleswick church (North Yorkshire) which was used to fetch water for baptism from the local holy well. The inscription around its middle reads: + One Lord + One Faith + One Baptism.

Animals

References to animals in holy well lore can be found in **Desecration and destruction** (dogs), **Fishes and frogs**, and **Healing** (cattle, horses, dogs, etc).

B

Baptism

Baptism is an important rite of the Christian Church, usually happening early in a child's life: it washes away original sin, and signifies the entry of that child into the Church. It has long been the custom in some communities for water from the nearby holy well to be fetched and placed in the church font, and then used in a baptism after being blessed by the priest (see **Holy water**) – and some wells may possibly have acquired their status as holy wells *because* they supplied water for the rite of baptism.

Examples of holy well water being used for baptism include the Normandy Well at Horsham (West Sussex), St Patrick's Well in Patterdale (Cumbria), and Ffynnon

The ancient font at Duloe church (Cornwall), decorated with carvings of dolphins and griffins, was originally located at St Cuby's Well and is believed to have been used by St Cuby for baptisms in the sixth century. It was removed by vandals in the 1820s, and later used as a garden ornament before being taken into the church in 1959 where it is now used again for baptisms with water from the holy well. Photo: Tristan Gray Hulse

Gadfarch at Abererch (Gwynedd), among many others. Indeed, some churches may have been located close to a spring for that purpose. (See **Wells inside and close to churches**) At Abererch (Gwynedd), when the use of the holy well water for baptism was ended, the congregation watched 'with considerable dread and misgivings'; clearly they felt that the holy well water was superior to that from any other source.

The earliest reference to baptism among the Celts is in St Patrick's *Letter to Coroticus*, dating from the mid fifth century, where the baptism takes place in a river; while the earliest surviving Celtic baptismal rite (Stowe Missal, *circa* 800) has baptism performed by affusion (i.e. pouring water over the head). Archaeological evidence from the Late Roman period in England suggests that sizeable lead tanks were used for baptism by **immersion**. There are in fact three basic types of baptism: immersion (the body partially submerged, plus affusion); affusion alone (water poured over the head); submersion (total immersion). There is no direct evidence that holy wells were intended to be, or were regularly used as, baptisteries, though from the seventeenth and eighteenth centuries Protestant sects like the Baptists did sometimes adopt holy wells for adult baptism by complete immersion.

There may be a parallel between the practice of **bowssening**, where the sick person would be immersed in a holy well in hopes that their illness (often madness) would miraculously disappear, and baptism by immersion, which symbolically washed away sin – or this parallel may equally be spurious: no one can be sure why such rituals developed. Also, the practice at some holy wells of applying holy water to the body in the hope of banishing illness echoes the rite of baptism, but again the parallel may be more apparent than real. In Wales at least, the principal real evidence for connecting the bathing ritual with baptism is found in fifteenth-century votive poems, and the link is therefore relatively recent, and literary in inspiration.

Country folk believed that a church baptism or christening (now interchangeable terms, though technically 'christening' is the anointing with the Chrism, one of the three kinds of holy oil, which forms a single element of the Catholic rite of baptism) would protect the child against diseases, as well as against ghosts, demonic forces, fairies and witchcraft, and would also ensure that a bad-tempered child would regain its good temper. (There is an echo here of the belief in fairy changelings, where a human child would be replaced by a sickly fairy child.) Water that had been used for baptism was also curative, and anyone whose eyes were bathed with this water would never see a ghost. The holy well at Ludgvan (Cornwall) had the unusual ability to prevent anyone who had been baptised in its water from ever being hanged.

Sources: Christening and baptism folklore: Roud 2003: 78–83. **Normandy Well:** Hope 1893: 165. **St Patrick's Well:** Hope 1893: 169–70. **Gwynedd wells:** Jones 1954: 82. **Ludgvan Well:** Hunt 1985: 21.

Bath

The city of Bath grew up around ancient hot springs: they produce 240 gallons (1,170,000 litres) of water at a temperature of 46C every day, and have been doing so for thousands of years. The first major development of the site was in Roman times when the baths of Aquae Sulis (the Roman name for the place, meaning 'the waters

The Great Bath: how the complex developed long after Roman times.

One of the paterae found at Aquae Sulis, possibly used to make offerings of holy water. Photo: The Roman Baths Museum, Bath

of [the goddess] Sulis') were constructed. This activity destroyed any earlier remains, but modern excavation has revealed evidence of a pre-Roman rubble and gravel causeway, along which the earliest pilgrims to the hot springs may have walked. This place was almost certainly a sacred place for the Celts, and eighteen Celtic coins, possible early offerings to the goddess Sulis, were discovered in the causeway and the mud of the spring. We can only imagine how the site must have looked in

Some of the artefacts and coins that have been found during excavations at Bath. Photo: The Roman Baths Museum, Bath

pre-Roman times: it has however been possible to determine the Roman and post-Roman activity in great detail, owing to the considerable remains available to modern archaeologists. The Romans constructed a huge complex of buildings, with warm and cold baths and a large bathing pool (the Great Bath). Presiding over the spring was the British healing goddess Sulis (who was also linked with the Roman goddess Minerva to form the joint deity Sulis Minerva – see the photograph of her cult statue in **Goddesses**) and altars dedicated to her have survived to the present day. The spring at Bath features in Rhigyfarch's *Life* of St David, and this is one of the very earliest references to any British holy well to have survived.

In its heyday thousands of pilgrims visited Aquae Sulis hoping to be healed. They threw coins and other **votive offerings** into the water, along with lead tablets bearing curses (see **Cursing**); other finds include gemstones, brooches and metal pans known as *paterae* which could have been used to make offerings of holy water. They are inscribed with the letters DSM or the words *Deae Sulis Minerva*, showing they were dedicated to the goddess. These items are all now on view in the Bath museum.

In the post-Roman period the baths continued in use, and they are now preserved within Georgian spa buildings which can be visited; audio-guided tours are available. Bath was also the location of numerous lesser-known springs, wells and spas, full details of which can be found in the chapter on Bath in Phil Quinn's book *The Holy Wells of Bath and Bristol Region*.

Sources: Excavation: Cunliffe 1995. **Sulis:** Green 1992: 200–2; Green 1995: 93–9. **Bath overview:** Quinn 1999: 73–106; Cunliffe 1995; Stewart 1981. **Visitor information:** www.romanbaths.co.uk

Bells

Bells have been used around the world in religious ceremonies for thousands of years, and so have developed a rich folklore. There are numerous links with water, and in some cultures bells would be rung to call for rain. Within the Catholic Church, going back to the eleventh century, bells could be baptised or washed with holy water by a bishop in a ceremony designed, among other things, to give the bell the power to drive away storms and terrify evil spirits and the Devil. As at the baptism of children, the bells were given names; and bells are still named today, in continuance of this practice, such as Big Ben.

The European folklore of bells often includes stories of bells being stolen from churches and sent to a watery grave in a pond or river. Sometimes the lore also mentions holy wells, and this is probably a distorted memory of the concealment of church bells during the Reformation and never recovered. However the church bells connected with holy wells all seem to have been hand-bells, not the consecrated ('baptised') bells that hung in church steeples. In Ceredigion the Devil is said to have stolen a bell from the church at Llanbadarn Fawr. While carrying it away, he rested by Ffynnon Gloch (Bell Well) near Llanarth church, and consequently that place is

A stained-glass window of St Teilo inside Bosherston church, Pembrokeshire, shows him holding his bell.

considered to be bewitched, with people standing there being unable to hear the church bells when they are ringing. A well at Corwen (Denbigh) went by the name of Ffynnon y Gloch Felen (Well of the Yellow Bell), referring to the discovery there, according to Edward Lhuyd's late seventeenth-century *Parochialia*, of 'an old brazen yellow bell' – probably a Celtic hand-bell from the church at Corwen, and possibly seen as a relic.

Bells were sometimes used in healing rituals, with the holy water being poured into the bell before being drunk from it. A gilt bell was preserved at Llandaff Cathedral (Cardiff) in the Middle Ages and it featured in a tale told of St Teilo (or alternatively of St Oudoceus) and his well close to the cathedral. He found some women washing butter there and on requesting a vessel from which to drink the well water they said they had nothing but the butter so he took some and shaped it into a bell and drank from it. It was miraculously changed into a metal bell and afterwards people believed that touching it would heal the sick. St Fillan's Bell, a Celtic hand-bell, was used during the procedure to cure insanity at St Fillan's Pool (Stirling): after immersion in the pool the patient would be laid down, tied up and left overnight in the nearby chapel, with the bell, believed to have curative properties, placed over his or her head. If next morning the patient was free of the ropes, there was considered to be some hope of a cure.

Sources: Folklore of bells: Leach 1984: 132–4. **Baptism of bells:** Addis & Arnold 1960: 71. **Ffynnon Gloch & Ffynnon y Gloch Felen:** Jones 1954: 130, 193. **St Teilo's Bell:** Doble 1971: 219–20. **St Fillan's Bell:** Miller 2004: 51.

Blood

Legends of bloody wells usually involve murder, as is the case in Dorset where there is a well at Powerstock which sometimes appears to have red water, because an unfaithful wife was drowned here by her husband. However the legend also comments that the redness could be caused by the dye from her petticoat! Red water in wells, or red staining on stones in wells, is unsurprisingly referred to as blood, and folklore explains its presence. The death of a saint is one explanation: if the saint was decapitated, the well sprang up where their blood flowed – sometimes with the additional detail that the water ran forever red with the saint's blood. Sometimes a stone in a well had red marks which were said to be the bloodstains of the martyred saint, as at *St Winefride's Well,* **Holywell** (Flint). Wells also ran red with blood after battles, after murderers washed their hands in them, after weapons were washed, and after severed **heads** were washed. The water of St Thomas's Well in Canterbury Cathedral (Kent) was rendered holy when some of Thomas Becket's blood was added to it after he was murdered in the cathedral in 1170, thus becoming a relic of the saint. Pilgrims visiting Canterbury would wear a small **ampulla** of the 'Water of St Thomas' around the neck, and the liquid was a celebrated medicine in the twelfth century. Not only was it drunk by the sick, and rubbed on the eyelids of the blind, but it was also used in magic rituals to identify thieves.

The real explanation for red water is either from iron in chalybeate springs, or from algae (see also **Mosses and other plants**). Any well named Red Well is very likely to have chalybeate water, such as that at Wellingborough (Northampton) which became famed as a healing spa, with King Charles I and his court staying there for nine weeks in 1626 to benefit the health of the Queen.

Here are a few particularly interesting examples of bloody wells. Tobar na Fala (Well of Blood) on Skye was considered to be the place where a young girl was killed by a water-horse – a legendary creature from Scottish folklore, the best-known of them being the Kelpie which haunted rivers and could appear as a shaggy man or as a young horse. In the hills above Llangollen (Denbigh) a giantess who ate human beings was fought and killed by St Collen, who washed away his bloodstains in a well which took his name, Ffynnon Gollen. The Priest's Well (Monmouth) in the hills above Hay-on-Wye is believed to take its name from monks who had fled into the hills at the Dissolution of the Monasteries, but had been hunted down and beheaded. Proof of this could be seen in the well, where there were stones blotched with red – the blood of the monks. The red faded to grey when the stones were removed from the water. Numerous examples were kept in local houses, and they would be shown off to the curious visitor by putting them back into water to make the 'bloodstains' reappear.

The shock of being pushed backwards into a pool of water may have cured a few people of their madness, but it seems more likely to increase it. Artwork: Anthony Wallis

Sources: Powerstock: Harte 'Dorset' 1985: 7. **Canterbury:** Sumption 2002: 83. **Red Well:** Thompson 1914: 227–30. **Tobar na Fala:** Forbes 1923: 427. **Ffynnon Gollen:** Jones 1954: 39. **Priest's Well:** 'Magic Stones – A Well Story from Present-day Hay', *Wood & Water* 8: 18; Jones 1954: 38.

Bowssening

This strange word (alternative spelling 'boussening') describes a violent procedure that was used at certain Cornish wells to try and cure the insane. One such well was St Nonna's at Altarnun, and the method was described by Richard Carew in the early seventeenth century:

> The water running from S Nuness well fell into a square and close walled plot which might be filled at what depth they listed. Upon this wall was the franticke person set to stand his backe towards the poole and from thence with a sudden blow in the brest tumbled headlong into the pond, where a strong fellowe provided

> for the nonce tooke him and tossed him up and downe alongst and arthwart the water, untill the patient by foregoing his strength had somewhat forgot his fury. Then was he conveyed to the church and certain masses sung over him upon which handling, if his right wits returned S. Nunne had the thanks; but if there appeared small amendment, he was bowssened (or dipped) againe and againe while there remayned in him hope of life or recovery.

St Gundred's Well at Roche and the holy well at *St Cleer* were two other Cornish wells reputedly used for bowssening.

A variant on bowssening was used at other places; for example, lunatics would be taken to St Maelrubha's Well on the island in Loch Maree (Highland) for immersion. In 1850 a boy who was mentally disturbed was taken by boat to the island and immersed in the well, then he was towed round the island three times tied to the boat with a rope; but this shock treatment did not seem to have cured his madness, perhaps unsurprisingly. The insane would also be immersed in St Fillan's Pool in the river in Strathfillan (Stirling) before being tied with ropes in the nearby chapel and left there overnight with a **bell** over their head; while in the far north of the Isle of Lewis (Western Isles) a similar technique was employed to cure madness but without the immersion. The lunatic was taken to St Moluag's church at Eòrapaidh (Eoropie) at nightfall and after he had walked seven times round the church sunwise he would drink water from the nearby well (Tobar Rònain/Tobar an Teampaill) and also be 'baptised' using water from the well. (Probably being splashed with the water was intended rather than baptism, since at that time everyone was baptised in infancy.) He would then be tied to the church altar overnight, and would be cured if he slept. Arthur Mitchell, who was the lunacy inspector for Scotland in the mid nineteenth century, wrote of this practice: 'One man who had been taken there, and whom I saw, had the good fortune to sleep, and was cured.'

Sources: Derivation: Hope 1893: 20. **Altarnon well:** Richard Carew, *Survey of Cornwall* (1602), quoted in Lane-Davies 1970: 8–9 & Hunt 1993 (Second Series): 296. **Cornish wells:** Hope 1893: 25. **Loch Maree & Strathfillan:** Miller 2000: 34; Miller 2004: 50–1. **Tobar Rònain:** MacLeod 2000: 23–4.

Bullauns

Also known as 'basin stones', these rounded stones with hollows in their surfaces are found only in Ireland, near old monasteries. No one is really sure what they were, but one practical guess is that they were used for grinding corn. However it is unlikely that they could have ground sufficient grain for use at large monasteries such as Glendalough or Clonmacnoise, and more efficient querns were in use in the Iron Age. Anthony Weir suggests that 'they were used to grind special ritual food in pre-Christian times, and were later Christianised.' He comments that 'The eating of ritual grains in the form of gruel is well-known in pre-Christian Europe, and in Ireland they may well have been ground in bullauns. In Christian times medicinal

Bullauns

The Deer Stone at Glendalough (Wicklow), to be found beside a path after crossing the river to the south of the cemetery.

herbs would certainly have been prepared on monastic sites, and bullauns would have served the purpose admirably.'

Michael Herity's suggestion is probably the most sensible: that the hollows in bullauns developed from the stones' use in prayer (or sometimes cursing) rituals.

> A custom widely observed to the last century [nineteenth] was the turning of so-called 'cursing stones', often rounded in shape, at places of pilgrimage. It is recorded that some of these stones were to be turned clockwise as prayer-stones, anti-clockwise as 'cursing-stones'; at some places the stones were passed around the body. These appear to be intimately connected with the traditional stational observance known as *an Turas* [pilgrimage rounds].
>
> It seems likely that *bulláns* can be explained as the result of constant turning of prayer- (alias cursing-) stones as part of the ritual of a penitential visit; it is eloquent that many hollows, as at Inishkeel... have been worn quite through.

Bullauns can still be found with the pebbles surviving in the hollows, and maybe their use as prayer- and cursing-stones also still survives. Other bullauns have healing connections: water often gathers in the depressions, and as a result some bullauns are regarded as holy wells. The water is usually believed to cure **warts** – an example of a bullaun with this reputation is to be found at Clonmacnoise (Offaly). As at more conventional holy wells, a ritual would be performed round the bullaun. For example, the Deer Stone at Glendalough (Wicklow) had to be visited on a Sunday, Tuesday and Thursday in the same week, and each time the pilgrim had to go round it seven times on his or her knees. The Deer Stone was so-called from a story that a deer, in answer to the saint's prayer, came and left some of her milk in the bullaun when St Kevin had no cow. An alternative version says she provided the milk to feed two orphaned babies.

Sources: Theory: Weir 1980: 55; Herity 1995: 298, 300. **Deer Stone:** Logan 1980: 108.

C

Celtic influence

It is now in many quarters an accepted 'fact' that many aspects of holy well belief and ritual date back many centuries, and indeed were 'part of an archaic Celtic inheritance'; but recent impartial research has shown that the oft-claimed Celtic influence is much less certain, and that the identification of the Celts as the originators of much of the lore and practice we today study has been embraced with over-enthusiasm. Indeed, all that the Celts may have had in common may have been their language, as it is now increasingly believed that the blanket term 'Celts' comprised a number of differing peoples rather than a specific and united Celtic race. Also, it is uncertain whether practices deemed 'Celtic' were true pre-Roman survivals, or actually introduced to Britain by the Romans themselves. Some of the later Northern European well practices and rituals probably originated in areas heavily influenced by the Romans, such as Italy, where similar practices pre-date those further north.

The Celts developed certain springs as healing shrines, most notably in France, but again the absence of finds pre-dating the Roman conquest strongly suggests that such practices developed post-conquest. The best-known of such shrines in Britain was that dedicated to Sulis Minerva at **Bath** (Somerset), where Celtic and Roman influences overlapped. The Celtic shrines had some common features: they were dedicated to Celtic gods and goddesses, the patients would give **votive offerings** which took the form of models of the diseased parts of their bodies (examples have been found in England at Bath, Muntham Court, Lydney and Springhead), and at some shrines a period of sleep (known as **incubation**) would be part of the healing process, the pilgrims hoping to see the god while asleep and be rewarded with advice on regaining good health (as is believed to have happened, for example, at Lydney in Gloucestershire). The practice of incubation came to the Celtic lands with the Romans, who themselves had imported it into Roman Italy from the Eastern Mediterranean. (See also **Heads; Roman water shrines**)

Sources:'Archaic Celtic inheritance': Carroll 1999: 16–17. **Celtic/Roman water rituals:** Webster 1995: 449–52. **Healing:** Green 1992: 132, 197–8.

Circumambulation

The customary ritual to be performed at many holy wells often included walking round the well one or more times, usually 'sunwise' or 'sunways' i.e. to the right, or clockwise. The opposite or backwards way was known as 'widdershins' or 'withershins'. Sunwise was believed to be lucky, whereas widdershins was unlucky. It was believed that witches deliberately turned left in their dancing or when casting spells and raising the Devil. At Chibbyr Undin on the Isle of Man, for example, visitors to the well would take a mouthful of water and hold it there until they had walked round the well twice sunwise. At Chibbyr Lansh, visited for the cure of sore eyes, the patients had to walk three times round each of the three pools at the site while saying in Manx 'In the name of the Father, and of the Son, and of the Holy Ghost' before putting the water on their eyes. At Ffynnon Ddeier, Bodfari (Denbigh), poor parishioners offered chickens after circumambulating the well nine times.

Circumambulation appears to have been a worldwide practice, according to John C. Irwin in this extract from a paper he presented at a conference of South Asian archaeologists.

> The rite of circumambulation and its associated taboos seem to have been common to the whole ancient world. Its usual explanation as a survival of sun-worship may be an oversimplification. It would perhaps be more accurate to say that the rite was primarily cosmogonic in origin and that it reflected the need once universally felt to live in harmony with cosmic forces represented in this case by the sun as ultimate generator of life. To circumambulate clockwise was to identify with the sun's diurnal course, regarded as life-enhancing and bringing luck. Anti-clockwise circumambulation was regarded as an identification with the sun's nocturnal course, and also with death and misfortune.

Circumambulation, the rounding ritual, or 'making rounds', was (and still is) particularly important at Irish holy wells; a colleague in Ireland noted early in the twenty-first century that 'Walking around the wells saying a rosary has become much more common and established over the past 10–15 years.' Pilgrims would walk round the well in a clockwise direction a set number of times, while saying certain prayers including Our Fathers, Hail Marys, Credos and Glorias, thus earning the remission of punishment for sin. At Irish well sites there were often other monuments in addition to the well itself: standing stones, piles of stones to which the pilgrim made a contribution, stone slabs, stone structures known as the saint's bed or grave

Pilgrims circling round, and kneeling at, St Columcille's Well, Rosaveel, Co. Galway; probably photographed during the late 1940s.
Photo: National Museum of Ireland.

– these together with the well were part of a sacred landscape, and would be included in the rounding rituals.

Rounding, in addition to being a means for the Catholic pilgrim to gain merit, could also be interpreted as a formal gesture of ritual reverence, and thus was also probably once common at holy wells in Wales and Scotland, not necessarily being confined to Ireland, even though it does not now feature largely in the surviving rituals at wells in the former areas. As in Ireland, it is possible that in Wales and Scotland, and also in certain areas of England, the holy well was originally only one element in a wider sacred landscape, and not the isolated phenomenon we see today.

Sources: Sunwise/widdershins: Roud 2003: 444–5; Simpson and Roud 2000: 211 (leftward movement), 295 (rightward movement). **Isle of Man wells:** Moore 1894: 224–5. **Ffynnon Ddeier:** Jones 1954: 105. **Worldwide practice:** Irwin 1979: 801–2. **Ireland**: Carroll 1999: 30–3, 58–60. **Modern Irish practice:** Comment from Allen Kennedy, 7 April 2005.

St Boniface's Well, Munlochy, a famous cloutie well always festooned with rags. Photo: Hamish M. Brown

Cloutie wells

'Clouties' are **rags** torn from the clothes of pilgrims who have visited the well in search of a cure. The sick person would dip the cloutie in the well water and then wipe the afflicted part of the body, before tying the rag to a tree or bush close to the well, and the theory is that as the cloth rots, so too will the illness wither and die. Nowadays clouties are much more common than they were even twenty years ago, appearing at wells where they were never seen until recent years, and all kinds of items are now being fastened on to the trees, not just rags from the visitor's clothing (rarely that now, I should imagine). These days handkerchiefs, tissues, scarves and ribbons are seen — clearly the modern pilgrim uses any scrap of material that may be to hand, and the ritual probably does not now relate to an ailment. The cloutie is simply another kind of **offering**, which acts as a subtle link between the pilgrim and the 'spirit of the place' — leaving something behind, be it a coin, or a flower, or a cloutie, has become the 'correct' thing to do at a holy well.

For readers interested in the origins of words, 'cloutie' is a Scottish variant of 'clout', meaning a shred of cloth, or a rag, and the same word as appears in the traditional saying 'Ne'er cast a clout till May be out'. The most famous Cloutie Well is St Boniface's Well, Munlochy (Highland) where there are so many rags that the area has become an eyesore.

Unfortunately there is a superstition which includes the warning that if you remove any rags, you will take on the ailments of the pilgrims who discarded them in the first place. This idea is similar to the belief that warts can be transferred from one person to another if the sufferer touches the **wart** with a stone and then throws it away in the belief that anyone picking up the stone will magically acquire the wart. At the wart well known as Ffynnon Cefn Lleithfan at Bryncroes (Gwynedd) a clout with grease on it was used when the wart was bathed, and the clout then had to be hidden under the stone at the mouth of the well, so it was not always the tradition that the rag should be hung on a bush or tree.

Alun Williams, then well-keeper at St Winefride's Well, Holywell, holds the coins he found in the well when it was emptied for cleaning in June 1993.

Sources: St Boniface's Well: Morris 1982: 169. **Transference:** Roud 2003: 485. **Ffynnon Cefn Lleithfan:** Rhys 1893: 61.

Coins

Pilgrims visiting holy wells in the centuries since the Industrial Revolution would most commonly offer **pins**, sometimes bent, to the waters; today coins are the most popular offering at holy wells and **wishing wells**. But the use of coins as offerings is definitely not a modern development, and goes back to Roman times. It seems that coin offerings in springs throughout the whole of north-west Europe began with the arrival of the Romans, and not before – in the same way that the whole cult of wells was brought to Britain from continental Europe. (See also **Deposition; Offerings; Votive offerings**)

Sources: Roman import: Sauer 2005: 22.

The water-goddess Coventina as depicted on a sandstone slab found in Coventina's Well at Carrawburgh. This slab can be seen in the Chesters Roman Fort Museum on Hadrian's Wall. Photo: Museum of Antiquities of the University and Society of Antiquaries of Newcastle upon Tyne.

Coventina's Well

Coventina's Well at Carrawburgh (Northumberland) was discovered by lead prospectors in 1876. It lay close to the Roman fort of Brocolitia (also Procolitia), and was a stone-built structure 7 feet deep, with an area of over 50 square feet.

Inside the well were found thousands of items that had been deposited there before the stone parapet had been demolished into it. These included twenty-four votive altars, some dedicated to the goddess Coventina; also inscribed slabs, one showing Coventina with an inscription below that included her name, another carrying a design with three nymphs (or a triple image of Coventina – illustrated in **Goddesses**); a stone head, bronze heads, and part of a human skull; bronze models of a horse, a terrier and a hand; bells, rings, brooches, pottery, glass, pins and many odds and ends; and around 14,000 coins, which may have been the shrine treasury, though some were probably offerings. Also many of the other items were likely to have been **votive offerings**, given by pilgrims hoping to find favour with the goddess, and relief from illnesses. The altars and slabs are most likely to have been placed in the well for safe-keeping when danger threatened: the care with which the items were placed in the well, the well-shrine then being demolished and the well sealed, suggests that the reason for the closure may have been to prevent the profaning of the well by the newly ascendant Christianity. Although the nearby Temple of Mithras was destroyed in the fourth century, the dates on the coins show that the well shrine was in use into

Cures and curses

A plate from the Illustrated London News *of 15 November 1876, showing Coventina's Well as it then was, plus a few of the thousands of artefacts that had been discovered during the excavation of the same year.*

Creation of wells

St Gwinear depicted on a kneeler in Gwinear church, Cornwall. According to a Life of the saint, circa 1300, he was beheaded by Theodoric, King of Cornwall, which explains why he is carrying his head. He had already created several holy wells in Cornwall and Brittany before being beheaded, but after beheading he again struck the ground with his staff and a new holy well flowed in which he was able to wash his head.

the fifth century. Today all that can be seen of Coventina's Well is a reedy swamp a few yards north-west of the Mithraeum.

In 1960 a second well was discovered only a few hundred yards away in a Nymphaeum (shrine of the nymphs), so in this small area were located three shrines: two wells and the Mithraeum, where a small goddess figure was found. Five Mithraea have so far been found in Britain, all in military locations: one in London, one at Caernarfon, and three on Hadrian's Wall at Carrawburgh, Housesteads and Rudchester. They were either built close to streams or actually over springs. The significance of water in the cult of Mithras, a god of Persian and Zoroastrian origin, is not clear, although the rites included a form of baptism.

Sources: Well excavation: Allason-Jones 1985. **Finds:** Morrell 1998: 35–6. **Coventina:** Green 1989: 156. **Nymphaeum:** Smith 1962.

Creation of wells

There are numerous legends describing the supernatural methods by which wells and springs came into being. Very often the well sprang up at the instigation of a saint, or following the dramatic death of a saint, as the following examples show.

1. A holy person, often but not necessarily a saint, struck the ground with their staff and water flowed. This is a very common saint's legend, and links back to the Old Testament story (Exodus) where Moses needed water for the people of Israel

A crude eighteenth-century depiction by Thomas Gent of the beheading of St Winefride, from his life of the saint, British Piety Display'd *(1743).*

who were with him in the wilderness. God ordered him to 'smite the rock' with his rod, and when he did so, water began to flow. One of the many saints who created a holy well in the same way was St Augustine at Cerne Abbas (Dorset); while Sir John Schorne, rector of North Marston (Buckingham) from 1290 to 1314, was said to have struck the ground when water was scarce during a drought – and Sir John Schorne's Well came into being.

2. A well sprang up where a saint lay down to sleep. An example was St Morwenna whose well was at Morwenstow (Cornwall). When the people were going to build themselves a church, she fetched a stone to be used as the font. On the way, she stopped to rest, and where she lay, the well started to flow. She took the stone and carried it to the place where the church now is. The parishioners had started to build it somewhere else, but every night the stones were moved to the new site, so they gave in and built it there.

3. The death of a saint by decapitation often resulted in the creation of a well where the head fell. In the case of St Winefride, who was beheaded by a thwarted suitor at **Holywell** (Flint), the famous *St Winefride's Well* began to flow where her head fell – but luckily the head was retrieved and popped back on to Winefride's neck by her uncle St Beuno, who happened to be close by, and she lived for many more years.

4. Where the body of a dead saint was laid temporarily, a well began to flow. In the case of St Kenelm, his body was being carried down to Winchcombe (Gloucester) and the bearers were tired and thirsty, so they laid their burden down and prayed to God for water, who obliged by creating a new spring; St Kenelm's Chapel was later built beside it. A second well began to flow in the Clent Hills (Worcester), where St Kenelm had been murdered (see *St Kenelm's Well*).

The ancient font in Morwenstow church.

An Irish story about St Cormac is a dramatic variation on the theme of a well forming where a saint lay down. It was prophesied that he would be killed by wolves, so he built a tower with no opening except at the top, where food was passed to him. One evening he saw two black snails coming up the tower wall and they seemed to be changing. He realised he was in danger and jumped out of the tower, but the snails, which were now wolves, chased him. Every time he fell to the ground, a spring burst forth – but still the wolves caught him and killed him. This legend explained the origin of several wells in Ballyboy (Kilcormack) parish (Offaly).

Many other examples of saints' involvement in the creation of wells can be found in **Saints and wells** and **Saints' deaths** (see also **Heads; Visions**).

Sources: Sir John Schorne's Well: Hope 1893: 5. **St Moorin's Well:** Hope 1893: 61. **St Kenelm's Well:** Hope 1893: 74. **St Cormac:** Logan 1980: 49.

Cursing

The practice of using wells to curse people goes back at least to Roman times. The evidence is in the form of inscribed lead or pewter tablets (in Latin: *defixiones*, showing the intention of binding or fixing) that were thrown into the water: more than 1,500 curse tablets are now known, and two-thirds were written in Greek, the rest in Latin. Half the latter were found in Britain, mostly in the Severn estuary area: at the spring of Sulis at **Bath**, and the temple of Mercury at Uley. Roman-era curse

The slate curse tablet found in Ffynnon Eilian on Anglesey in 1925 had a wax effigy pinned to it. The figure was missing its left arm, and it may have been intended to represent 'RF' whose initials appear on either side of it, RF being the curser's victim. The original tablet is now in the Gwynedd Museum and Art Gallery, Bangor. Artwork: Anthony Wallis

tablets are also recorded from other places in England, suggesting the practice was once widespread. Roman curse tablets show four major motives for the curse: theft of goods owned by the curser (usually cursing the thief, and sometimes asking for the return of the goods – in which case the goods themselves are vowed to the deity); a desire for successful outcome of a lawsuit (cursing the opponent); success in love (cursing a rival); and cursing charioteers and their horses.

In addition to cursing being practised at ancient Roman well sites, one of the magical powers ascribed to some holy wells was the ability to bring about ill luck to anyone you might wish to curse. It was believed that curses could be whispered to the Devil's Whispering Well near Bishop's Lydeard church (Somerset). At Ffynnon Eilian (Anglesey) one method of cursing used was similar to that of the Roman curse tablets: a piece of slate (3 inches by 2 inches) found in the well had letters scratched on it and a wax figure pinned through its centre. At the same well, another cursing method was to impale a frog with a skewer, stick corks on the ends, and then float it on the well. So long as it remained alive, the cursed enemy would suffer. Also on Anglesey, another cursing well was Ffynnon Gybi where the names of those being cursed were written on paper which was hidden under one of the banks of the well. **Pins** were also sometimes used in cursing rituals, bent pins being thrown into the water of the holy well close to Llanllawer churchyard (Pembroke) by people cursing their enemies, and straight pins were used if the wishes were good. Pins were also offered by people cursing their enemies at Ffynnon y Gaer (Gwynedd).

Perhaps the best-known cursing well in Britain was Ffynnon Elian at Llanelian-yn-Rhos (Conwy). It was originally a healing well, created according to legend by St

Roman curse tablets found at Bath. The message had to be written in the correct language to be successful, and it was inscribed on a sheet of pewter and placed in the water either flat or rolled up, as shown here. The opened curse is the 'Theft of Vilbia' curse, found in 1880, and the text begins 'May he who has stolen VILBIA from me become as liquid as water...' Photo: The Roman Baths Museum, Bath.

Elian who prayed for water when he became thirsty while travelling. He also prayed that whoever came to the well with faith would obtain his wish, but he certainly would not have intended the wishes to be evil ones. The legend of St Elian was first recorded *circa* 1698 by Edward Lhuyd in his *Parochialia*, at which time the well was entirely beneficent. By Thomas Pennant's time, in the late eighteenth century, the well was still principally curative, but cursing was also recorded. However thereafter the well gained a powerful reputation as a cursing well, and by *circa* 1810, in Pugh's *Cambria Depicta*, it was noted only for cursing. The people who ran it found themselves in control of a lucrative business, and the most famous of these was Jac Ffynnon Elian, who twice went to prison for his involvement in the cursing business in the early nineteenth century.

An involved ritual had to be performed when laying or lifting a curse at Ffynnon Elian, but as noted below, the detail of the ritual might vary. To lay a curse, the victim's name was written in a book, and his/her initials scratched on a slate, or written on parchment which was folded in lead to which a piece of slate was tied, and then placed in the well while curses were uttered verbally. Alternatively a pin was thrown into the well while the victim was named. The well-guardian read some passages from the Bible, then handed the curser a cup of water, some of which was drunk and the rest thrown over the curser's head. He or she spoke the curse which they wished for, while the ritual was repeated twice more. Sometimes a wax effigy with pins stuck into it was used, and the well-guardian would speak secret curses, the effigy being dipped three times and then left in the well. Wax effigies were a late addition to the ritual, a theme clearly borrowed from contemporary ritual magic.

Seemingly there was no hard and fast ritual which must always be followed. The well-guardian may have varied the ritual according to his or her whim, or according to what the curser was able to pay. Whatever form the ritual took, it seems to have impressed both cursers and cursees, or else neither would have paid the large sums that they did. To curse someone cost one shilling, and ten shillings was charged to lift a curse; in 1820 five shillings was charged for a curse, and fifteen shillings to lift it. The rituals for lifting curses were equally involved, and were probably survivals of the earlier healing rituals, as they are familiar from descriptions of other wells. They included a reading of psalms and other Bible texts, walking three times round the well, and the emptying of the well by the guardian so that the lead and slate with his or her initials could be found and removed. Sometimes the slate was ground into dust, mixed with salt, and burned on the fire. The cursee also had to take some well water home and drink it while reading psalms.

Although we can see today that the whole performance of cursing was nothing but mumbo-jumbo, to the people who took part it was very serious indeed, and the use of biblical texts somehow set the seal of authenticity on it. There are reliable records of the effect on the cursee of being 'put in the well': they became ill, or began to behave in an irrational way. A woman from Dolanog (Powys) was bedridden for years after being cursed, only rising again when the person who cursed her was dead. The Reverend Elias Owen, a well-known collector of North Wales folklore, met this lady, and also wrote of another victim whom he met in the early 1870s when holding a funeral service at Trefeglwys (Powys). He was an old gentleman who had not left his home for years and years, after having been 'put in the well' as the result of a love affair when he was young. When he asked the well-guardian how the curse could be counteracted, he was told that it would not harm him so long as he remained within the bounds of his own property. Thus he lived, a bachelor all his life, and never left his home until he was carried a corpse to the churchyard.

In the late nineteenth century the use of Ffynnon Elian as a cursing well finally ceased. The stone structure was demolished, and there is now no trace of any of the buildings that once made up the well complex. But its influence clearly spread far and wide while it was active, for the Montgomeryshire (Powys) victims cited above lived 50 miles away, which was a considerable distance 150 years ago. The reaction of the victim to being 'put' into Ffynnon Elian was likely to have been the same as that experienced in Roman times by those 'put' into the sacred spring at Bath, and the belief in the efficacy of the ritual likewise was the same. The practice continued at Bath for at least two centuries, so obviously someone believed that it worked. However, after the practice died out at Bath, there seems to be no evidence for cursing rituals at wells before the second half of the eighteenth century. Although the two sets of rituals, at Bath and Ffynnon Elian, are not directly linked, the basic unchanging nature of the human psyche means that the two have common factors and similar outcomes, even though separated by 1,500 years. Other Welsh examples, such as Ffynnon Eilian (Anglesey), did not become cursing wells until after Ffynnon Elian (Conwy) was destroyed, but it seems likely that those later Welsh examples were direct imitations of the proceedings at Ffynnon Elian. That there was a need to curse is an interesting reflection on contemporary culture, when other

The Altar of Cursing on the island of Inishmurray off the Sligo coast. Anyone wishing to place a curse had to circle the altar three or nine times, saying the right prayer, and turn a stone as he passed. If the person cursed were guilty, the curse would fall on him; but if he or she were not guilty, the curse would return and fall on the person who placed it.

more acceptable, and legal, methods of justice and retribution were largely unavailable to the poor and disadvantaged.

There were also specific wells whose role was to undo curses or purify bewitched objects, such as Ffynnon Fair at Llanfairfechan (Conwy) where bewitched or cursed articles would be bathed. On occasion cursing could be beneficial: there was a Welsh well that could cure cancer if the sufferer washed in the water, cursed the disease and dropped pins around the well. But the visitors were an annoyance to the farmer whose land it was on, and it had been drained by 1880.

The transformation of a holy well such as Ffynnon Elian, initially used to cure illness but gradually becoming a cursing well until eventually that was its only use, could be a demonstration of the progressive disintegration of the **well cult** observable throughout the eighteenth century. A similar pattern may be observed in Ireland, where prayer-stones gradually became cursing-stones and the general behaviour at so many of the ritual sites progressively declined, leading the clergy to suppress many of them in the late eighteenth and early nineteenth centuries.

Sources: Bath: Tomlin 1988; Cunliffe 1995: 53–5. **'Theft of Vilbia' curse:** Tomlin 1988: 112–13. **Devil's Whispering Well:** Tongue 1965: 219. **Ffynnon Eilian:** Jones 1954: 118. **Ffynnon Gybi:** Jones 1954: 118. **Ffynnon Elian:** Jones 1954: 119–23; Parry 1965: 185–96. **Powys victims:** Owen 1882: 132–3. **Welsh cursing wells:** Jones 1954: 117–23.

D

Deposition

This term refers to the deliberate placing of objects in a permanent location, usually hidden, in this instance in water – springs, wells, pools, bogs, streams, rivers. Objects were frequently ritually placed or discarded in bodies of water in prehistoric times, and the impulse remains to the present day, though it is now reduced to throwing a coin into a holy or wishing well. It is impossible to prove a direct link between the intentions of the 'depositor' in prehistoric times and the 'depositor' in the early twenty-first century, but the fact remains that the custom of throwing gifts or offerings into wells continued through Roman times (see **Coventina's Well**) and right through the centuries until today, when people still throw **coins** into wells. If anything, the custom has strengthened in recent years as holy wells are being rediscovered.

Archaeologist Francis Pryor suspects that 'the practice of making offerings to the waters has origins that probably extend back into Mesolithic times', being able to cite examples from the Neolithic, Bronze and Iron Ages. The earliest in his experience was an unused jadeite axe clearly intentionally and carefully deposited in the water beside the Neolithic trackway in Somerset known as the Sweet Track. Offerings of valuable metalwork were also found at Flag Fen, a watery Bronze Age landscape near Peterborough which Pryor has excavated. In Ireland, an artificial pool inside an earthwork known as The King's Stables at Tray (Co. Armagh) was excavated in the mid-1970s and dated to the late Bronze Age. Sherds of pottery, animal bones, and part of a human skull were found, leading the excavators to suspect that this too was a site of ritual deposition. Archaeologists who have studied prehistoric deposition have come to the conclusion that different types of deposit were made in different places, suggesting that a structured procedure was being enacted, rather than items being deposited randomly. Miranda Aldhouse Green has interpreted deposition as a sacrificial act, with the sacrificial gift being transferred from the human world to the supernatural world by first damaging it to render it useless in the human world and then making it inaccessible by either burying or immersing it.

In the Iron Age (2–3,000 years ago) larger and more valuable offerings were thrown into lakes and rivers. Beautiful examples of Celtic craftsmanship, such as shields and lunulae (crescent-shaped gold ornaments), have been found in the rivers Thames, Witham, Trent, Bann, Shannon and others, too often to have been carelessly lost. Hoards of metalwork found in lakes or buried in once water-covered areas demonstrate that water had a central role in pre-Christian beliefs and rituals. In Shropshire drainage operations uncovered a small hoard (spearheads and sword fragments) near Bishop's Castle and another at Clungunford (animal bones, spearheads, sword fragments and other objects).

Such finds have been repeated countrywide, but one of the most spectacular hoards came from **Llyn Cerrig Bach** on the island of Anglesey. 150 objects were found, during a period beginning in 1943, when the military airfield at Valley was about to

Some of the items found in Llyn Cerrig Bach, with most of the different kinds of objects being represented. Artwork: Anthony Wallis

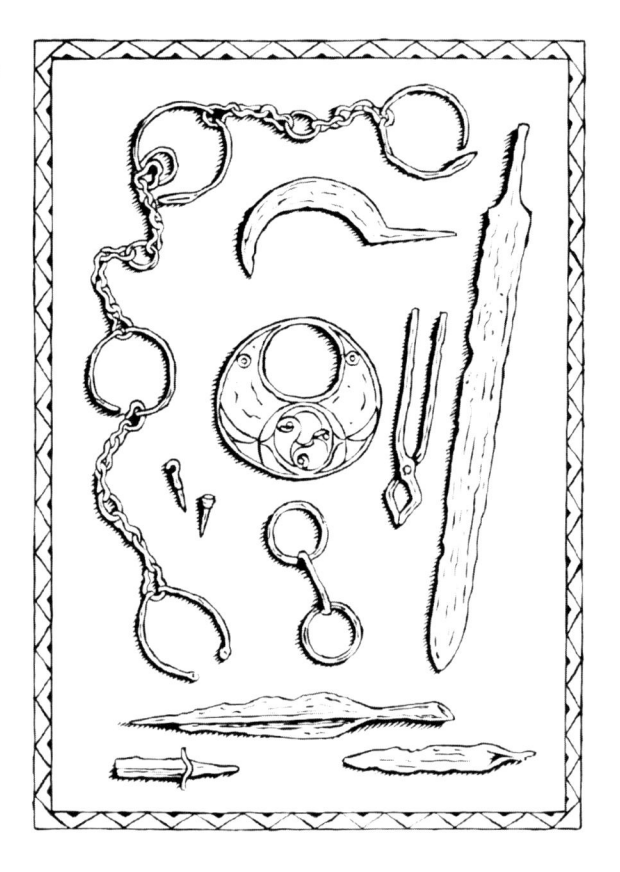

be built. In preparation of the ground, peat from nearby bogs was spread over the sand. As the peat was being spread, metal objects and bones were found, and so a thorough search was made. There may well be more metalwork lying deeper in the bog, and buried under the runways, both sites now inaccessible. Weapons (swords, spears, daggers, scabbards and shields), chariot fittings and harness constitute the bulk of the material discovered, with also some ox, sheep, pig, horse and dog bones (no human remains), the remains of two well-used bronze cauldrons, a broken trumpet, iron bars (perhaps currency bars) and two iron gang-chains used to link captives by the neck. The items were dated from the second century BC to the first century AD, with the gang-chains dated to the first century AD. It is possible that a major offering was made in AD 60, when the Romans were advancing on Anglesey, the last stronghold of the Druids who were a powerful Celtic priesthood. They may have desperately invoked the aid of the gods by means of this huge ritual offering – but in vain. Llyn Fawr in South Wales was another sacred lake where deposits of bronze and iron objects were made during the first millennium BC, possibly as offerings to the gods.

Another aspect of deposition is the deliberate placing of holy water with the intention of bringing about a desired result. **Ampullae** containing water brought by pilgrims from **Walsingham** (Norfolk) have been found buried at the edges of fields in various Midlands and Southern England locations, and one such ampulla, when its contents were analysed, was found to contain herbs as well as water, suggesting that the concoction was ritually prepared and blessed, with the prime intention of taking it home to deposit in a field, to protect or encourage the growing crops. The impulse behind this field burial may go back thousands of years to at least the later Mesolithic period (8500–4000 BC): excavations during 2004 near Midsomer Norton (Somerset) revealed that small circular pits had been dug at the edge of a tufa deposit, with flint blades, fossils, and a handmade tufa ball deposited inside them, possibly offerings left by Mesolithic hunters. (See also **Offerings; Pins; Rags; Votive Offerings; Wishing wells.**)

Sources: Prehistory: Pryor 2004: 131, 132, 282; Merrifield 1987: 23–30. **King's Stables:** Hamlin & Lynn 1988: 19–21. **Distribution:** Bradley 2000: 53–5. **Sacrifice:** Green 2001: 24. **Llyn Cerrig Bach:** Lynch 1970: 249–77; Green 1994: 5–8. **Llyn Fawr:** Green 1992: 134. **Mesolithic:** 'Hunters Respect White Magic', *British Archaeology*, 82 (May/June 2005): 6.

Desecration and destruction

The regular seeker-out of holy wells today will soon see that destruction is sadly common, though thankfully balanced by a considerable amount of restoration too. Prosaic neglect is one form of destruction; more colourful are the folklore tales involving desecration and what befell the desecrators. One such tale concerned Gilsland Spa in Cumbria. Reportedly, the owner of the land decided to build a house over the spring, with the intention of selling the healing waters and making himself a tidy profit. But as soon as the house was built, the spring dried up; as soon as the house was pulled down, the water came back again. In an Irish example, the rector ordered that St Catherine's Well at Killybegs (Donegal) be filled in, whereupon it came up through the floor of his house instead. At St Nun's Well, Pelynt (Cornwall), a farmer decided to take away the granite trough into which the water flowed and tried to drag it using a team of oxen, but the task was arduous and it took a long time to drag the trough uphill to the waiting cart. On reaching it, the chains holding the trough snapped and it rolled back downhill to its former place. Not only that, the wealthy farmer from thenceforth never prospered; indeed this tale says his 'reward' was instant, with his oxen falling dead and he himself being struck lame and dumb. Also in Cornwall, any stones removed from the chapel at St Cleer well mysteriously found their way back again during the hours of darkness.

Some wells appear to have had the ability to self-destruct, or move, if the rules were broken. A large cave on the island of Harris (Western Isles) contained two wells, the water of one of which should never be tasted by dogs. Anyone visiting the cave had to be careful to tie up their dogs, because if a dog were to sample the water, the well would soon dry up. However the dogs need not go thirsty, because the other well was called the dogs-well and its water should only be drunk by dogs. Dead animals being thrown into two Welsh wells resulted in the water drying up or only appearing intermittently: such events were believed to be a punishment for desecrating a well.

The troublesome trough is just visible in this nineteenth-century depiction of St Nun's Well, Pelynt.

Tobar an t-Solais (Well of Light) in Mellifont parish (Louth) moved its location, accompanied by many lighted candles, after butchers washed cattle intestines in it. People who polluted or closed wells sometimes received personal punishments: one man was cursed with cancer, and his descendants too. The man who filled in St Catherine's Well at Staffordstown, Lusk (Dublin) found that his cattle died as a direct result of his actions; while another Co. Dublin man who cut down a sacred tree at St Fintan's Well in Sutton went home to find that his house had burned down. Interfering with a well could also affect the weather. In Ireland it was believed that if the mud at the bottom of Tobar na Suil on the mountain Slieve Sneacht was stirred up, the pilgrim on descending the mountain might find himself enveloped in mist, rain or even snow.

Another aspect of desecration was the accidental neglect of the well by its guardian, who left it uncovered with disastrous results. The well overflowed, often drowning a town and all the people in it, and forming a permanent lake. (For some examples of this, see **Overflowing**.)

Sources: Gilsland Spa: Hope 1893: 43. **St Catherine's Well:** Logan 1980: 67. **St Nun's Well:** Hope 1893: 17–18. **St Cleer Well:** Hope 1893: 25–6. **Dogs-well:** MacLeod 2000: 42. **Welsh wells:** Jones 1954: 116–17. **Tobar an t-Solais:** Logan 1980: 67. **Dublin wells:** Skyvova 2005: 29–30. **Tobar na Suil:** Logan 1980: 63.

Divination

Wells were sometimes used to try and foretell the future, and even to influence future events. Perhaps it was their otherworldliness, their being on the boundary between the mundane human world and the world of supernatural beings, that led people to believe the future could be espied there. A tradition recorded in the Quantock Hills in Somerset around 1912 demonstrates a belief that wells had magical powers that could be used: 'If you want something very badly go down to the spring at night and whisper it three times, then sign a criss-cross above the water and you will get what you asked for in some way, *but you may not like it.*'

At Gulval Well (Cornwall) it was believed that you could find out whether an absent friend was dead, sick, or in good health: 'If the party be living, and in health, the still quiet water of the well-pit, as soon as the question is demanded, will instantly bubble or boil up as a pot, clear crystalline water; if sick, foul and puddle water; if the party be dead, it will neither bubble, boil up, or alter its colour.' Also in Cornwall, people would visit the holy well of Our Lady of Nance at Colan on Palm Sunday, carrying a palm cross in one hand and an offering for the priest in the other. The cross was thrown into the well and if it floated that person would expect to stay alive for the rest of the year, but if it sank, their death was foretold. Tobar Anndrais (St Andrew's Well) on the Isle of Lewis (Western Isles) could also be used to predict whether a patient would die. A wooden dish was used to take some of the well water to him or her, and then the dish was laid gently on to the water in the well. If it turned sunwise, the patient would recover, but if it turned the opposite way, he or she would die. At Ffynnon Bedrog in Llanbedrog parish (Gwynedd) it was believed that the victim of theft could learn the name of the thief. He must first kneel by the well and 'avow his faith in it'; then he had to throw a bit of bread into the well and name the suspect. If it was correct, the bread would sink. So the procedure would continue until a piece of bread sank and the thief was unmasked.

The place-name Fritwell or Fretwell, which occurs in Oxfordshire, Yorkshire, Shropshire and Nottinghamshire, seems to have originally meant 'a spring used for divination'. Some wells had permanent residents in the form of fish or eels, and these

The Lambton Worm, by now too large to get into the well, as depicted by Herbert Cole in 1906.

THE LAMBTON WORM

were sometimes involved in divination rituals (see **Fishes and frogs**). See also **Love magic; Prophecy.**

Sources: Quantocks tradition: Tongue 1965: 25. **Gulval Well:** Vaux 1902: 357. **Our Lady of Nance:** Meyrick 1982: 34. **Tobar Anndrais:** MacLeod 2000: 28. **Ffynnon Bedrog:** Rhys 1893: 61–2; Jones 1954: 114. **Fritwell:** Hough 1996–7: 65–9.

Dragons

The most dramatic well legends tell of dragons and giant serpents living in wells, growing ever larger, until slain by a brave knight. Probably the best known of these was the story of the Lambton Worm in Durham, which began its existence as an ugly newt-like creature fished from the River Wear by the heir to the Lambton title when he should have been in church. He threw it into a nearby well, which still bears the name of Worm Well.

In time the worm grew so large it had to leave the well and during the day it coiled round a rock in the River Wear, by night it encircled Worm Hill near Fatfield. It laid waste the countryside in its search for food, and eventually had to be despatched by the Lambton heir on his return from fighting in distant wars. In order to outwit it, he had sharp blades fastened to his suit of armour and stood on a rock in the river holding his sword. When the dragon tried to suffocate him by coiling around him it was badly wounded by the blades and as it lost blood it also lost energy, so that the knight was eventually able to use his sword to cut it in two, the severed part being carried away in the river so that the dragon could not reunite its parts and so died.

Another famous northern dragon, the Dragon of Wantley (South Yorkshire), lived close to a well until slain by the knight More of More Hall; and in Northumberland a dragon guarded the three wells at Longwitton, thus stopping people from using the well water to cure their ailments. Guy, Earl of Warwick, a famous knight, heard

The Dragon of Wantley being attacked in a sensitive place by More of More Hall. The top of the well which the dragon frequented can just be seen at the bottom right of the drawing.

about the dragon while travelling through the land, and confronted it at the wells. He fought it, but however much he injured it, it came back for more. He eventually realised that it was dipping its tail in one of the wells and receiving healing and strength from the water; so he leapt between the dragon and the well and stabbed it in the heart. In Herefordshire a dragon living in the Dragon's Well at Brinsop was slain by St George, this event being depicted on the tympanum of the nearby church. In Leicestershire a griffin was guarding a well at Griffydam, and stopping the villagers from fetching water, until it was shot by a passing knight. The dragon that guarded a well near Pittempton (Angus) devoured nine maidens before it was killed by Martin, the lover of one of them, this story explaining the name Nine Maidens' Well. The scaly flying snake, a dragon by any other name, of Brawdy parish (Pembroke) would fly from St Edrin church tower to the marshes near Grinston, and at night it would coil up at the bottom of Grinston Well.

In Ireland it was the saints who battled with the giant serpents and routed them. The well Tobar Barry sprang up where St Barry's knee touched the ground while he was chasing the serpent known as the Oll Phiast which lived on the hill of Slieve Badhan near Strokestown (Roscommon). He had thrust his crozier at it just before it disappeared for good into Lough Lagan, and this was when his knee touched the ground and the well appeared. He blessed it and it became a holy well.

The Lambton Worm began its life as a small creature living in a well; some holy wells had sacred fishes or eels living in them around which folklore and rituals were woven. See **Fishes and frogs** for more details.

The Drumming Well at Harpham, sadly neglected today.

Sources: Lambton Worm: Hope 1893: 68–71. **Dragons at wells:** Cleaver 1985: 25–8; Simpson 1980: various: see index entry 'wells'. **Longwitton:** Binnall & Dodds: 64–5. **Brinsop:** Sant 1994: 24. **Grinston Well:** Jones 1954: 215. **Tobar Barry:** Logan 1980: 51.

Drumming wells

A few wells got this name because of the sounds that issued from them, most notably the Drumming Well at Oundle (Northampton), where the noise was reported to be 'like strokes upon a drum... at nearly equal intervals of time'. It could sometimes be heard 60 yards away, and the longest period of drumming recorded was ten days without stopping, in June 1704. The well seems to have been particularly 'active' during the eighteenth century, but it stopped drumming altogether early in the nineteenth century. Beeby Thompson gave as his explanation that the well acted as a 'resonating tube' for sounds arising in certain conditions which caused air to be 'expelled by compression from rock crevices into the well, through a water-seal, periodically, in bubbles'. The local people tended to view the mysterious drumming as having powers of prediction, and one account published in 1744 in the *Northampton Mercury* tried linking the drumming to events of national importance: 'It first beat Jan. 18th, 1700–1, which year was remarkable for the Death of King James II... It beat again, June 4, 1701, and usher'd in the Commencement of a glorious War; wherein we humbled the Power of France... But the Beating, Dec. 7, 1702, of the Drumming Well seem'd to prophecy that the Bavarian... should soon be drumm'd out of all his Dominions...' and so it continued with numerous other highly stretched connections between the drumming and historical events.

The drumming that issued from the Drumming Well at Harpham (East Yorkshire) was believed to foretell the death of the head of the house of St Quintin, the Lords of Harpham. This followed an accident some centuries ago, when a drummer boy was knocked into the well by the squire and drowned there. His demented mother, also known as a seer, prophesied: 'Squire St Quintin, you were the friend of my boy, and would still have been his friend but for this calamitous mishap. You intended not his death, but from your hand his death has come. Know, then, that through all future ages, whenever a St Quintin, Lord of Harpham, is about to pass from life, my poor boy shall beat his drum at the bottom of this fatal well! It is I – the wise woman, the seer of the future – that say it.' The boy's body was removed from the well and buried, but, as his mother had foretold, his drum could be heard in the well on the evening before the death of the head of the house.

Phil Quinn described hearing the 'tattoo' issuing from Drumhill Spring in the parish of Stowey-Sutton (Somerset) which can be heard from 20 metres away: 'Upon approaching the well closer the sound can be very impressive and somewhat disconcerting!' He also heard drumming at St Alphege's Well at Charlcombe (Somerset); and noted that a spring in Hutton parish (Somerset) was known as Ludwell (the loud well) on account of the noise it made.

Sources: Oundle: Thompson 1913 (June): 81–3; Thompson 1913 (September): 107–10. **Harpham:** Hope 1893: 196–8. **Somerset wells:** Quinn 1999: 63–4.

E

Ebbing and flowing wells

Some wells seemed to echo the tides in that they would periodically ebb and flow. One such was Ffynnon Leinw at Cilcain (Flint). Descriptions of its behaviour appeared in books such as the twelfth-century *Itinerary* of Giraldus Cambrensis and the sixteenth-century *Britannia* of William Camden and *The Breviary of Britayne* by Humphrey Lhuyd, the last writing: 'In Tegenia is a well of marvellous nature which being 6 miles from the sea in the parish of Kilken, ebbeth and floweth twice in one day. Yet have I marked this of late, when the moon ascendeth from the east horizon to the south (at which time all seas do flow) that then the water of this well diminisheth and ebbeth.'

Another famous ebbing and flowing well noted in a classic historical source is that at Giggleswick (North Yorkshire), said to ebb and flow at varying intervals, sometimes several times within an hour. Michael Drayton mentioned it in his poem *Polyolbion* (1613): 'At Giggleswick, where I a fountain can you show, That eight times a day is said to ebb and flow.'

Other wells with the ability to ebb and flow included St Gundred's at Roche Rock (Cornwall), and Tullaghan Well (Sligo) which was mentioned by Gerald Barry in his twelfth-century description of the Wonders of Ireland. It was on top of a mountain and some distance from the coast, yet its waters ebbed and flowed like the tides of

The Ebbing and Flowing Well at Giggleswick.

the sea, or so it was claimed. More believable were the five ebbing and flowing wells on the shore at Weston-Super-Mare (North Somerset): they were, somewhat surprisingly, said to be full at low tide and empty at high tide.

Sources: Ffynnon Leinw: Davies 1959: 64–5. **Giggleswick:** Hope 1893: 201–3. **St Gundred's Well:** Hope 1893: 24. **Tullaghan Well:** Logan 1980: 49–50. **Weston-Super-Mare:** Quinn 1999: 197–8.

Eye wells

Many holy wells were believed to have **healing** powers, but not all wells could heal all illnesses, and very often a well would be visited in hopes of curing one specific ailment and no other. The complaint which crops up most often in the lore of wells is sore eyes, and this indicates that many people must have suffered eye problems of one kind or another.

Some eye wells are known by that name; and occasionally the well may even resemble an eye. One such was Ffynnon Lygad (Eye Well in Welsh), a spring on the north-east side of the rocky outcrop known as Clegyr Boia close to St Davids (Pembroke). It is a 'small eye-shaped hole naturally occurring in the rock-face' beside a steep and narrow path, and its water was reputed to be helpful for eye troubles. It was in addition an **ebbing and flowing well**, and children would look at it to judge the state of the tide, the sea being close at hand. The fact that this particular eye well actually resembled an eye may provide a clue as to why some wells were given this name and why they were believed to have the power to cure

This drawing of St Winefride's Well by Thomas Dineley (1684) is the second earliest surviving depiction of the well at Holywell and shows the eye well at the bottom right. It was later drained and covered, and the site is now under the steps by the well pool.

sick eyes. Without conducting proper scientific experiments it is impossible to know whether the water of eye wells really does benefit sore eyes, and if it does, whether the reason is (a) that cold water is itself soothing; (b) that the water contains certain minerals or other qualities that somehow influence the eye; (c) that the process is psychological, resulting from suggestion and/or faith in the saint to whom the well is dedicated.

Professor Rhys noted that 'the regular Welsh word for the source of a river is *llygad*, Old Welsh *licat*, "eye"', and gives three examples including Llygad Llychwr, 'the source of the Loughor river' close to Carreg Cennen Castle (Carmarthen). He conjectured that 'the well or spring was regarded as the eye of the divinity of the water', which would explain why in the Irish *Book of Leinster* it was told that anyone who gazed into Trinity Well, the source of the River Boyne (Kildare), would bring about 'the instant ruin of his two eyes'.

Some 'eye wells' were springs close to larger holy wells; there was even one at *St Winefride's Well*, **Holywell** (Flint), as noted by Thomas Pennant in the late eighteenth century:

> On the outside of the great well, close to the road, is a small spring, once famed for the cure of weak eyes. The patient made an offering to the nymph of the spring, of a crooked pin, and sent up at the same time a certain ejaculation, by way of charm: but the charm is forgotten, and the efficacy of the waters lost.

Sources: Ffynnon Lygad: Trier 1995: 22. **Theories:** Binnall 1945: 361–4. **Irish and Welsh rivers:** Rhys 1901: 390–1. **Holywell:** Pennant 1796: 223–4.

F

Fairies

Those places in the landscape where water flows from the earth could be seen as places where contact might be made with the supernatural realm of the Underworld or Otherworld. It was at such liminal places that otherworldly beings were sometimes seen, such as the Little People. Folklore records them frequently dwelling in underground homes such as burial mounds, cairns and hillocks. Sometimes fairies were believed to live beneath wells, such as at Llanreithan (Pembroke), and this belief may be a possible folk memory of the Otherworld or Fairyland. A shepherd lad on the hill of Freni-fawr in the Preseli hills (Pembroke) actually visited Fairyland and lived in a palace there for a while, though he was warned never to drink from a fountain or well in the garden where golden fishes swam. His curiosity eventually got the better of him, he tasted the water, and instantly found himself back on the bare hillside with the sheep.

Other Welsh wells believed to be fairy haunts were Virtuous Well at Trellech, the Fairy Well north of Abergavenny (both Monmouth), and the Fairy Well at Laugharne (Carmarthen).

In Somerset the fairies were considered to be guardians or spirits of the wells, and there were ten fairy wells in the county. Gifts had to be left for the fairies whenever a well was visited: a rag, a pin, or a coin, were most popular. Some wells were named for the fairies, but without any relevant folklore having survived, such as, for example, the Fairy Well at Aikton (Cumbria). West Country fairies were often known as pixies or piskies, and one of the names of St Nun's Well at Pelynt (Cornwall) was Piskies' Well. **Pins** were once thrown into the well basin 'to get the goodwill of the Piskies', according to a local workman questioned in the nineteenth century. The Pin Well north of Wooler (Northumberland) was believed to have a fairy guardian, who

Cures and curses

had to be propitiated by a gift, usually a crooked pin, a button, or a coin. The fairies who lived at the well in the grounds of Edenhall mansion (Cumbria) owned a vase which was stolen by the mansion's butler: it became known as the 'Luck' of Edenhall after the fairies chanted to the thief: 'If that glass should break or fall, Farewell the luck of Edenhall!'

Puck, the shape-shifting hobgoblin, is linked with several wells, such as one bearing his name in Wiltshire: Puckwell, in Puckwell Coppice at West Knoyle. There was also a Puck Well at Aynho (Northampton). The name of Robin Round-Cap Well in Holderness (East Yorkshire) also refers to a fairy figure, a kind of hobgoblin who did domestic chores. This Robin haunted a Holderness farm and appears to have been a nuisance rather than a help, so that the farmer decided to move house and leave

The shepherd lad who was transported into Fairyland from Freni-fawr was unable to resist the temptation of the forbidden well. Illustration by T.H. Thomas for Wirt Sikes' British Goblins.

The Luck of Eden-Hall.

It comes in murmurs up the stairs,—
    A low, a sweet, a mellow voice,—
And charms away the lady's cares,
    And bids the mother's heart rejoice.

'Sleep sweetly, babe!' 'twas heard to say;
    'But if the goblet break or fall,
Farewell thy vantage in the fray!—
    Farewell the luck of Eden-Hall!'

Though years on years have taken flight,
    Good-fortune's still the Musgrave's thrall;
Hail to his vantage in the fight!
    All hail the LUCK OF EDEN-HALL!

The 'luck' of Edenhall is the vessel to the right with the fairy standing inside it. From The Book of British Ballads *edited by S.C. Hall (1853).*

Robin behind. But as the family left, a friend enquired, 'Is tha flitting?' Before the farmer could reply, a voice piped up, 'Ay, we're flitting!' Realising that he could not shake Robin off, the farmer returned to his home. But afterwards Robin was enticed into the well by the use of charms, and he cannot escape, which is why the well bears his name. It is probably the same as a well at Garton, where a hob named Robin was imprisoned by the aid of charms for ninety-nine years and a day, with ninety-nine nails hammered into the mill door to attest to this.

The White Wells at Ilkley (Bradford) were visited by a host of tiny fairies who were seen there by the well-keeper in the nineteenth century. Dressed in green and only 18 inches tall, they were bathing fully clothed. He shouted out in surprise, and 'away the whole tribe went, helter skelter', leaving no trace behind. More details of this event, and other wells throughout the UK which were believed to be fairy haunts, can be found in my book *The Traveller's Guide to Fairy Sites*.

Sources: Fairy dwellings and Welsh wells: Bord *Fairy Sites* 2004. **Somerset:** Tongue 1965: 22. **Fairy Well, Aikton:** McIntire 1944: 4. **Piskies' Well:** Hope 1893: 19. **Pin Well:** Hope 1893: 102–3. **Edenhall:** Bord *Fairy Sites* 2004: 105. **Puckwell (Wiltshire):** Jordan 1998: 18. **Puck Well (Northampton):** Thompson 1915: 67. **Robin Round-Cap Well:** Nicholson 1890: 80–1. **Garton well:** Smith 1923. **White Wells:** Bord *Fairy Sites* 2004: 98.

Fertility

The water of some wells was believed to be able to promote fertility, and newly married women would resort to them to drink the water. Pizien Well at Wateringbury (Kent) was traditionally visited by the whole wedding party for this purpose. The Bride's Well near Corgarff (Aberdeen) was visited by the bride and her 'maidens' on the evening before the wedding. They bathed her feet and upper body with water from the well, to ensure she had a family, and she would put a few crumbs of bread and cheese into the well to keep her children from ever being short of food. After a woman had been married for a few years and no children had arrived, she would sometimes resort to a well with a reputation for solving the infertility problem, such as the Borewell at Bingfield (Northumberland). Childless women would drink from this well and silently wish for a child, their wish being granted within a year.

In Ireland too women would resort to holy wells in hopes of becoming fertile, a practice considered superstitious by the Catholic authorities, as demonstrated in a seventeenth-century ruling: 'Also forbidden are those practices that involve a striving to have children and such, since such practices smack more of superstition than devotion.' This order was probably aimed at the clergy: although a formula of blessing intended to promote conception was part of the marriage rite, the authorities could not condone the performance of any rites that hinted at magic or folk-religion.

Sources: Pizien Well: Martin 1985: 28. **The Bride's Well:** Gregor 1892: 68. **Borewell:** Balfour 1904: 2. **Ireland:** Carroll 1999: 45.

Fishes and frogs

Some wells were believed to be home to magical fish, such as the Annat, a small fish thought to be immortal which lived in the Well of the Annat (Tobar na h-Annait) on Skye. One big sacred trout lived in Tobar Bhan in Glen Elg (Highland). An old woman, Anne MacRae, used to clear the well periodically, and keep the approach strewn with gravel from the seashore. She had 'great regard' for the trout – but it disappeared early in the twentieth century when its custodian died. Several Welsh wells held sacred trout; the appearance of the trout that lived in Ffynnon Beris at Llanberis (Gwynedd) during bathing was regarded as a good omen. A newspaper report in 1896 noted that two new fishes had just been put into Ffynnon Beris, the last of the previous two having recently died. Anyone standing in Ffynnon Gybi, Llangybi (Gwynedd), would be cured if a large eel coiled round their legs – but it was believed that the well lost most of its healing virtue when a man removed the eel. The pilgrims who visited St Ciaran's Well at Castlekeeran near Kells (Meath) on the first Sunday in August would all try to get a glimpse of the sacred trout which lived in the well, but since it supposedly only appeared for a short time after midnight, they would gather round at that time and use lights to try and spot it. Sacred trout and/or eels were believed to live in numerous Irish wells.

Tobar Vacher (St Machar's Well) near Corgarff (Aberdeen) miraculously acquired fishes as a result of a miracle performed by the saint. At a time when there was a local famine, the priest himself had no more food, and he went to the well and cried to St Machar for help. Arriving home, he told his servant to go to the well at sunrise, walk three times round it, in the name of the Father, Son and Holy Ghost, but without looking into it. She must then draw some water. She followed these instructions, and found three fine salmon swimming in the well, which provided food for the priest and his servant until other supplies became available. An angel kept St Neot's Well at St Neot (Cornwall) always stocked with two fishes as food for the saint, though he could only take one each day. On one occasion when he was ill and lacking his appetite, his servant cooked both fishes in different ways. When St Neot realised what had happened, he threw them back into the well and prayed for forgiveness, whereupon they were both restored to life. Taking one out and cooking it, St Neot instantly regained his health on tasting it.

Fishes and eels living in wells sometimes played vital roles in divination rituals. Pilgrims would apparently wait for several days at Ffynnon Elaeth, Amlwch (Anglesey), for the eel to appear, and then the meaning of its movements would be interpreted by a person who lived nearby. The movements of small eels in Crochan Llanddwyn, a well on Anglesey, were interpreted by an old woman from Newborough: they foretold the supplicant's love and marriage prospects. Eel-like in appearance, but definitely not an eel, was the so-called 'worm' that inhabited Worm Well (Durham): it was a dragon which wreaked havoc before being killed (for the full story see **Dragons**); as too did other dragons that lived in or at holy wells.

The significance of fishes in the folklore of holy wells shows that at least some of that lore goes back many centuries and probably to prehistoric times. The salmon symbolised wisdom and knowledge in the Irish and Welsh mythologies, as most

A fine early nineteenth-century depiction of the trout that lived in the Golden Well at Dorstone (Hereford) hangs on the wall of Peterchurch church not far away.

famously demonstrated in the Irish tale of Finn the hero, who was given the Salmon of Knowledge to cook. He burned his thumb on the fish while it was on the grill and in this way gained knowledge, also gaining wisdom by eating the flesh of the fish. The salmon had itself gained knowledge by eating nuts from nine hazel trees growing by a well at the bottom of the sea. Other legendary fishes can be found in the Lives of the Irish Saints, and a recurring tale describes how a sacred trout was taken from a well and put on a gridiron to cook. On feeling the heat, it flew back into the well, but thereafter the marks of the gridiron could be seen on its side. People who caught and ate the sacred fishes in holy wells would be expected to suffer as a result.

The Frog Well at Acton Burnell (Shropshire) was believed to be home to the Devil and his imps in the form of three frogs. The largest was identified as the Devil, but he always stayed at the bottom of the well and was rarely seen. An Irish nun remembered that in the mid-twentieth century members of her community would visit St Patrick's Well near Ballyhaunis (Mayo) on the pattern day. They sometimes had to stay there for several hours until the Reverend Mother said she had seen the immortal frog which lived in the well. Only when she saw the frog could she be certain that her request would be granted.

Sources: Tobar na h-Annait: Forbes 1923: 427. **Tobar Bhan:** MacGregor 1935/1948: 112–13. **Welsh wells:** Jones 1954: 108–10. **New fish in Ffynnon Beris:** *Liverpool Mercury*, 18 November 1896, quoted in Rhys 1901: 366 fn. **St Ciaran's Well:** Logan 1980: 44–5. **Tobar Vacher:** Gregor 1892: 69. **St Neot's Well:** Hope 1893: 29–30. **Ffynnon Elaeth:** Jones 1954: 110. **Ffynnon Ddwynwen:** Jones 1954: 111–12. **Symbolic fish:** Green 1992: 184–5. **Irish fish:** Logan 1980: ch.X. **Frog Well:** Hope 1893: 146. **St Patrick's Well:** Logan 1980: 126.

Two in a series of stained-glass windows in the church at St Neot (Cornwall) showing the story of St Neot and the fishes: to the left, the sick St Neot in his bed telling his servant to cook a fish; to the right, the servant cooking both fishes beside the well. Depictions of saints' wells are rare in the medieval and late medieval art of the British Isles. Photo: Roy Fry

Flower of the well

This refers to the first water drawn from a well on New Year's Day. In Northumberland at Crowfoot Well, Birtley, the first person at the well on that day drew water and kept it in a bottle. It was believed to stay fresh all year through, and to bring good luck to the house. He or she would throw in a flower (if there were any around on 1 January!) or a piece of grass or straw, to show later arrivals that the flower of the well had already been taken. Also in Northumberland, the same procedure was followed at three wells at Wark on Tyne, but in addition the first visitor would also drink from the well and be granted extraordinary powers such as the ability to fly through the air or pass through a keyhole.

In Scotland the girls from the farms were in friendly rivalry to be the first on New Year's morning to get the flower of the well from the spring, and on their way they would chant:

>The flower o' the well to our house gaes,
>An' I'll the bonniest lad get.

At some Scottish wells the 'cream of the well' was drunk on the first Sunday of May, and at Redbeard's Well on the Hill of Craigour at Durris (Aberdeen) the youths who climbed up to the well on that day would, after drinking the well water, cut their names or initials in the turf beside the spring.

Wales also had well customs relating to New Year. One belief was that well water drawn between 11 and 12 p.m. on New Year's Eve (and on Easter Eve) would turn into wine. In parts of Pembrokeshire, the first water drawn early on New Year's Day would be taken to various houses by children and sprinkled over the rooms and people using sprigs of holly and other evergreens. At other wells in Wales the first water of the year was known as the 'crop of the well', and the well would be decorated with box or mistletoe when the water was drawn. This happened at Disserth (Powys), where the woman who came first to the well on New Year's Day would 'reap the crop of the well' and be known as 'a queen'. However, the water would then 'lose its virtue' for a year.

Sources: Crowfoot Well: Binnall & Dodds: 22; Hope 1893: 107. **Wark on Tyne:** Binnall & Dodds: 71; Hope 1893: 106. **Scottish girls:** Mackinlay 1893: 23. **Redbeard's Well:** MacDonald 1908: 472. **Wales:** Jones 1954: 91–2. **Disserth:** Howse 1991: 16.

Folklore

Many folk beliefs about wells and well water are eccentric but not inherently impossible. But there is one class of folk tale that was clearly intended purely as a joke. An example comes from Wiltshire where, below the white chalk hill figure of a horse to be seen on the hill-slope near Bratton village, there are the Bridewell Springs. The name may commemorate a local bride of centuries past, or it may derive from the name of St Bride (also Brigid or Bridget), but a nineteenth-century form was the Briddle Springs. The story told locally was that when the Bratton church clock strikes midnight, the white horse goes down to Briddle Springs to drink. The joke embodied in the saying is that Bratton church does not have a clock, so, even apart from the impossibility of the white horse ever going anywhere, the midnight call would never come.

Names sometimes give rise to folklore as people try to explain an old name. Chattle Hole in Wiltshire, which once had a spring at the bottom, may derive from Chadwell meaning 'cold spring'; another option links the name to 'chapel' making Chapel Hole. The story devised to explain this name was there was once a chapel being built at the site, but the Devil opened up the earth and swallowed it. A spring at Bingfield in Northumberland was also famed for having swallowed something. It was known as Hell's Cauldron because of the water's boiling motion, and one day, or so the story ran, a team of oxen yoked to a cart were working on top of the hill above the spring when they were startled and began to run downhill towards the Cauldron. A pole from the cart collided violently with the ground, causing a new spring to burst forth. The oxen continued downhill at full tilt, afterwards leaving the mark of their

A contrived explanation for the name Chattle Hole or Chapel Hole: the Devil opened up a hole to destroy a chapel. Artwork: Anthony Wallis

passage in the form of the new spring's watercourse. On reaching the Cauldron the oxen, the cart and the driver 'sank for ever' – except for the horns of the oxen, which soon afterwards were thrown out by the surging water. Another Northumberland well which appeared to boil was the Silver Nut Well near Otterburn. Its name came from the tree debris and hazel nuts from ancient forests, preserved and silvered by some property of the water, which would come up to the surface. Reputedly a man with a horse and a cart full of hay once disappeared into the well.

The occasional tales of underground passages must also be taken with a pinch of salt, since such passages would normally have been difficult and expensive to construct. Of one such passage believed to have once linked Longthorpe holy well with Peterborough Cathedral, 'by which the monks of the Abbey of Burgh, it is said, used to come to bathe in the pool' (the holy well was an elaborate structure with genuine underground chambers), Beeby Thompson gave as his opinion that 'there never was such a passage; to make one under the intervening water meadows would require very considerable engineering skill and much money, and certainly the builders of this crude hermitage could never have done it.' (However he did allow the possibility of an underground passage 'to some near building on higher ground'.)

In 1964, when workmen were placing telephone kiosks in the Cathedral square in Peterborough they did find an underground passage; however it turned out to be something to do with eighteenth-century fire precautions.

Folklore sometimes tells of wells that have moved from one location to another. St Fillan's Spring at Comrie (Perth & Kinross) moved from the top of the hill Dunfillan, to the foot of a rock a quarter-mile away; while a well on the isle of Islay moved there from the opposite isle of Colonsay (Argyll & Bute) after it was abused by a woman washing her hands in it. Most of the wells which moved did so to escape being profaned in this and other ways. Perhaps the most extraordinary case of a moving well, at least so far as distance was concerned, was the well of St Fergus on the hill of Knockfergan somewhere in the old county of Banffshire (Aberdeen) which moved there from Italy!

Folklore also records some genuine oddities, such as the well on the island of Barra (Western Isles) which, it was locally believed, produced cockle embryos. There are sixteenth and seventeenth century firsthand accounts of the 'certane litill Cockles' to be found in the well; though early in the twentieth century Alasdair Alpin MacGregor believed he had found the answer to the mystery, saying that the water in the spring 'is charged with calcium carbonate, which is deposited on sand grains and similar objects, thus giving rise to the superstition that the water contained minute cockles.' The Well in the Wall at Checkley (Stafford) was believed to 'throw out' small bones like those of sparrows and chickens – except in July and August.

Sources: Bridewell Springs: Jordan 1998: 18. **Chattle Hole:** Jordan 1998: 19. **Hell's Cauldron:** Binnall & Dodds: 21–2. **Silver Nut Well:** Binnall & Dodds: 205. **Longthorpe:** Thompson 1913 (September): 114–15; Parish 2002. **Moving wells:** Mackinlay 1893: 21. **Cockles:** MacLeod 2000: 68–70. **The Well in the Wall:** Hope 1893: 156–7.

Footprints

Most especially in Ireland, the footprints of the saints are to be found at many holy wells. The stones bearing the impressions which the pilgrims identify as the footprints (or sometimes, hand-prints, finger imprints, or the imprint of the saint's head, his knee, or even his bottom) play their part in the rituals to be performed at each sacred site, along with the other structures there, which would usually include a holy well, and often a tree, a pile of pebbles to which each pilgrim would make a contribution, and perhaps also a cross or pillar-stone.

Not unexpectedly, Patrick is the saint who most often left his imprint on stones in Ireland. His knee impression was on a large stone at St Patrick's Well, Clonfad (Monaghan) and the pilgrims would kiss the stone, bow to it, and walk round it three times, during their procession through the stations. There was also another stone at the bottom of the well which bore the mark of the saint's foot. His knee-prints were also to be found on a stone at St Patrick's Well at Oran (Roscommon), and his finger

Our Lady's Footprint, close to her well above Llanfair, near Harlech (Gwynedd).

imprints were on a healing stone below Tobernalt Well (Sligo). People with back pain would lie on it in search of a cure, and it was believed that by placing one's fingers in the four impressions in the stone, you could acquire power from the saint. The footprint of the Virgin Mary was to be found on a stone, no longer extant, at Our Lady's Well south of Stow church (Scottish Borders); while in Wales she also left her footprint, and her knee-prints, close to her well above Llanfair near Harlech (Gwynedd).

Also in Gwynedd, she left her hand imprint on a rock close to Ffynnon Fair (St Mary's Well) on the Lleyn Peninsula. In the same Welsh county, St Tydecho left his fingermarks at the bottom of a rock hollow known as Ffynnon Dydecho (St Tydecho's Well) in the hills above Llanymawddwy. St Columba's footprints were left on a rock near the holy well and ancient chapel of Keil in Kintyre (Argyll & Bute).

Sources: **St Patrick's Well:** Ó Mórdha 1975: 283–4. **St Patrick impressions:** Bord *Footprints* 2004: 189–90. **Our Lady's footprints:** Bord *Footprints* 2004: 77. **St Tydecho's fingermarks:** Bord *Footprints* 2004: 91. **St Columba's footprints:** Bord *Footprints* 2004: 195.

Fortune-telling

Details of the ways in which people used holy wells to foretell the future can be found under **Divination; Love magic;** and **Prophecy.**

G

Ghosts

Certain wells were believed to be haunted by a white lady ghost – but why a 'white' lady? Does this refer to the traditional belief that ghosts are pallid, insubstantial creatures, or does the white lady of the holy well appear as a white mist (perhaps because that is what she is)? The well at Ashmore (Dorset) called Washers Pit had a white lady ghost, and one story told how the cook from a nearby big house had a dream and rode to the well, arriving in time to save a lady dressed in white whom

A headless woman in white haunted the Goblin Well. Artwork: Anthony Wallis

she found hanging from the ash tree above the well. In Somerset, when the Hungerford family were living at the manor house in the village of Wellow, they believed that when any calamity was about to strike them, a 'fair white lady' would appear at St Julian's Well north of the parish church. A white lady haunted the Lady Well at Whitton Lea, and another frequented the Cattle Well at Detchant (both Northumberland).

The idea of a well being haunted by a white lady may have become attached to those wells known as Lady Well when the original meaning of that name (i.e. a well dedicated to the Virgin Mary) was no longer understood by the local people. Lady Wells that are located near castles are especially prone to becoming the haunt of a white lady, who has migrated there from the castle. White ladies are also sometimes involved with hidden **treasure**, and the white lady who haunted the Goblin Well near Mold (Flint) promised 'a precious store of sparkling gems' to a young man who encountered her there, if he would return at midnight on the following day armed with a pick and shovel in order to dig up the jewels she said were buried by the well. All she needed was a certain necklace because if she could retrieve it, her head could be re-attached. This was a ghost with a terrible problem: she had been decapitated and now carried her head tucked under her arm!

The Atwick holy well (East Yorkshire) is a roadside pool near the church. It was believed to be haunted by a 'boggle' which took the form of a hooded, one-eyed woman.

Not all holy well ghosts took the form of white ladies. Female ghosts were sometimes dressed in another colour, like the green lady that haunted Marcross well (Vale of Glamorgan), watching people tying rags to the thorn bushes. Penylan Well in Cardiff was haunted by a woman in 'sombre garments' at twilight: she once told a man that she could be released from bondage if he held her by the waist and made no sound. He tried to hold her, but could not keep silent, and she fled, crying, 'Two hundred years more before I shall be free.' A similar story is told of the grey lady that haunted Taff's Well (Cardiff), and another grey lady at St Denis's Well, Llanishen (Monmouth) was held in bondage because of her evil deeds. She used to follow drovers for a mile or so, and then return to the well.

The ghost that was seen by a milkmaid near a spring in South Wales was the complete opposite of a white lady: it was a black man! The girl, Anne Jenkins, went one evening to milk the cows and when passing through a wood she saw the eerie figure standing by a holly tree. Her dog barked at it, and it then poked out a long black tongue, which sent the dog running back to Anne in fright. She fetched her cows in, only looking at the holly tree again after she had passed it, and she saw the 'monster' again – 'very big in the middle and narrow at both ends'. The ground seemed to tremble under its feet as it walked away in the direction of a spring called Ffynnon yr Ysbryd (meaning 'spirit well' or 'ghost well'), which was already known to be haunted. It whistled loudly as it crossed over a stile, and then disappeared. The location of this well was in Trevethin parish near Pontypool (Torfaen).

Some wells were simply thought of as spooky, haunted by some indefinable atmosphere or presence – in Wales the words *bwci*, *bwgan* and *bwbach* used in association with wells indicate an undefined ghost, spirit or bogeyman. The *bwgan* of a north Powys well lived among the roots of a tree growing over the well: he would get up to mischief if the water level dropped. In the same area, it was customary to get rid of an evil spirit by sealing it in a bottle and dropping it into a deep well, for example at Llanllwchaiarn, Newtown (Powys).

Some Welsh wells were haunted by ghostly horses, these possibly being the legendary *ceffyl-dwr* (similar to the Scottish Kelpie, a water-horse who was an evil spirit in equine form). Late in the nineteenth century a vicar and his son saw a white horse walking on its hind legs before vanishing into the well in Oxwich churchyard (Swansea). A horse, plough and ploughman disappeared for ever into the bottomless well Ffynnon Ddôl Erw Llyw near Abergele (Conwy) (see also **Folklore**); and anyone near the well at Gerddi Bach Trewilym (Pembroke) at night would hear the sound of a galloping yet invisible horse.

Sources: Washers Pit: Harte 'Dorset' 1985: 7. **St Julian's Well:** Harte 'Somerset' 1985: 11. **Lady Well:** Binnall & Dodds: 72. **Cattle Well:** Parsons 1933: 301. **Meaning of Lady Well:** Parsons 1933: 302. **Goblin Well:** Holland 2005: 28. **Glamorgan wells:** Jones 1954: 126–7. **Ffynnon yr Ysbryd:** Sikes 1880: 177–8. **Bwgan:** Jones 1954: 131–2. **Atwick Boggle:** Nicholson 1890: 78. **Horses:** Jones 1954: 132–3.

Goddesses

The recent growth of modern paganism has encouraged a preoccupation with the goddess figure, and consequently it has become fashionable to espy her everywhere. For example, there are a few wells where the water flows from the breasts of a carved female figure, and the automatic assumption is that she represents 'the goddess of the well'. An example of this occurred at St Anne's Well close to Llanmihangel church in the Vale of Glamorgan, where there is a stone slab carved with the head and shoulders of a woman. This has been interpreted by some people as a depiction of St Anne, in her perceived role as goddess-guardian of the well, especially as the water once flowed through two holes pierced in the slab roughly where her nipples would be. But the design of the image shows it to be of no great age, and it may simply have been a neo-classical garden ornament. That is to say, there is no

The small stone image of a mother goddess found at Caerwent. Photo: Newport Museum and Art Gallery.

evidence whatsoever to support the idea that the figure was ever intended to depict a goddess – or even a saint. Not only that, one David Jones, writing in 1890, told how, despite having known the well for fifty years or more and being well versed in the traditions of the parish, he had never heard of its being dedicated to St Anne. The carving is still in place at the well, but is not immediately visible as it becomes silted up. Mysteriously, an identical figure, now in a grotto in the garden of Plas Llanmihangel across the road, may also have come from the holy well.

A similar female figure was sited at the spring known as Old Woman's Spring, in Chinkwell Wood near Brill (Buckingham): the water used to flow from the breasts of the stone figure. Evocative though such figures might be, it is dangerous to equate them with goddesses, since when dispassionate research is undertaken there is precious little evidence to be found that links female saints with pre-Christian goddesses. The interpretation of St Anne, for example, as the supposed Irish mother goddess Ana/Anu can easily be disproved with some basic research. The earliest 'evidence' for Ana as a goddess in pre-Christian Ireland is basically a single sentence in Cormac's *Glossary* (Cormac mac Cuilennáin, died 908), a compilation from the end of the ninth century; everything else supposed about her has been evolved by modern commentators. This hardly suggests that she was a major figure (a 'mother goddess') in the earlier mythology. The linking of Anne and Ana through their names

Water-nymphs (or triple Coventina) holding vases of water and pouring out streams of water. This carving was found in Coventina's Well on Hadrian's Wall. Photo: Museum of Antiquities of the University and Society of Antiquaries of Newcastle upon Tyne.

is also unsustainable: for one thing, the cult of St Anne developed in the West so late that it is impossible that any cult of such a minor figure as Ana could have survived the intervening centuries, which would have been necessary if St Anne was to 'succeed' Ana. Anne's cult was truly popular in the West only in the final centuries of the Middle Ages.

Carvings of goddess figures have been found at some Roman shrines and wells, for example a single figure of a mother goddess was found deep in a well close to a Romano-Celtic temple at Caerwent (Monmouth).

At **Coventina's Well** on Hadrian's Wall, in addition to the single image of the British water goddess Coventina depicted earlier, a stone relief was found in the well which shows either the goddess and two nymphs or three images of Coventina herself – the Romano-Celtic mother goddesses (*matres*) were often portrayed as three seated women, and they were sometimes associated with healing springs. Three goddesses were depicted on a plaque found at **Bath** – they may represent the mother goddesses known as the *Suleviae*. Also found at Bath was a life-size gilded bronze head of the goddess Sulis Minerva, which was clearly once part of a complete statue, maybe even the cult statue from the temple. The name of the goddess Sulis Minerva shows how Sulis, the Celtic goddess of healing who may already have been 'in residence' at Bath before the Roman period, and the Roman goddess Minerva, had eventually become regarded as one and the same.

Sources: St Anne's Well: Davis 2003: 47; Jones 1890: 152–3. **Old Woman's Spring:** Valentine 1985: 23. **Coventina:** Green 1995: 99–102. ***Suleviae:*** Green 1995: 105. **Caerwent:** Green 1995: 65, 111.

The head of the cult statue of the goddess Sulis Minerva from Bath.
Photo: The Roman Baths Museum, Bath.

Guardians

The idea has been put forward that some wells had human guardians who acted as 'the representative of an ancient priesthood of the well', this custom being a survival from pagan times. One well with a so-called guardian was Ffynnon Deilo in Pembrokeshire, where a member of the Melchior family, living in the adjacent farmhouse, had in her possession the surviving remains of St Teilo's Skull, the use of which was essential to the correct performance of the well ritual. (For more information see **Skulls**.) Other wells once believed to have had a guardian include *Ffynnon Gybi* at Llangybi (Gwynedd), where the remains of a small stone cottage still

On the right is the ruined cottage that adjoined the well building at Ffynnon Gybi, Llangybi, where the keeper or caretaker of the well would have lived.

adjoin the ruined well building; also Crochan Llanddwyn (Anglesey), Ffynnon Sarah at Derwen (Denbigh) and Ffynnon Elian at Llanelian-yn-Rhos (Conwy) (see **Cursing**).

However, there is no evidence to support a belief in an hereditary guardian of the well who promulgated pre-Christian rites, and it is far more likely that the women who were on hand to help pilgrims and other visitors seeking cures did so because they were simply the people on whose property the well stood. They may also have been poor, and reliant on the tips they received from visitors. They probably did feel an affinity with the well and a desire to help the sick people who came there – but there is no evidence that their involvement was hereditary or that they were acting in any way as a 'priestess' of a pagan religion. St Teilo's Skull was not present at Ffynnon Deilo until the mid-seventeenth century, and so the vital ritual involving the drinking of the well water from the skull could not have begun any earlier: the Melchior 'guardianship' was thus a relatively late development.

Quite possibly some of the self-appointed 'guardians' were women with psychic powers, which they were able to use for the benefit of pilgrims to their well. In Cornwall the holy well at Gulval was watched over by an old woman through whom enquiries concerning the health of friends were put to the well. She was 'intimately acquainted with all its mysteries', and until her death in the mid-eighteenth century she seems to have drawn many visitors to the well, some seeking information on lost goods and livestock. She may have used clairvoyance, or perhaps nothing more than a good knowledge of people, and local goings-on, to answer the questions visitors to the well put to her.

There were also etherial guardian spirits at some wells and springs which had to be placated or else the consequences would be severe. Tobar-Fuar-Mòr (Big Cold Well) at Corgarff (Aberdeen) was fed by three springs, each curing a different disease. Their guardian spirit lived under a large stone between two of the springs, the stone being known as the Kettle Stone because gold, which had to be offered to the spirit in order to bring about a cure, was placed by her into a kettle below the stone. It was believed that an accident, or even death, would befall anyone who tried to rob the spirit. A group of lads who, with great difficulty, moved the stone, found no kettle of gold. On their way home they were met by an old lady who, when she heard what they had done, told them they would all die within a few weeks. (But whether this actually happened is unknown to me.)

Also near Corgarff was Tobar-na-Glas a Coille (Well in the Grey Wood) and close by a small knoll where lived a spiteful spirit known as the Little Grey Man (Duine-glase-beg). He watched over the well and made sure that everyone who drank from it dropped a pin or other piece of metal into the water. If anyone failed to do so, and afterwards tried to take some water, the spirit would search out that person and ensure that they died of thirst. Similarly, a 'well' on Ben Newe in Strathdon (Aberdeen) also had to be provided with some small object before any water was taken, or else the traveller would not reach the foot of the hill alive. The 'well' was a circular hollow in a rock on top of the hill that always contained water, and when visited by W. Gregor in 1890 he found in the 'well' 'several pins, a small bone, a pill-box, a piece of a flower, and a few other objects'.

Sources: Survival of priesthood: Hulse 'St Teilo' 1994: 14–16. **Corgarff wells:** Gregor 1892: 67–8. **Ben Newe well:** Gregor 1892: 69.

H

Heads

The lore and legend of the human head is a fascinating study in its own right; however, it is safe to say that, despite its appearance in numerous modern books on the Celts, there does not appear to be any reliable evidence for the existence of a specific 'head cult'. In the context of holy wells, both severed heads and **skulls** make an appearance in the folklore. There are numerous legends telling how water began to flow at the place where a severed head fell to the ground. One example was the story of St Osyth or Osith, who was an obscure Anglo-Saxon princess who founded a convent at Chich (Essex) and died there *circa* 700. But according to legend she was murdered, beheaded by pirates because she refused to commit idolatry, and where her head fell, a fountain of water sprang up. Despite having been decapitated, St Osyth got up, picked up her head, and walked to the church three miles away. Afterwards, it was claimed, she haunted her well, the church, and Nun's Wood, still carrying her head in her hand. (Further examples of wells appearing where saints were beheaded can be found under **Saints' deaths**.)

This depiction of a Celtic warrior with the severed heads of his vanquished victims, from John Speed's seventeenth-century History of Britain, *illustrates the Celt's supposed preoccupation with heads; but a tendency to decapitate one's enemies does not equate to cultic worship of their heads.*

The severed head whose fall triggered the creation of a well need not necessarily be that of a saint. St Catharine's Well at Newark (Nottingham) began to flow, according to legend, where the knight Sir Everard Bevercotes was slain by his jealous rival. There are Scottish tales of men being beheaded and their heads washed in the water of a holy well. Two specific examples are Tobar nan Ceann on Barra (Western Isles) and The Well of the Heads at Loch Oich (Highland). The last prince of Wales, Llewellyn ap Griffith, was killed at Cilmeri (Powys) and it was said that his severed head was washed in a spring which, according to Adam of Usk, 'Throughout a livelong day did flow in an unmixed stream of blood.'

The other kind of head linked with holy wells is that carved from stone, through the mouth of which the water often flows. There is one still to be seen at *Ffynnon Beuno*, Tremeirchion (Denbigh); however, although this appears at first glance to be a head only, when the plants are moved a half-length figure is clearly visible. In addition, the flow of water through the mouth is merely an overflow from the bath behind the wall and does not come direct from the spring.

There is a head at Diana's Well in woods on Witton Fell (North Yorkshire) where the water flows from the mouth – this head is thought to be a gargoyle taken from nearby

Traces of an upper body can just be made out below the strange head at Ffynnon Beuno, Tremeirchion.

Jervaulx Abbey. White Wells on Ilkley Moor (West Yorkshire), famous for a fairy visitation in the early nineteenth century (see **Fairies**), has a stone head in the stone walling of the plunge bath, through which water flows. The water at Boilton Spa, Grimsargh (Lancashire), believed to cure consumption, used to flow through the mouth of a carved human head. At St Helen's Well, Eshton (North Yorkshire), there were until recently three stone heads under the water, which could be felt by kneeling on the curb stones and feeling the three stones with hollowed tops.

Sometimes stone heads at wells have been identified as the saints after whom the wells are named, such as St Tydecho at Ffynnon Dydecho (at Foel, formerly Garthbeibio, in Powys) and St Oswald at St Oswald's Well, Oswestry (Shropshire). Some of these were probably the focal point of rituals, as at St Oswald's Well which performed as a **wishing well** if a precise ritual was followed. The wisher had to visit the well at midnight, lift some well water in the hand, drink some of it while wishing, and then throw the rest of the water over a certain stone at the back of the well which had a crowned head carved on it, believed to be a depiction of 'King Oswald'. This well is doubly relevant in the context of heads, because according to tradition, St Oswald was decapitated at Oswestry in 641 by Penda, king of Mercia.

Sources: Head cult: Critical discussion of the supposed 'head cult' can be found in Hulse 'St Teilo' 1994: 14–16. **Heads as trophies:** Green 2001: 95–7. **St Osyth:** Hope 1893: 72–4. **St Catharine's Well:** Hope 1893: 116. **Tobar nan Ceann:** MacLeod 2000: 64–5. **Llewellyn:** Jones 1954: 54. **Celtic heads:** Billingsley 1998. **Yorkshire wells:** Whelan 1998: 16–18. **Boilton Spa:** Darwen 1988: 27; Taylor 2002: 34. **St Oswald's Well:** Hope 1893: 145.

The head carved on the ancient wooden door to St Ambrew's (or St Ambrusca's) Well at Crantock, Cornwall, was gradually fading from view as the years passed, here photographed in 1974. The door has since been replaced with a new one, still bearing a mysterious head.
There is no folklore involving heads linked with this well, so far as I know, and the head may have been intended to depict the saint.

Healing

The water of a great many holy wells was believed to have medicinal properties and this eventually became a major reason why people visited them. There were numerous other reasons for visiting holy wells of course, as is shown elsewhere in this book, but the focus of visits turned to healing in the repressive anti-superstition climate of the post-Reformation period. Also because of a lack of proper healthcare, people continued to visit holy wells in pursuit of healing when the other reasons to visit them had been made obsolete by education, Church pressure, etc. Bathing for cures, as opposed to simply drinking the water, almost certainly developed from biblical examples, such as the curing of Naaman's leprosy after he was ordered by Elisha to wash in the River Jordan, and the occasion at the Pool of Siloam when Jesus healed a blind man. From the earliest times of pilgrimage to the Holy Land, pilgrims continued to visit these places and bathe there, and it is probable that the bathing rituals at British holy wells developed from examples such as these.

Most wells were credited with the power to heal only one or two ailments, those most often mentioned being: weak and sore eyes, scurvy, jaundice, 'obstructions', scrofula or King's Evil (swelling of the glands), leprosy, consumption, epilepsy, rheumatism, sprains, broken bones, skin diseases, rickets, warts, toothache, and lameness. Other ailments mentioned for one or two wells include cancer, fever, ague, indigestion, piles, gravel, coughs, paralysis, drunkenness, mental problems, deafness, melancholy, baldness, and sterility (see also **Fertility**).

In past centuries a great many people sought healing at their local holy well. Artwork: Anthony Wallis

Each well had its own specific practices which must be followed if a successful cure was to result, and these varied widely. (See **Rituals** for some examples.) Usually the well water was drunk and/or applied to the body, either to the afflicted part only, or totally by means of bodily **immersion**. The procedure did not necessarily have to happen at the well, and some of the water could be carried away to treat at home a person who was too ill to attend. Often there were specific rituals to be followed when carrying water home, such as that it must be carried in silence, and the container must not be put down until the bedside was reached. The bathing and drinking at the well were usually accompanied or followed by a prayer or a vow or an offering, as the pilgrim attempted to make psychic contact with the spirit or saint or deity or guardian of the well – whoever they believed to be responsible for granting cures.

Sometimes the cure would affect people not suffering from the particular affliction, such as happened at Tobar Mhàraig on the island of Harris (Western Isles), a well which was acclaimed for being able to restore lost appetite. People who were not suffering from that would find that they too were feeling hungry after drinking the well water, even though they had eaten only a short time before. Very rarely, the water of a holy well was believed to be positively harmful and should *not* be drunk!

A recent photograph of a pilgrim applying water from Doon Well (Donegal) in search of a cure for leg cramps. Photo: Allen Kennedy

One such was St Chad's Well at Stowe, Lichfield (Stafford), which would give you 'a fit of the "shakes"[ague]'. The water of Tobar Aibheog at Lismullyduff (Donegal) was not for domestic use, and anyone trying to boil the well water in their kettle would find they could not make it boil and the inside of the kettle would be 'stone dry'.

An early description of the curative powers of a holy well comes from the *Life* of St Cadog of Llancarfan (Vale of Glamorgan) written in the late eleventh century by Lifris, and concerns a well created in Cornwall (probably St Cadoc's Well at Harlyn Bay near Padstow) by St Cadog when he struck his staff on the ground: 'For if any sick person drink from that fount, trusting firmly in the Lord, he will receive soundness of belly and bowels, and he will throw up in his vomit all slimy worms out of himself.' St Cadog later revisited the well and topped up its power with water he had brought all the way from the River Jordan, presumably in some sort of ampulla (see **Ampullae**). The most detailed account of healing at a holy well anywhere in the British Isles in the pre-modern period is the *miracula* section added to the anonymous *Vita prima* (First Life) of St Winefride dating to the first half of the twelfth century and describing cures at *St Winefride's Well*, **Holywell** (Flint).

People who knew of a local well with a reputation for healing would not necessarily resort to it even though its powers were specific for the ailment they suffered, because it was considered superstitious to do so. One such case concerned Ffynnon Arthur in the parish of Llanfihangel Ynghwnfa (Powys), famed for curing bruises. A local man hurt his leg playing football, and the flesh wasted away until it was nothing but skin and bone. After two or three years he decided to try the well water, as a last resort, and began to bathe in it daily. The result was a perfect cure, and the vigour of the man was noted by the folklorist Reverend Elias Owen when he visited the well at the end of the nineteenth century. Other nineteenth-century users of holy wells resorted to them with much more enthusiasm, as a visitor to Monkton (South Tyneside) discovered one fine morning when he rose early and strolled to Bede's Well. Sitting there enjoying the birdsong, he saw an Irishman walking very fast to the well and then filling a bottle with well water and drinking it.

> 'A fine morning, sir,' said our friend. 'Sure and it is,' replied the man; 'and what a holy man St Bede must have been! You see,

> when I left Jarrow, I was as blind as a bat with the headache, but as soon as I had taken a drink just now, I was as well as ever I was in my life.' So he filled his bottle once more with the precious liquid, and walked away, bidding our informant good-morning.

It is difficult to know how many people still, in the early years of the twenty-first century, visit holy wells in genuine search of a cure for some ailment, but it may be more than is generally realised. The most famous holy wells, for example *St Winefride's Well* at **Holywell** (Flint), certainly still receive a steady stream of genuine pilgrims seeking cures, many of whom still bathe in the well as well as drinking or applying the water, but the same probably cannot be said of most of the minor rural wells. One account of a local cure was recorded by Lady Fox, wife of the archaeologist Sir Cyril Fox, in 1935 when she visited Ffynnon-y-Flameiddan (the inflammation spring) or the Breach Well near Llancarfan in the Vale of Glamorgan. A local farmer, Mr Williams, showed her the spring and told her that his wife had been cured of erysipelas (a skin disease) by means of its water.

> During the dry summers of 1933–5 it was unaffected by the drought. When I visited the well in August 1935, three old rag-pieces of dish cloth and calico and a piece of brown wool were tied to the overhanging branches, by the source. The treatment as described by Mrs Williams consisted in using the water for drinking to the exclusion of all other fluids, in applying [water to] the affected part and in tying a rag preferably from the under clothing by the well. Erysipelas, I was told, was not uncommon in the parish. The well was resorted to especially when medical treatment failed. The rags at the well, however, were becoming less numerous.

In Ireland, some time before 1968, Bearnárd Ó Dubhthaigh tape-recorded the recollections of Francis Boyle concerning his local holy well, Tobar Aibheog (at Lismullyduff, Donegal). At that time belief in the efficacy of the well was still strong, as Doyle explained.

> Anyone that ever had a toothache and went into that wee well and made the station or whatever prayers you like to say yourself and take 3 sups of water out of the well, the toothache died away – there was no more bother with it. There were several other cures in the well, if you had any ailment. That is if you had the right belief in it.

> I knew a fellow... Byrne. Anyway, he was going about two or three weeks with a toothache in a bad way. And one night, in the middle of the night, he was so bad that he jumped out of bed in his shirt and he opened the door and went out. The woman waited a while and there was no word of him coming in so she got alarmed. She got up and felt around for a light. She could not see him at all and she did not know what road to go to look for him.

An mid twentieth-century photograph of a paralysed man entering the water at St Winefride's Well, Holywell, in search of a cure.

He went down into the well in the middle of the night and made a station. And, finally, he came in the lane and him with nothing on but a shirt and in his bare feet. He went in home and sat down at the fire like a cat and he fell asleep. He did not waken until the next evening and never found a sting of a toothache since.

(The last two sentences have strong echoes of the practice of **incubation** which was often practised at wells as part of the healing ritual.)

Some wells were famed for healing animals, and Doulting in Somerset had two of them: sick cattle or those that had been 'overlooked' (by witches) were taken to St Aldhelm's Well, while St Agnes' Fountain was used to cure cattle paralysis (though it never cured cattle that had been stolen). The Lepers' Well at Fritham (Hampshire) was, as its name suggests, originally noted for curing leprosy, but it later became known as Iron's Well, and people took their dogs there to be cured of mange, which is, like leprosy, a skin disease. The well even had a special contraption on top so that you could drop your dog into the chalybeate water, and a place where it could scramble out. In Ireland it was customary to drive cattle and horses through specific lakes, pools and rivers in order to keep them healthy and fertile, such places often being regarded as 'holy wells' or having water from a holy well running into them.

On one occasion the water of a holy well was believed to have cured an animal even though it was not taken there for that reason. On the Isle of Man one Thomas

Moore, who owned the farm named Ballalonney, where the holy well called Chibbyr Baltane was situated, commented that:

> We had a pony and trap when we were younger... The pony got sick and very poor in flesh, so we put the pony in the field where the well was, as we thought to die; but to our surprise the poor pony got very fat and fine looking. He had no grass to eat to make him fat, so that it was altogether the water of the well that made him so fat and well.

Several Welsh wells were believed to have curative powers over animals, including cows with warts on their udders, dogs with mange, sick horses, cattle, sheep and pigs. Tobar Thiobartain, a well on South Uist (Western Isles), on the other hand, was mortally offended when someone brought a horse to it for healing, and thereafter lost its healing powers.

The well in the churchyard of St Edrins (Pembroke), claimed to cure madness, reacted in a similar way to being visited by an animal, though in this instance the well dried up. A farmer took his mad dog to the well where it drank the water and was cured – but the farmer died. After the water dried up, its healing power transferred to the grass growing round the base of the church walls and the grass would be eaten in a sandwich in order to obtain a cure. Francis Jones' grandmother remembered a boy who had been bitten by a dog being given a grass sandwich, presumably because they feared he might have caught rabies from the dog.

The water from the Head Well at Whitchurch (Buckingham) was not only taken to the sick, but also used to ascertain whether a sick person would recover. A piece of their clothing would be placed in the well, and if it floated, recovery was likely, but if it sank, there was no hope. (See also **Divination**.)

Whether the water from holy wells really has ever cured anyone of a genuine ailment (as opposed to an hysterical one) is a debate I do not intend to enter into. Many people have claimed cures – records of hundreds of cures are on file at *St Winefride's Well*, **Holywell** (Flint). But sceptics are of course doubtful – and indeed have long been doubtful. The following account written by someone named Granger was published as a footnote in an early nineteenth-century book.

> I was myself a witness of the powerful workings of imagination in the populace, when the waters of Glastonbury [presumably the Chalice Well spa] were at the height of their reputation. The virtues of the spring there were supposed to be supernatural, and to have been discovered by a dream to one Matthew Chancellor. The people did not only expect to be cured of such distempers as were in their nature incurable, but even to recover their lost eyes, and their mutilated limbs. The following story, which scarcely exceeds what I observed upon the spot, was told me by a gentleman of character. 'An old woman in the workhouse at Yeovil, who had long been a cripple, and made use of crutches, was strongly inclined to drink of the Glastonbury waters, which

she was assured would cure her of her lameness. The master of the workhouse procured her several bottles of water; which had such an effect, that she soon laid aside one crutch, and not long after the other. This was extolled as a miraculous cure; but the man protested to his friends that he had imposed upon her, and fetched the water from an ordinary spring.' I need not inform the reader, that when the force of imagination had spent itself, she relapsed into her former infirmity.

People who believe that they have genuinely been cured by the application of water from a holy well are not likely to be swayed by such sceptical pronouncements. John Trelille, a Cornishman who was cured at *Madron* holy well, would surely be among them. In 1640, after being crippled for sixteen years, he followed advice given to him in his dreams and went to the well, washing in its water and sleeping on the saint's bed close by, whereupon he was completely cured. More recently, pilgrims visiting Irish holy wells were quite sure that cures were to be obtained there, as shown by Jimmy McPhillips who was aged 80 in 1975 when Father Bernard Maguire spoke to him. He remembered visiting St Patrick's Well at Clonfad (Monaghan) when he was a boy, early in the twentieth century: 'Dozens of people used to come every Sunday when I was a boy; my father used to send me down to make the cure.' He told how this was done 'by rubbing the water and reciting 3 Paters, 3 Aves and 3 Glorias.' His cousin was cured of double joints in the knee by having the water rubbed on his knees and prayers said; and Hughie Fay had his paralysed arm cured: 'God bless you, long life to you,' he said to Jimmy: 'I can raise my arm.' There seems little doubt, as the records of cures at St Winefride's Well show, that many people have obtained lasting relief through the use of water from holy wells.

Sources: Ailments: Jones 1954: 98–9. A list of Somerset healing wells with the ailments each cures can be found in Tongue 1965: 218–19. **Procedures:** Jones 1954: 100–6. **Tobar Mhàraig:** MacLeod 2000: 43. **St Chad's Well:** Hope 1893: 159. *Life* **of St Cadog:** Wade-Evans 1944. **Ffynnon Arthur:** Owen 1898: 308–9. **Bede's Well:** Hope 1893: 109–10. **Breach Well:** Bowen 1988: 12–13. **Tobar Aibheog:** Ó Dubhthaigh 1968: 275–6. **Curing animals:** Tongue 1965: 219. **Lepers' Well:** Hope 1893: 77. **Irish cattle:** Logan 1980: ch.XI. **Chibbyr Baltane:** Paton 1941: 191. **Welsh animal wells:** Jones 1954: 106–7. **Tobar Thiobartain:** MacLeod 2000: 61–2. **St Edrins:** Jones 1954: 105–6. **Head Well:** Valentine 1985: 26. **Holywell cures:** Hulse *Father Ryan's Diary.* **Scepticism:** Caulfield 1813. **John Trelille:** Hope 1893: 11. **St Patrick's Well:** Ó Mórdha 1975: 284.

Holy water

It seems relevant to point out that holy well water is not the same as holy water. 'Holy water' refers to water that has been blessed by a priest according to a ritual formula sanctioned by the Church, and it can be taken from any source, from a mains supply via a tap, or from a holy well, or even from a puddle. Holy well water

The holy water stoup in the porch of Llanidan old church on Anglesey. Despite the church no longer being used, it was claimed that the stoup always contained some water, even though there was no apparent source of supply.

is not holy water until it has been so blessed – but water from holy wells has been, and often still is, taken to the church specially for use in the rite of **baptism** after being blessed.

By virtue of coming from a well designated holy, holy well water was credited with being different, special, imbued with the power to bless. In the village of Carnguwch (Gwynedd), the early twentieth-century residents remembered when a vessel containing water from the holy well was kept behind the church door and a little brush was used to sprinkle some over everyone who entered the church. All Catholic churches have a vessel of holy water beside the door, and the practice at Carnguwch appears to be a direct survival of pre-Reformation practice.

Sources: Carnguwch: Jones 1954: 82.

Holywell

The well located in this small Flintshire town (Welsh name Treffynnon – 'well town') was once so important that the town was even named after it. *St Winefride's Well* is a vivid example of a thriving holy well, one that is still visited by approximately 30,000 pilgrims annually, many in sincere hopes of being cured, as has been the case for at least 900 years. Many miraculous cures have been claimed and documented, and sick people still bathe in the well.

St Winefride's Well differs from most other holy wells in its size, one could almost say its grandeur. Whereas most holy wells are small, perhaps with a rudimentary stone covering, perhaps just a damp hole in the ground, St Winefride's Well has, in addition to the large enclosed well basin where the water continually bubbles up, a large exterior bathing pool; the well is also enclosed in an elaborate early sixteenth-century stone building with a chapel on the upper floor. Many original carvings echoing the nature of the building, e.g. a sick person being carried on a helper's back, still survive, and close attention to the stonework also reveals graffiti left by pilgrims of earlier centuries.

According to legend the well came into existence when Gwenfrewi (the more familiar versions of her name, Winefride, Winifred, and Wenefred, are derived through Latin and English from this Welsh name), a seventh-century virgin, was harassed by Caradoc, a prince's son, who tried to rape her. Enraged by her refusal, he cut off her head as she fled to the church. Where her head fell, a spring began to flow – and St Beuno, her uncle, was fortunately at hand to restore her head so that she was able to resume her life with no ill-effects save for a thin red line which remained visible around her neck – and which can sometimes be noted on depictions of Winefride as a saint. She became a nun and lived for the last fifteen years of her life at Gwytherin, a remote North Wales village. After her death, a cult grew up centred on her relics, which were moved to Shrewsbury Abbey in 1138. Thousands of pilgrims visited both Holywell and Shrewsbury in medieval times. King Henry V walked on **pilgrimage** from Shrewsbury to Holywell in 1416, and Edward IV is said to have done the same. Not even the Reformation was able to halt the pilgrimages to Holywell, which have continued to be as popular as ever through the centuries to the present day.

St Winefride's Well as it appeared 300 years ago, in 1713. It is still easily recognisable, though the scene is not now so rustic, and there is a modern road to the right of the well building and not a winding track.

The best example of pilgrim graffiti at St Winefride's Well.

In addition to the well, chapel and bathing pool, there is also a small converted mid-Victorian gatehouse beside the pool which houses a statue of the Virgin and Child (where pilgrims leave offerings of rosaries draped over the figures) and a colourful stained-glass window depicting saints Winefride and Beuno sitting together by the well. The well has a permanent custodian and regular opening hours, and has recently undergone an extensive programme of maintenance and renovation. There is now a museum housing items connected to the history of the well, such as pilgrim banners, as well as displays recording details of the well's history. Visitors can take away bottles of well water, and buy souvenirs of St Winefride in the well shop. Despite all the recent developments, St Winefride's Well retains its primary function as a holy well, where many people still come to bathe for cures. There is also a daily service, with veneration of St Winefride's relic, during the pilgrimage season (from Pentecost to the end of September).

Sources: Cures: Hulse *Father Ryan's Diary*. **St Winefride and the history of Holywell:** Hulse *Father Ryan's Diary*.

The heading of a broadsheet dated 1776, describing the well and depicting St Winefride.

Cures and curses

I

Immersion

There were three kinds of immersion: immersion for the purposes of Christian **baptism**; ascetic immersion practised by saints and monks and other holy people wishing to undertake an act of penitence; and immersion for healing purposes. Ascetic immersion could take place in a river, a stream, a pond, a tub of cold water – or in a holy well. It was best if the water was ice-cold, since the practice was often performed 'to overcome the lust of the flesh'. St Monenna, a sixth-century Irish abbess, would recite the psalms at night, standing up to her breasts or her shoulders in a well. Some holy wells were reputed to have acquired their 'holiness' from such acts of ascetic immersion, for example Ffynnon Ddyfnog, Llanrhaeadr (Denbigh), where St Dyfnog stood each night under the well's outflow, reciting the psalms. Ascetic immersion was a regular ritual practice performed by pilgrims to *St Winefride's Well*, **Holywell**, into the late nineteenth century, and it is still found in Ireland, for example as part of the Lough Derg pilgrimage ritual.

Children would sometimes be immersed, both for their general good and for specific healing purposes. Aristotle recorded that the Celts had a custom of 'plunging their newborn children into a cold river', which doesn't seem a desirable practice unless you are trying to toughen up the infant from the very start. In Wales children from

One of the series of windows in St Neot church, Cornwall, depicting scenes in the life of St Neot, shows him sitting with his feet in his holy well, reading the psalms. This is a rare, possibly unique, British medieval example of this iconographic motif. The Life of St Neot tells how he was wont to stand in the fountain repeating the entire psalter, 'as an act of self-mortification'. Artwork: Anthony Wallis

Rhaeadr (Powys) were dipped in 'a small rill [streamlet] called Bwci's Wave', believed to possess 'a mysterious virtue'. Rituals specifically intended to be used to heal sick infants often involved immersion, or dipping, in a holy well, as for example at *Madron Well* (Cornwall). In order to cure rickets, children would be taken to the well on the first three Sundays in May, stripped naked, and plunged into the water, the person holding them having to stand facing the sun. After the dipping the children were passed nine times round the well from east to west, and after dressing were laid on St Madron's Bed, a grassy mound beside the altar in St Madron's Chapel, which may represent the traditional site of the saint's tomb. It was considered a good omen if they slept, or if the well bubbled. At Ffynnon Ddier in Bodfari (Denbigh), to prevent a child crying in the night it would be dipped up to its neck at three of the corners of the well. Chickens would be offered at this time, a cockerel for a boy and a pullet for a girl, and it was also part of the ritual to walk nine times round the well. Such **circumambulation** was a survival of pre-Reformation ritual practice.

Adult immersion in a holy well for healing purposes also occurred, sometimes voluntary, when the patient simply walked into the well, but sometimes involuntary. Involuntary immersion was a favourite 'cure' for madness, the procedure being known as **bowssening** in Cornwall; presumably the rationale was that the shock of being suddenly pushed into the cold water would bring the lunatics to their senses. It somehow seems doubtful that it ever worked.

Sources: Ascetic immersion: Gougaud 1927: Pt 2 Ch.2. **St Dyfnog:** Jones 1954: 35. **Immersion of children; Bwci's Wave:** Jones 1954: 81. **Madron:** Quiller-Couch 1894: 125–38. **Ffynnon Ddier:** Davies 1959: 62.

Incubation

Part of the healing ritual at some holy wells, especially in Wales, was the period of incubation, that is, time spent by the pilgrim asleep in a room at the well set aside for that purpose, or at some other place near to the well, during which it was believed that the saint would visit the sick person and activate the healing process. This was a procedure almost certainly borrowed from the Classical world, via the Romans, along with other practices (see **Celtic influence**), it being a feature of numerous shrines around the Mediterranean, for example in Greece, Rome, Asia Minor, Egypt, etc., established there by *circa* 400. The practice is likely to have been transferred relatively early to Wales, by *circa* 500, as an integral aspect of the cult of saints, and it survived at some Welsh wells into the nineteenth century.

One of the most elaborate Welsh rituals incorporating incubation took place at Llandegla (Denbigh) where people suffering from epilepsy would visit Ffynnon Degla in search of a cure. The complicated ritual involved a cockerel or a hen (the sex of the bird was matched to that of the patient) and took place at the well and then the church, where the sufferer would have to lie under the communion table covered with a carpet and with the church Bible as a pillow until daybreak. Almost certainly,

An early twentieth-century drawing of St Canna's Chair from S. Baring-Gould and John Fisher, The Lives of the British Saints, *vol.2. It still survives, but to the casual observer it looks like any other abandoned block of stone.*

sleeping under the altar took the place of the original medieval incubation at or on the saint's tomb, which was destroyed at or soon after the Reformation.

Among other Welsh locations, incubation was also practised at Ffynnon Beuno, Clynnog Fawr, as recorded in Pennant's *Tours in Wales*, at *Ffynnon Gybi*, Llangybi, and at Ffynnon Celynin, Llangelynin (all in Gwynedd). Since most wells were not large or elaborate enough to boast of a separate room where incubation could take place, local farmhouses were often used instead, a bed being set aside for that purpose. Sometimes there was a special saint's bed, or chair, or other stone formation close to the well where the sick person was taken to lie after treatment at the well. At Llangan (Pembroke) visitors to St Canna's Well might try to sleep afterwards on nearby St Canna's Chair; while at Llangybi (Ceredigion) the sick person visiting Ffynnon Gybi would afterwards be taken up the hill behind the well and there placed under Llech Gybi, 'Cybi's slab', actually the remains of a prehistoric burial chamber. If they slept, 'it is an infallible sign of recovery: if not, death'.

Sources: History of incubation: Hamilton 1906. **Ffynnon Degla:** Jones 1954: 104. **Canna's Chair:** Jones 1954: 15. **Llech Gybi:** Edward Lhuyd's *Parochialia* quoted in Jones 1954: 15.

L

Llyn Cerrig Bach

This Welsh lake has already been mentioned in **Deposition** as the site of a major find of Iron Age objects presumed to have been thrown into the lake as offerings to the gods. But it merits its own entry because what happened there has links to the folklore which later developed at holy wells, and also because it is an atmospheric place worth visiting (despite the proximity of the neighbouring air base).

The incubation ritual at Llandegla (Denbigh) required the patient to spend the night in the church, sleeping under the altar with the Bible for a pillow. Artwork: Anthony Wallis

The discovery of a large quantity of metalwork and bones only came about because of the construction of the Royal Air Force base at Valley on Anglesey. Peat was being taken from a nearby peat bog for use in the creation of runways in the early 1940s, and while it was being spread over the sand the first objects were found and collected together by the workmen. Everything came from the peat bog to the west of the present-day lake known as Llyn Cerrig Bach ('the lake of the small stones or rocks'): in the Iron Age the lake would have been larger. The objects were all below a cliff (possibly described in the lake name) that would have been about eleven feet above the level of the lake, clearly providing an ideal platform from which to throw the objects into the water.

One hundred and forty-four objects were found, and it is probable that more remain undiscovered in the peat. Weaponry such as swords, spears, a dagger, scabbards and parts of shields, iron tyres and decorative bronzework from light chariots, horse bits and other related metalwork, iron currency bars, smithing tongs, sickles, remains of bronze cauldrons and a bronze trumpet, and iron gang-chains which were used to link captives at the neck: these had all been thrown into the lake. (Some of the items found are illustrated in **Deposition**.) Much of the metalwork was broken, probably intentionally in the same way that **pins** were sometimes bent before being thrown into a holy well, possibly to render them unusable and thus symbolically converting

Llyn Cerrig Bach, Valley, Anglesey.

them from tool to offering. Professor Miranda Aldhouse Green has noted that damaging bronze or iron objects by snapping or bending them demanded 'the expenditure of considerable force' and this 'would seem to reflect violence of a kind, akin to the sacrificial act of killing.' Much of the metalwork was connected with warfare, and it is possible that at least some of the objects may have been deposited after battles had been won, as thank-offerings to the gods.

Large quantities of animal bones (but no human bones) were also found in the lake: ox, sheep and pig probably represent the remains of ceremonial feasts, while horse and dog bones may have come from sacrificed animals. Llyn Cerrig Bach was clearly once an important sacred lake, in use for several hundred years, and possibly of national rather than simply local importance. It could have been of major importance to the Celtic Druids who held their last stand against the Romans on the island of Anglesey. The metalwork contains nothing dated later than AD 60, and this was the year when Suetonius Paulinus invaded Anglesey and defeated the Druids in a battle by the Menai Strait. Some of the deposits may represent the Druids' last-ditch attempt to call the gods to their aid.

Llyn Cerrig Bach is on the northern edge of Valley Airfield a few miles south-east of Holyhead in the west of Anglesey, and a mile south of Caergeiliog, beside a minor

An engraving depicting the massacre of the Druids by the Romans; after a painting by R. Smirke.

road. Its location is shown by a descriptive plaque on a boulder; there is roadside parking. OS map reference: SH 306765.

Sources: Iron Age metalwork: Lynch 1970: 249–77, including drawings of many of the finds; Green 1994: 5–8. **Killing objects:** Green 2001: 22–4, 50.

Love magic

One form of **divination** practised at holy wells by young people unsurprisingly concerned love and romance. St Agnes' Well at Cothelstone (Somerset) was one that was visited by would-be lovers (St Agnes was a Roman virgin martyr who refused to consider marriage, preferring to devote her life to God), and St Agnes Eve (the night between 20 and 21 January, the 21st being her feast day) was the traditional time for love divination. As one story about the practice so quaintly phrased it: 'And it come to a St Agnes Eve when maids creepy over to her well at Cothelstone and whisper their heart's desire when 'tis dark, and if St Agnes do fancy the maiden she'll send a husband that year.'

Madron holy well (Cornwall) was another place where young girls would try to find out if they would soon be married. They would visit on the first Sunday in May and throw two pebbles, pins or straw crosses into the water, and if they sank together, the answer was positive. Another version was that two pieces of straw fixed with a pin would be floated on the water and any bubbles forming would be counted, that number being the number of years before any marriage would occur. Bubbles also featured in another Cornish ritual at Alsia Well in St Buryan parish which would be visited by young girls who wanted to learn how soon they would find a lover. They would drop a pebble or a pin into the water and the number of bubbles rising as it sank would be the number of years they had to wait.

Crochan Llanddwyn (the Crochan cauldron) was a spring in the sand dunes near Newborough on Anglesey, which now survives as a small pool in the forest that was planted on the dunes. An old woman from Newborough used to predict the love lives of young visitors to the spring, by means of the movements of the eels which lived in it. William Williams, writing *circa* 1800, told how his mother had gone there when a girl and spread her handkerchief on the water, whereupon two eels appeared. The old woman told her that her husband would be a stranger from southern Caernarfonshire: and her prophecy came to pass.

There was a well in Northumberland where girls could even get to see the face of their future husband – if they were lucky. They would visit the Collie Well at Hartley on St Agnes Eve at midnight. Kneeling by the well with their hands behind them, they would sing:

> Agnes sweet and Agnes fair,
> Hither, hither, now repair,
> Bonny Agnes, let me see
> The lad who's to marry me.

At that point the face of the lucky man would appear reflected in the water. This would also happen at St Caradog's Well, Haverfordwest (Pembroke), but the woman had to throw three pins into the well on Easter Monday and then gaze intently at the water. One woman saw 'the evil face of a hairy monster'!

Young people would frequent the Silver Well at Llanblethian (Vale of Glamorgan) in order to test their lovers' fidelity, which they would do by collecting blackthorn points (by breaking them from the bush, not cutting them) and throwing them into the well. If the point floated, the lover was faithful, but if it sank he or she was unfaithful. A point which whirled around showed that the lover was cheerful, but if it stayed still he or she was stubborn and sulky. At Ffynnon Gybi at Holyhead (Anglesey) girls would use their handkerchiefs with the same intention, spreading them on the surface of the water (or they could use a rag or a feather). If the cloth moved to the south, they knew that their lover was honourable; if it moved north, the opposite was true. Usually it was girls and women who sought reassurance at holy wells, but some wells were visited by couples in search of good luck for their marriage.

Love magic

Trying to discover who one's husband would be was not always a happy affair, as a woman following the ritual at St Caradog's Well learned when she saw an evil face. Artwork: Anthony Wallis

Once they were married, the bride's first concern, if she lived at St Keyne in Cornwall, would be to get to the holy well and be the first to drink the water, thus obtaining mastery in the household. This belief was set out in a poem by Robert Southey, about a man who hurried to the well after his wedding in order to drink of the water first, so that he would 'be Master for life'. But he was too late:

> I hasten'd as soon as the wedding was done,
> And left my Wife in the porch;
> But, i'faith, she had been wiser than me,
> For she took a bottle to Church.

Possibly a similar belief attached to a holy well in Hay-on-Wye (Powys), also dedicated to St Keyne. C.G. Portman, who early in the twentieth century collected information on the holy wells of the town, saw the eighteenth-century diary of a man living across the river in Clyro which told how a newly married woman secretly went off to Hay in her wedding dress, to get to the well and drink the water, unknown to her husband, so that she could 'rule over him'. Portman also knew an old lady living in Hay who said whenever she heard of a domestic squabble, 'Oh, he [or she] got to the well first'; and when speaking of a wedding she would say, 'Tom or Nell? First to the well.' The same belief was found at other Welsh wells; and in South Wales it was

St Keyne Well, Cornwall.

the custom for a newly married wife to drop pins into the well at her new home when she first entered it, in order to ensure good luck during her first year of marriage. It was believed that failure to do so resulted in bad luck.

Sources: St Agnes Well: Tongue 1965: 23–4. **Madron well:** Quiller-Couch 1894: 132. **Alsia Well:** Hunt 1985: 20. **Crochan Llanddwyn:** Jones 1954: 111–12. Jones mistakenly confuses this well with Ffynnon Ddwynwen on nearby Llanddwyn Island. **Collie Well:** Binnall & Dodds: 32. **St Caradog's Well:** Jones 1954: 111. **Silver Well:** Bowen 1988: 12. **Ffynnon Gybi:** Rhys 1893: 62; Jones 1954: 111. **Hay-on-Wye:** Portman 1907. **South Wales:** Jones 1954: 113.

M

Miraculous powers

Some wells and springs were believed to possess powers that one would not normally associate with water. For example, the spring on Dartmoor (Devon) that John Fitz came across when he got lost while riding with his wife on the moor, which provided him with much needed refreshment, also appears to have had the power to show him the way, for no sooner had he drunk from it than he found he was no longer lost. He may have been pixy-led, with the water having the ability to break the spell which caused him such confusion. In his gratitude he had a memorial stone erected at the well, which thereafter became known as Fitz's Well.

Old Peter Dodd's Well (now lost) at Westhoughton (Lancashire) was believed to be able to foretell the weather. In the nineteenth century the well was covered by a stone grid containing holes, and if the weather was going to be fine, a piece of paper held over one of the holes would be drawn through into the well. If however rain was coming, the paper would be blown upwards. Farmers at harvest time would ask, 'What does the well say? Is it blowing up or down?'

On New Year's Day the first visitor to Lower (or Riverside) Well in Northumberland who took the first draught of water, known as the **flower of the well**, was believed to acquire the power to pass through keyholes and fly through the air, an achievement which they would retain for the whole year. (For details of other miraculous powers, see also **Desecration and destruction; Divination; Healing**.)

Sources: Fitz's Well: Hope 1893: 63. **Old Peter Dodd's Well:** Taylor 2005: 23. **Lower Well:** Hope 1893: 106.

Modern use of holy wells

That people still credit holy-well water with magical powers is shown by their actions. For example, in 2003 it was reported that athletes from Anglesey who were travelling to Guernsey to compete in the Island Games were taking with them a vial of water taken from *St Seiriol's Well,* Penmon. Each delegation at the games would take a bottle of water from its island, and as Anglesey's head of leisure, Aled Roberts, said, 'During the opening ceremony the water will be mixed together in a fountain. The Olympics has its flame and we have water as our emblem. Naturally, we are hoping it will bring us some good luck.' The fountain is kept running throughout the games; it presumably symbolises a link with each competitor's home country.

People still superstitiously acknowledge the power of **wishing wells** by throwing in a coin and making a wish; and this impulse is either being passed on from one generation to the next, or is instinctive, judging by various modern water-cult practices that have been recorded, such as that at the Ladywell at Speen (Berkshire) where children would throw a coin into the water and make a wish for success in a school test or exam. In Ireland students are developing the habit of leaving at wells the pens they have used in exams, presumably as votive offerings in hopes of ensuring a successful outcome. Also seen recently as offerings at Irish holy wells are children's comforters, inhalers, and identity cards; whereas elsewhere in Britain the new style of offering tends to the natural, such as flowers, crosses made of twigs, and other simple objects gathered from close by.

I recently came across a new slant in the spiritual use of water, in the form of a 'pebble pool'. This was seen in Holy Trinity church, Llandudno (Conwy) (and also in Llanrhos church in the same diocese) and it took the form of a small bowl (the pool)

Pebble Pool inside Holy Trinity church, Llandudno, photographed in 2005.

of water, beside which was a supply of large coloured glass beads. An explanatory leaflet tells us that 'each pebble placed in the pool represents a prayer', and that 'before you place the pebble in the water, you may wish to take it in your hand and find a quiet place in our church and say this prayer [quoted in the leaflet], or say the prayer as you drop the pebble into the water'. Once a week the pool is emptied and the pebbles placed on an altar in the church, with prayers being said. The pebble pool takes the place of candles purchased and lit by pilgrims, which are now being seen in many more Protestant as well as Catholic churches, but which are in this nervous age also beginning to be seen as a fire risk. It is interesting that fire is being replaced by water – and the use of the pebble pool of course echoes the custom of dropping offerings (in some cases pebbles) into holy wells.

There is a growing interest in visiting holy wells throughout Britain and Ireland, and the fact that people leave offerings – of whatever kind – shows that they are not merely visiting, but are also attempting to interact with the spirit of the place. The growth of Internet use has also enabled people to learn more about holy wells, and also to participate in other sacred water projects, such as the 'Project of love and thanks to water' initiated by Harmonik Ireland, whereby they were aiming 'to purify water on Earth by our prayers of love and thanks'.

Sources: Island Games: Greenwood 2003. **Ladywell:** Bayley 1995: 5. **Ireland:**

Personal communication from Allen Kennedy, April 2005. **Pebble pool:** Leaflet 'The Pebble Pool' from Holy Trinity church, Llandudno. **Project of love and thanks to Water:** www.harmonikireland.com (Irish Holy Wells).

Mosses and other plants

At a few wells, plants naturally growing there have been drawn into the folklore of the well. There were two types of moss that formerly grew in the bathing pool at *St Winefride's Well*, **Holywell** (Flint). One was known as St Winifred's Hair – this long-branched moss was identified as *Jungermannia asplenioides* – and it was collected by pilgrims and dried. Later it would be moistened with water from the well and used as a poultice for the cure of sprains and other physical problems. This practice continued into the twentieth century and, like the water itself, and pebbles from the well-bottom, the moss functioned as a third-class relic of the saint. The same species of moss also grows (or grew) in other Welsh holy wells, and it can still be seen in Ffynnon Fair, Cefn Meiriadog (Denbigh).

The other moss which grew at St Winefride's Well was *Byssus jolithus*, which produced what appeared to be bright red stains on stones in the well. Throughout the Middle Ages these marks were said to represent indelible bloodstains resulting from Winefride's martyrdom. Occasionally the moss would shape itself into 'miraculous' pictures on the stones; and in addition it smelled of violets or incense. The two mosses growing at St Winefride's Well were named in Thomas Pennant's *A Tour in Wales* (1784), and their names came from Linnaeus.

At St Arilda's Well, Oldbury on Severn (Gloucester), the water is said to be red with the saint's **blood**, commemorating her martyrdom by beheading, an act performed by a man whose advances she spurned. The reddish staining on the stones in the well which gave rise to the legend in fact comes from a freshwater alga by the name of *Hildebrandia rivularis*. This grows only in water at a certain temperature; and pools where the well water flows, under the shade of trees, are also a favoured spot for the 'blood'.

Sometimes plants growing close to a holy well are favoured for medicinal purposes, as was the case in Glen Elg (Highland) where the local people who used the well called Tobar Bhan used to gather watercress and also a herb known as 'flower of the three mountains' growing beside it, which they then used for healing. The other significant plant found growing at holy wells is, of course, the tree, and for more information on their importance in holy well lore, see **Trees**.

Sources: St Winefride's Well: Pennant 1784. **St Arilda's Well:** Bradshaw 1998: 13. **Tobar Bhan:** MacGregor 1935/1948: 112.

This late-eighteenth century depiction of St Winefride's Well by Moses Griffith includes a sketch of the moss known as St Winifred's Hair.

N

Names

In some of the areas covered by this book, well names are often found in the original language of the area, so that in Wales the name *ffynnon* is often seen, this being of course the Welsh for 'well'. In Scottish and Irish Gaelic the equivalent word is *tobar* (or *tober, tubber, toubir*). On the Isle of Man, you will find the Manx word *chibbyr*. In Cornwall *venton* or *fenten* occurs, this being the same as the Welsh *ffynnon*. Both *ffynnon* and *venton* are derived from the Latin *fons* – spring or source – which is another factor suggestive of the distinct possibility that the well cult as we know it in these islands was essentially a creation of the Late Classical or Early Christian period, adopted from Europe as part of a fully formed cult of the saints.

The development of well names over the centuries, and sometimes their precise meaning, is a complex affair. Many holy well names commemorate the saint to whom the well is dedicated, or some other person associated with it (e.g. Robin Hood's Well), or else the place where the well is located, or a notable feature of the well or its surroundings ('spout', for example – in Welsh *pistyll* – to describe one whose water spouts forth; or **ebbing and flowing well** for one with those properties), or the traditions practised there (e.g. Rag Well, Pin Well), or the ailment it was believed to cure (e.g. Eye Well), or some folklore connected with it – for example, Hart-Leap Well, Boar's Well. But occasionally the name is a real curiosity, and a few examples follow.

The name of the Whistlebitch Well at Utkinton (Cheshire) was thought locally to have described the whistling sound the water made as it came out of the ground, although its true derivation is unknown. Its pre-Reformation name was St Stephen's Well, while *circa* 1600 it was known as the New-Found Well.

An early engraving dated 1600 of the once-famous New-Found Well, later called the Whistlebitch Well.

NEWES OVT OF Cheshire of the new found Well.

Imprinted at London by F. Kingston for T. Man. 1600.

The name of Peg o' Nell's Well at Clitheroe (Lancashire) has two possible derivations. In the most popular, Peg o'Nell was the spirit of the well, the ghost of a servant at nearby Waddow Hall, who died while fetching water from the well after her mistress expressed a wish that she would fall and break her neck. Thereafter, whenever something went wrong at the hall, it was blamed on Peg's curse. The other possibility is that the name came from a headless statuette by the spring, which possibly represents St Margaret of Antioch (Peg or Peggy is of course a pet name for people christened Margaret). Peg also pops up elsewhere, such as at Peggy's Spout, a spring near Top Lock in Lancashire, and Peggy Well near Bradford: she may be a memory of an ancient water goddess – a water spirit inhabiting the River Tees was known as Peg Powler.

Another possible 'goddess' figure was Mother Red Cap, who gave her name to a spring at Harlestone (Northampton) – or was she one of the Little People? A creature named Redcap was a malignant Northumberland goblin; a better-natured Redcap lived in Perthshire, while the Dutch redcaps were brownies.

The Starwell near Biddestone (Wiltshire) gets its name (used by travelling people; its other name is more prosaically Holy Well) from the tiny star-shaped fossils which can be found there. They come from the sea creatures called crinoids, but local folklore says they are petrified flowers which dropped from the elder trees which grow round the spring.

Sources: Well-names: Harte 2000; Skyvova 2005: 9. **Whistlebitch:** Hulse 'Whistlebitch' 1994: 24; Crawshaw 1995: 28. **Peg o' Nell's Well:** Nelson 1998:12. **Peggy:** Hilton 1997: 18. **Mother Red Cap:** Thompson 1915: 72. **Starwell:** Jordan 1998: 17.

O

Offerings

A common offering to the spirit of the well during the last couple of centuries (but not before the Industrial Revolution, of course) was a household pin, usually bent (see **Pins**), but today people do not carry pins and now coins are the most common item to be thrown into wells.

Coins were also offered in earlier times – groats, pennies and farthings, all coins no longer current – and also **rags**, buckles, buttons, thorn-points, flowers and stones. At the end of the nineteenth century a visitor to Chibbyr Uney (St Runy's Well) on the Isle of Man noted that visitors either dropped coins in the well or left three white pebbles close to it, the pebbles being substituted for coins by the poor. Another visitor a few years later found a large pile of white pebbles close to the well. White quartz pebbles were associated with burials, which is probably why fishermen would not have them in the ballast in their boats. White or quartz stones were also left as offerings at some Welsh wells, a custom of some probable antiquity since they were also found in prehistoric tumuli (burial mounds) and at early Christian sites, such as on the altars of Manx keeills (chapels).

Also on the Isle of Man, a visitor to Chibbyr yu Argid noticed 'bits of Latin prayers scratched upon the rocks', which is an earlier version of the messages (prayers and requests) written on pieces of paper that modern pilgrims sometimes leave at holy wells. Pilgrims often feel the urge to leave something of themselves in the form of a written inscription, hence the graffiti (usually initials and dates) that have been carved on tree trunks, or on stone walls where there is a building at the well. Pieces of cloth are also left (see **Cloutie wells; Rags**); and some unusual offerings have included eggs, horses, fowls, human hair (all in Wales). A colleague living in Ireland has noted recent changes in the kinds of objects left as offerings there: 'Recently, apart from leaving children's comforters, inhalers, ID cards, etc., students have been leaving the pens they used in exams.' (See also **Votive offerings; Wishing wells**.)

Opposite top: *Pebbles left as offerings at St Fechín's Well, Omey Island, Co. Galway. Photo: Ann and John Welton.*

Bottom: *A wide variety of items left as offerings at Fanad holy well, Co. Donegal, can be spotted in this photograph including inhalers, pens, comforter, watch, baseball cap, St Brigid's Cross. Photo: Allen Kennedy*

Offerings

Llyn Glasfryn: Grace's Well is in the bushes by the shore and now overgrown. The standing stone in the foreground, when seen from the big house nearby, resembles 'a female figure hurrying along, with the wind slightly swelling out her veil and the skirt of her dress'. It was remembered by a resident of the big house that when he was a boy (possibly mid-nineteenth century) the stone was partially white-washed and an old bonnet and shawl would be placed on this 'would-be statue'. The field in which the stone stands was known as Cae'r Ladi (the Lady's Field), and the legends surrounding the stone, the lake, and the well are very complex, involving a ghost, a mermaid, a woman who was changed into a swan, and a terrifying figure called Morgan who lived in the lake.

Sources: Types: Jones 1954: 92–3. **Chibbyr Uney:** Paton 1941: 186. **White stones:** Jones 1954: 95–6. **Chibbyr yu Argid:** Paton 1941: 189. **Unusual:** Jones 1954: 93, 96. **Modern Irish:** Comment by Allen Kennedy, 7 April 2005.

Overflowing

In Welsh folklore there are several instances of a well overflowing because of neglect by the person who looked after it. The usual story was that a female guardian who was supposed to cover the well at night failed to do so and it overflowed, resulting in the formation of a lake or the drowning of a town. Llyn Glasfryn near Llangybi (Gwynedd) was formed when Ffynnon Grassi (Grace's Well) was left uncovered: the door was always supposed to be kept shut except when water was being drawn.

Folklore records that Bala Lake formed when a local holy well was left uncovered and overflowed.

Grassi may be the one who left the well uncovered, and after the lake formed she could be heard moaning and weeping as she wandered about the field.

The great lake at Bala (Gwynedd) was also the result of an uncovered well, Ffynnon Gywer at Llangower; and, among other Welsh examples, it was a man named Owen (Owain Glyndwr?) who forgot to replace the flagstone over a well on Mynydd Mawr at Llanarthney (Carmarthen), resulting in the formation of Llyn Llech Owen (the lake of Owen's slab). On a much larger scale, the whole of Cardigan Bay, once dry land, was allegedly submerged when a well was left uncovered.

There are also similar inundations recorded in Irish folklore, one of them concerning the origin of the River Boyne. There was a special well on Carbury Hill (Kildare) in the garden of King Nechtan which was forbidden to women, but the king's wife Boan went there and walked three times round it anticlockwise (see **Circumambulation**), causing a grave insult to the well, the water from which rose up and chased her out to sea, where she drowned: the water flow became the River Boyne. Loch Gamhna on the Cavan–Longford border was formed when a woman washed dirty clothes in a well. A calf jumped out and ran towards the valley, the water following behind and creating the lake.

Sources: Welsh inundations: Rhys 1901: Ch.6. **Llyn Glasfryn:** Rhys 1901: 367–75. **Irish inundations:** Logan 1980: 48–9.

P

Petrifying wells

The best-known petrifying well in Britain must be that at *Knaresborough* (North Yorkshire), but it is not the only well believed to possess the strange quality of apparently turning to stone any object immersed in its water. Another petrifying well is St Cuthbert's or Cubert's Well, strangely located inside a cave on the shore of Holywell Bay (Cornwall). These two wells could not be more different, but both could be classed as wonders within the field of holy wells. T. Quiller-Couch waxed quite lyrical when describing St Cuthbert's:

> This well has Nature only for its architect, no mark of man's hand being seen in its construction; a pink enamelled basin, filled by drippings from the stalactitic roof, forms a picture of which it is difficult to describe the loveliness. What wonder, then, that the simple folk around should endow it with mystic virtues?

The apparent petrifaction which occurs at some wells is caused by the water being calcareous (containing calcium carbonate or lime) so that anything coated in it hardens and appears to be made of stone, a classic demonstration of this being the teddy bears and other objects hung up at the Knaresborough petrifying well. Such wells are commoner than generally realised, and other examples include a spring above Stowey church (Somerset), the Wor Well at Tetbury (Gloucester), and several springs in Lincolnshire such as the Petrifying Springs at Dragonby and Whitton, and the Witch Hole Spring at Goulceby.

Sources: St Cuthbert's Well: Hope 1893: 34; Quiller-Couch 1894: 54–7. **Stowey and Tetbury wells:** Quinn 1999: 194–5, 3. **Lincolnshire springs:** Thompson 1999: 22, 24, 39.

Pilgrimage

A pilgrimage can be either a small, personal affair, comprising oneself and maybe one or two other like-minded pilgrims, or a large-scale organised event. The practice of pilgrimage is now thought of as predominantly an Irish tradition, and indeed it has survived most purely in Ireland, where Catholicism remained the dominant religion. However before the Reformation, there was no difference in the pilgrimage tradition in Catholic countries, and in late medieval times England was especially famous for its pilgrimage tradition.

In Ireland the pilgrimage event focused not just on a particular holy well but usually encompassed a variety of 'stations' at the pilgrimage site, such as a tree, a carved stone, a heap of stones that the pilgrims would add to, a saint's footprint visible in a rock, or a saint's bed, a medieval church or chapel, a High Cross, all equally as important as the holy well. The routine would normally centre on 'rounding', or

Some of the objects hung in the water flow at the Knaresborough petrifying well, which have slowly 'turned to stone'.

circumambulation, of the stations, which was done all the while saying the Rosary and the prescribed Paters, Aves and Glorias. The whole procedure could take some time, especially if there was also a sacred mountain to climb, such as Croagh Patrick (Mayo). The Lough Derg (Donegal) *turas* (pilgrimage) lasts three days (though a one-day option has just been introduced); earlier, it lasted nine days, and in the Middle Ages it lasted fourteen or fifteen days. The classical *turas* at Ballyvourney (Cork) consisted in making the same set of rounds daily for twenty-one days, and this was still being done occasionally up to fifty years ago. Before modern transport, a pilgrimage could take weeks or months in total, if getting to and from the pilgrimage site is also considered.

Pilgrimages are generally linked in the popular consciousness with the Middle Ages, but they have always been popular, and in the early twenty-first century they are continuing to grow in popularity throughout the United Kingdom. Some are small local pilgrimages held just once a year, other locations such as Holywell and Walsingham are the focus of large, regular pilgrimages. There is an annual

Pilgrimage to St Winefride's Well, Holywell, in June 1987.

pilgrimage in South Wales from the Cistercian Abbey at Llantarnam to St Mary's Well at Penrhys (Rhondda), following a route taken by pilgrims in the late medieval period; and there are also regular organised pilgrimages to *St Mary's Well* (Ladywell) at Fernyhalgh (Lancashire). In West Penwith, the most westerly part of Cornwall, the Three Wells Walk is an annual event which began in May 1989 when a few friends met up at Sancreed and walked to Carn Euny Well, then to Sancreed Well and finally to *Madron Well.* Their intention was to use ancient footpaths, which would have been used in earlier times to reach the wells, and they worked out a route using tracks which linked the wells in a figure of eight, covering twelve miles in total. They also turned the walk into a pilgrimage, 'collecting water from each of the wells in turn and finally placing it in the last well in a simple blessing ceremony.'

A number of organised pilgrimages to *St Winefride's Well* at **Holywell** (Flint) are held throughout the summer months, some including processions through the town, the largest of these being the Annual National (Welsh) Roman Catholic Pilgrimage when many hundreds of pilgrims walk through the town behind a colourful display of banners, and with the saint's relic in its reliquary, on 22 June (if a Sunday) or on the Sunday immediately following this date.

The other most impressive pilgrimage at Holywell is the Annual Pan-Orthodox Pilgrimage held on the first Saturday in October, when icons are carried in the procession. There are regular pilgrimages to the Anglican and Catholic shrines at **Walsingham** (Norfolk) throughout the year, with more details to be found on the informative Walsingham website.

Some wells are known as pilgrims' wells: these may have simply been on a well-known pilgrimage route, such as St Edith's Well at Kemsing (Kent) close to the Pilgrim's Way leading to Canterbury, or they may have been themselves the focus of a pilgrimage.

Sources: In Ireland: Logan 1980: 21–34. **Three Wells Walk:** Straffon 1995: 7. **St Winefride's Well:** Kerridge 1998 (Spring): 21–5. **Walsingham:** www.walsingham.org.uk

Pins

The use of pins of one kind or another as **votive offerings** goes back into prehistory. At the same time as valuable weapons were being deposited in water, so too were pins, but whereas the weapons seem to have been dropped into deeper water from boats, pins and small ornaments have been found in shallow water, as if they were deposited from the bank of a lake or river. These early 'pins' may have been some sort of brooch or cloak-fastening; in fact, they were almost certainly not 'pins' as we understand the word, but were really offerings of jewellery. In more recent times the pins deposited in holy wells were probably chosen as offerings because they were easily available and also cheap, and so the dropping of pins into holy wells is probably a relatively modern custom which only developed after the Industrial Revolution with the mass production of pins and needles.

The pins which were dropped into wells were often bent, perhaps with the intention of exorcising the evil spirit that afflicted the person who offered the pin. When Ffynnon Faglan (St Baglan's Well) at Llanfaglan (Gwynedd) was cleaned out in the mid-nineteenth century, two basins-full of pins were found, all of them bent. When the well was in use, it was a wart well and the method used was to wash the wart in the well water, prick it with a pin, bend the pin and throw it into the well. The same procedure was followed at Ffynnon Gynhafal (Llangynhafal, Denbigh), but see **Warts** for a different procedure followed in Ireland. Ffynnon Gwynwy near Llangelynin (Conwy) was also a wart well where many crooked pins were deposited: nobody would touch the pins lest they 'caught' the warts attached to them.

Possibly the custom of bending a pin before dropping it into a well is a survival of the once-common practice of bending a coin at a moment of crisis. It was then offered as a promise to the saint to take the coin as an ex-voto to his or her shrine when the hoped-for event, be it a cure or whatever else, occurred; in the meantime it 'belonged' to the saint and once bent could not be used as currency. If the coin was bent in connection with sickness, it would be bent while being held above that part of the body which was thought to be ailing. Finds of bent coins, bent pilgrim tokens of pewter, and bent daggers and knives, in river mud, suggest that the practice was more widespread than is generally realised, and that ritual bending was not uncommon. A folk belief about bent pins was that they were 'lucky': 'crooked things being considered, according to long-standing tradition, as lucky things, as our grandmothers were wont to carry crooked sixpences in their purses.' However,

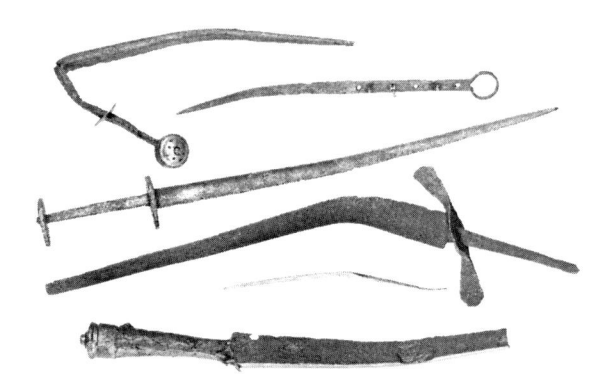

Some early sixteenth century knives and daggers, which had been deliberately bent or broken before being thrown into the River Thames from St Paul's Stairs in the City of London. Photo: Museum of London

Professor Miranda Aldhouse Green has interpreted the bending of iron and bronze objects such as swords and spears before they were deposited in a sacred pool or river as acts of ritual sacrifice. Perhaps such practices as these in prehistoric times were the origins of the later custom of bending pins and coins before using them as votive offerings.

A few Irish 'wells' are located in tree stumps, and that at Coney Island (Armagh) was called the Pin Well, since offerings of pins were stuck into the tree bark. There was also a tree well at Magheringaw (Antrim) where pins were stuck into the bark.

Sources: In prehistory: Bradley 2000: 53–4. **Ffynnon Gynhafal:** Jones 1954: 175. **Ffynnon Faglan:** Hartland 1893: 453. **Ffynnon Gwynwy:** Rhys 1893: 59. **Bending pins & coins:** Finucane 1977: 94–5; Duffy 1992: 183–5; Merrifield 1987: 91–2, 109–12. **'Crooked things':** Vaux 1902: 365. **Sacrifice:** Green 2001: 50–1. **Irish tree wells:** Logan 1980: 119.

Prehistory

The earliest evidence for water cults in Britain is suggestive rather than clear-cut, and relates to the time when earth and stone structures were first being built, beginning around 6,000 years ago. Some prehistorians have noted possible relationships between early structures and water: for example, in his book *The Stone Circles of the British Isles*, Aubrey Burl points out that 'Where an avenue of stones is associated with a stone circle it almost invariably leads from a source of water, indicating the importance of water in the ceremonies that took place in the rings.' And in *From Carnac to Callanish* he again comments on the apparent link between 'major ritual centres' and water:

> Avenue after avenue led from water to a stone circle: Broomend of Crichie from the River Don; Callanish from the direction of Loch Roag; the short Stanton Drew avenues from the River Chew; the extension at Stonehenge from the River Avon; the Kennet avenue from the springs and streams in the Kennet valley. The

Silbury Hill in Wiltshire, when autumn rain has filled the surrounding ditch.

> Beckhampton avenue crossed the Winterbourne brook. What rites were involved in these hydrographic associations remains unknown. Rituals of purification and fertility are not unlikely.

More recently, Francis Pryor has provided further evidence for the significance of water to people in the earliest prehistoric times. In *Britain BC* he discusses Mesolithic sacred landscapes which, he suspects, 'were marked out by paintings on natural rocks, and by special trees, ponds, springs or streams'. He also notes other instances where prehistoric sites are linked to water, including cursuses (linear earthworks) that cross water or end near boggy land that was probably originally open water, as for example the Newgrange cursus at the Bend of the Boyne in Ireland where there is also a strange structure known as the Monknewtown 'ritual pond', an earth enclosure 100 feet across which still holds water.

While this book was being written, the discovery was announced of a prehistoric ceremonial road in Wiltshire with a rammed flint surface, wider than many modern roads and more substantial than any other Neolithic track in Europe. It ran from the timber circle at the Durrington Walls henge down to the River Avon, thus probably linking the river, Durrington Walls, and nearby Woodhenge and Stonehenge in one complex, possibly a funerary monument. As archaeologists reinvestigate and reassess even the most well-known prehistoric monuments, the evidence for a clear link between early religions and water seems stronger than ever.

Following recent reassessment of that important prehistoric monument (and largest man-made prehistoric mound in Europe) known as Silbury Hill (Wiltshire), archaeologists have come to realise that water was important in the hill's functioning (though as yet it is not clear what the monument's significance was). It has a 165 by 85 metre 'cistern' or 'tank' attached to the ditches that surround it, and although no one is sure of the tank's purpose, in some parts of the world, such as India, similar tanks are focal points of ritual and ceremony. The mirror-like quality of the standing water – which when viewed from the summit of Silbury Hill would reflect the sky – may have been important; so too may the appearance that the water had captured the sun on its surface; also there may have been the belief that the water provided a link to the underworld: all these may have played a part in whatever rituals were practised at Silbury. Even today, and especially in winter, the ditches can be filled with water for long periods; and there are also springs (or wells) in the vicinity, one in the south-west ditch terminal being still used in the nineteenth century.

Some holy wells are in close proximity to prehistoric sites, but this may be purely coincidental. In Somerset St Sativola's Well at Wick lies close to a large earthen burial mound or tumulus: mothers would take their children and wash them in the water to cure skin and eye ailments, and sailors would use it to cure scurvy after being away at sea. Cromlechs (the remains of stone burial chambers, with a huge capstone supported table-like on upright stones) were located close to at least two wells on the St Davids peninsula (Pembroke), Ffynnon Penarthur (the Well at the end of Arthur's land – nothing to do with the famous King Arthur) and Naw Ffynnon (Nine Wells), though both cromlechs have now disappeared. At the latter site, there was a gory 'tradition' that 'in pagan times twelve maidens each under twelve years of age were burnt alive as a sacrifice on the stone altar there'; but such a tradition is found nowhere else, the content does not ring true, and indeed the reference to a 'stone altar' shows that the 'tradition' is relatively modern – and certainly fictional. A cromlech on the Gower peninsula of South Wales, known variously as Coetan Arthur (Arthur's Quoit) and Maen Ceti (Stone of Ceti), was, according to legend, a place of pagan worship until St David split it with his sword and then ordered a holy well to flow, thus christianising the site.

Some stones close to holy wells play a part in the rituals practised there and are described as the saint's stone or chair or bed. For example, people visiting St Canna's Well (Pembroke) seeking cures would drop a pin in the well, drink the water or bathe in it, and then sleep on St Canna's Chair not far from the well. (See also **Incubation**.) Some of these stones which became included in well rituals may originally have been part of prehistoric ritual sites, though such a direct link is rarely easy to prove. Francis Jones noted sixty-two examples of wells associated with megaliths in Wales, and fourteen wells close to tumuli, and many other instances of wells and antiquities being in close proximity can be found in England, Scotland and Ireland – but, as noted earlier, it is simply not possible to draw any conclusions from such proximity, and the nature of water cults in prehistoric Britain is a subject in need of serious research.

Sources: Siting of monuments: Burl 1976: 78; Burl 1993: 72; Pryor 2004: 176, 216–17, 282. **Ceremonial road:** *Yorkshire Post Today*, 15 October 2005. **Silbury Hill:**

Coetan Arthur, on the Gower Peninsula (Swansea).

'A Green Hill Long Ago', *British Archaeology*, 80 (January/February 2005): 12–19. **Significance of water:** Green 1992: 223. **St Sativola's Well:** Harte 'Somerset' 1985: 9. **St Davids Peninsula:** Trier 1995: 17–22. **Maen Ceti:** Jones 1954: 41. **Sacrifice:** Jones 1954: 26. **Wales:** Jones 1954: 14–18.

Prophecy

Prophecy differs from other methods of foretelling the future, such as **divination** or fortune-telling. Prophecies are usually uttered by people famed for their powers in that field, such as Nostradamus, or the biblical prophets such as Elijah and Isaiah, and concern historical events on a large scale, as opposed to the small-scale and personal nature of divination and fortune-telling. A famous Scottish prophet was known as the Brahan Seer: he was Kenneth MacKenzie, born at Uig on the Hebridean island of Lewis and believed to have lived in the seventeenth century. Unusually, one of his prophecies concerned a well, Tobar Tath (Taah) on Skye, and part of it in translation from the Gaelic said: 'There is the well called Tobar Taah, A well where yet there shall be war... ' And it told of men's deaths there, with 'the dead bones of well grown men' strewn on the white beach. But whether the Seer's prophecy about the well ever came true, no one seems to know.

It was sometimes believed that the odd behaviour of a holy well foretold some momentous national event, such as occurred at St Helen's Well, Rushton Spencer

Mother Shipton inn sign in Knaresborough, not far from the petrifying well.

(Stafford), which would sometimes run dry after overflowing for several years. This would always happen at the beginning of May, and in wet as well as dry seasons, and was believed to foretell a calamity. It happened before the Civil War began, before Charles I was executed, before the corn scarcity in 1670, and in 1679 when the Popish Plot (a supposed Catholic plot to murder Charles II) was discovered. A spring at Warlingham (Surrey) was said to flow only before important events, such as the restoration of Charles II to the throne in 1660, the plague in London in 1665, and the Revolution of 1668. The problem with this belief is that national events are taking place all the time, and if we tried to follow the same reasoning today we would be hard-pressed to know which of the many newsworthy events the spring was foretelling! The well at Ashill (Somerset) would sometimes appear to ebb and flow, and this was believed to presage some national disaster.

The price of corn was somehow foretold from the behaviour of two Midland springs, the Corn Spring at Atherstone (Warwick) and Dudley's Spring at Allesley (Coventry). A shortage of corn was foretold by a dry stream suddenly starting to flow near Hindon (Wiltshire), and another Wiltshire stream also forecast 'a dear year of corn'. This preoccupation with the supply and price of corn may seem quaint today, but of course in the seventeenth century people were very reliant on local food supplies and everyone suffered if the crops failed, unlike today when we import food from all corners of the world and have completely lost any sense of self-sufficiency.

A Warwickshire holy well between Whitmarsh and Radford foretold coming events through the medium of a church bell which had accidentally fallen into it when it was taken there from the old church to be 'reconsecrated' (according to a *History of Warwickshire*); more likely this is a garbled memory of the ancient ritual whereby a bell was washed in holy water, referred to as the 'baptising' of the bell, and it may have been taken to the well as part of the ritual. People would throw stones into the well at night, and 'in the morning their questions are answered by the sounding of the bell.' (See also **Bells**.)

The famous *Dropping Well*, a **petrifying well** at Knaresborough (North Yorkshire), also happens to be the birthplace of the famous prophetess Ursula Sontheil, better known as Mother Shipton, who was born in 1488 in a cave only yards from the well. Many books were published containing what were said to be her prophecies, but none appears to involve the well or its seemingly magical powers.

Sources: Tobar Tath: Forbes 1923: 428. **St Helen's Well:** Hope 1893: 156. **Warlingham:** Hope 1893: 164. **Ashill:** Harte 'Somerset' 1985: 3. **Corn springs:** Hope 1893: 168, 170. **Church bell:** Hope 1893: 168–9.

R

Rags

Rags were – and still are – often tied to trees and bushes at holy wells by those who came seeking a cure. The whole point of the rag was that it was supposed to be a piece of cloth from the clothing of the sick person. Leaving behind something that was formerly close to the sufferer symbolised separation. The rag symbolised the illness – the sufferer separated himself from the rag, and therefore from the illness – and on leaving the well left both rag and illness behind. There was also a belief that as the rag rotted, so too would the ailment disappear. Francis Jones noted that the earliest reference he had come across to the custom of leaving rags at wells dated back to 1618, when Christ's Well at Menteith (Stirling) was 'all tapestried about with old rags'.

At one Isle of Man well, Chibbyr Beltain, it was customary to say, when tying 'a bit of clout' (i.e. a rag) on to a briar by the well: 'I lift the water for the good of such and such a certain man, in the name of God, the Son, and the Holy Ghost.' At Ffynnon Elian (Conwy) the rags were customarily tied to the bushes using pieces of wool – natural wool, presumably the tufts left on brambles by passing sheep – and at some wells the wool actually took the place of rags.

(For more information on the use of rags or clouts see **Cloutie wells**.)

Sources: **Symbolism**: Carroll 1999: 34. **Christ's Well:** Jones 1954: 94–5. **Chibbyr Beltain**: Paton 1941: 192. **Ffynnon Elian:** Rhys 1893: 57.

A rag-bush at Doon Well, Co. Donegal. Photo: Allen Kennedy

Rejuvenation

The water from holy wells sometimes has apparently magical powers, even the ability to bring the dead back to life, according to legend. The tale told of the holy well at Garendon near Loughborough (Leicestershire) – known as the Monk's Well, or Holy Well Haw – involved a young woman who fled from Groby Castle to escape an unwanted suitor, and eventually collapsed exhausted, or even died, beside the well, where she was discovered early the next morning by a monk from the nearby hermitage. He carried her to the well and prayed over her while sprinkling her with well water – whereupon she came back to life, and after her eventual marriage she and her husband made a pilgrimage to the well.

The powers of rejuvenation attributed to some other wells are not quite so dramatic as at the Monk's Well, but useful nevertheless. One such, known as the Well of Youth, was on the remote island of St Kilda. A man leading a sheep on a lead came across a water source he did not know about, and drank from it, immediately feeling young again. He ran to the village to tell everyone, leaving the sheep at the well. When he went back, there was no sheep and no well to be seen: apparently he should have left a piece of iron at the well, and then neither it nor the sheep would have disappeared.

Sources: Holy Well Haw: Trubshaw 2002: Garendon. **The Well of Youth:** MacLeod 2000: 80.

The unconscious woman is carried to the Monk's Well where the water revives her. Artwork: Anthony Wallis

Relics

A relic of a saint can be a part of the saint's body, or a fragment of his or her clothing – anything which has been in contact with the saint, in fact – and such relics were believed to have special healing powers as well as creating a bond between saint and pilgrim if touched or kissed.

The widespread belief among the Catholic population in the power of saints' relics explains why in the early eleventh century a woman who had gone blind had a dream in which she was told that her sight would be restored if she washed her eyes in water that St Cuthbert's relic (part of his shroud) had been dipped in. Her son called a monk to the house, and finding that the old woman had total faith in the cure, he called for water to be brought from a nearby holy well – at Hartley in Northumberland. But strangely, the relic could not be made wet by immersion in the water. The monk drank the water himself and immediately lost all weariness and weakness. When the old woman's eyes were washed, she instantly regained her sight – the relic's contact with the water, even though the relic itself remained dry,

Pilgrims venerate the relic of St Winefride by kissing the reliquary in which the relic, one of the saint's bones, is held. This happens every year, but this photograph was taken during the National Pilgrimage to St Winefride's Well, Holywell, in June 1987.

had transformed the holy well water into a 'relic' itself. The significance of the relic remaining dry may be that although the water is transformed by the contact, the relic is unaffected and thus retains its integrity. There are many references in early sources to the technique of multiplying relics by touching objects, as well as water, to the original relic.

The eighth-century historian Bede, and many others, gave examples similar to the story of St Cuthbert's relic. It was once common to dip saints' relics into water, with a blessing, and then to use the water for healing purposes. The following story from the Isle of Man is also based on the belief that contact between water and a saint's relic can endow the water with healing powers, though in this case it was the contact between the water and the tomb wherein the bones once lay, which was enough to render the water holy. The bones themselves had long gone, but the mere fact that they had once been there was enough to sanctify the place.

The bones of St Maughold were believed to rest in a stone sarcophagus in the cemetery of St Maughold's church on the Isle of Man. However the coffin no longer contained any relics, only a continual supply of water from a spring which was 'sweet to the draught, wholesome to the taste, and it healed divers infirmities.' People visited this spring for its healing water, and various attempts were made to take away the stone, by people such as the King of the Norwegians who, when he subdued the island, wished for a constant supply of sweet water. But however deep they dug, the stone was found to be fixed even more deeply in the ground. The records concerning the spring in the sarcophagus date back to the twelfth century – in the early nineteenth century a sarcophagus was discovered in the right location when a new grave was being dug, but there was no spring, though various stone drains were found, suggesting that there was once a water supply close by.

The tradition connected with St Maughold's bones may have developed from a practice once common in Early Medieval Irish Christianity. Following continental examples, saints' bones were often placed in stone tombs or shrines that had small holes, so that items such as pieces of cloth could be briefly placed inside to make contact with the bones and thus become secondary relics. At some of the continental shrines, perfumed oil or water was poured into the shrine so that it could run over the relics and then run out through a hole at the base, where the liquid would be collected again and used as a relic. Possibly Celtic Christians attempted to reproduce this practice by allowing the waters of a sacred well (or of a well that became sacred by virtue of this practice) to flow over a stone reliquary containing some relic of the local saint, and something similar to this may be how the tradition of St Maughold's bones came into being.

For more information on relics, see also **Ampullae; Blood** (St Thomas's Well), and **Creation of wells** (holy wells that flowed in saints' graves).

Sources: Hartley: Balfour 1904: 3. **St Maughold:** Moore 1894: 223–4, quoting from *Trias Thaumaturga,* Sexta Vita S. Patricii, cap. cliii, 98, 99, 116.

Revelry

Certain wells were the focus for annual celebrations, such as, in the Penrith area of Cumbria, Shaking Bottle or Sugar Water Sunday, when on the four Sundays in May people would go to the four local holy wells and mix the water with liquorice or sugar and drink it while singing May carols. At Greystock the children would walk in procession to their well on Bottle Shaking Sunday, clutching bottles of liquorice water which, on reaching the well, they would shake until the contents frothed and they then drank it. Annual fairs and markets were held at the same time, and in the early nineteenth century the clergy tried to suppress the festivities because of the mischief that took place, but some survived into the early years of the twentieth century. Also in Cumbria, on the second Sunday in May the youth of the parish of Bromfield would gather at St Cuthbert's Well to have fun competing in various

Cures and curses

Young couples would share a quiet moment and drink sugared water together at Trinity Well. Artwork: Anthony Wallis

sports. Despite the fact that no strong drink was consumed there, the church curate decided that the Sabbath was being profaned and put a stop to the annual jollity.

At Hinderwell in North Yorkshire Ascension Day was known as Spanish Water Day when the children would take bottles containing liquorice to St Hilda's Well and mix it with well water before drinking it. At the Spo (or Spaw) Well near Rochdale (Lancashire), the first Sunday in May was Spo Sunday, when 'spo' was made from a mixture of the well water and stick liquorice shaken in a bottle. The emphasis on May for all these celebrations suggests that they are residual Rogations/Beating the Bounds celebrations: the principal feature of both was a procession around the parochial boundaries and its main features, which often included holy wells. In Carmarthenshire Palm Sunday was the chosen time to drink sugared water, and in Kidwelly the parents of the children who were taken to Ffynnon Stockwell on this day even kept special mugs for the event. They would put brown sugar into them and take the children to the well where they would add water from the well and drink the syrupy liquid.

As shown from the wide geographical spread of these traditions, of which the above are only a small sample, the custom of drinking sweetened or flavoured water on a certain day was a popular one. It would be interesting to know when the custom began, since until the eighteenth century or even later, sugar was a rare and expensive commodity. The custom may celebrate the new availability of sugar and the other sweeteners used: being able to have a small quantity of this much-prized substance would be considered a special treat. Another possibility is that the Church authorities encouraged the drinking of sweetened water in the hope that it would replace alcohol at public holiday times. When this didn't work, and nor did the other objectionable features stop, such as dancing, they made every effort to suppress the holidays altogether.

Sometimes the act of gathering to drink sweetened water also had a deeper significance. Trinity Well near the summit of Golfa Hill near Welshpool (Powys) was visited on Trinity Sunday when the custom was for young men and women to go there to 'plight their troth'. They would drink from the same cup of water taken from the well and mixed with a little sugar, before 'the silent thinking and wishing... took place'. Married couples would also go to the well to 'drink and pledge each other their continued love'. The ritual at the well may have been a silent one, but afterwards at the public house down below the young people 'Kept the Well' with music and dancing well into the night. Folklorist Reverend Elias Owen spoke to an elderly lady whose memory of the revelries extended back to the early nineteenth century and she told him that in addition to the festivities at the public house, the drinking of beer and gin also took place in the churchyard, and things were sold there, until the parson brought all that to an end.

Sugared water was not an invariable component of well-side revelry. There was an annual gathering of local people at St Bede's Well near Jarrow (South Tyneside) on Midsummer Eve, with bonfires, music, sports and dancing. The well was locally famous as a healing well, especially for babies and children, but may have been chosen as the site of the Midsummer revels simply because it was a location everyone knew, and there was a suitable open space beside the well, rather than being chosen for the sanctity of the site. Sugared water does not appear to have featured in the festivities at Irish holy wells either, which were known as patterns or patrons, these names connecting the events with the wells' patron saints. Several thousand people might attend an annual pattern, and after the rounding rituals they would eat and drink and engage in singing and dancing, etc. A description of such a pattern in the early nineteenth century, at St Bridget's Well at Kilmanaheem (Clare), demonstrates the mingling of spiritual and secular pursuits:

> The last Sunday in July is a patron day, when a number of people assemble at Lahinchy: they amuse themselves with horse racing on the strand, dancing, etc... On Saturday evening preceding this Sunday, numbers of people, male and female, assemble at St Bridget's well, and remain there the entire of the night. They first perform their rounds, and then spend a good part of the time in invoking this saint Bridget over the well, repeating their prayers

and adorations aloud, and holding conversations with the saint,
etc. When this ceremony is over, they amuse themselves until
morning by dancing and singing, etc.

Late in the eighteenth century, Irish bishops started to issue edicts banning the clergy from getting involved in patterns, and even with the intention of banning the patterns altogether. This was not because they disapproved of the people's religious activities at the holy wells, but that the patterns often became too unruly, with too much drinking, too much fighting, and too much licentiousness. In 1761 Thomas Burke, bishop of Ossory, referred to the 'mobbing, rioting, cursing, swearing, thieving, excessive drinking and other great Debaucheries [that] are constantly practised at St. John's Well near Kilkenny', all of which by association brought the Catholic religion into disrepute.

Sources: Shaking Bottle Sunday: Page 1990: 6; Park 1987: 8–9. **Bromfield:** Hope 1893: 40. **St Hilda's Well:** Hope 1893: 195. **Spo Well:** Taylor 2005: 42–3. **Ffynnon**

Photographed in the mid twentieth-century, a regular pilgrim to St Winefride's Well, Holywell, kneels on the stone of St Beuno and prays. She was not ill, but nevertheless felt the need to show reverence, and afterwards felt herself 'a worthier woman'.

At Clonmacnois in County Offaly, a group of pilgrims kneel with reverence around an ancient stone, possibly the one that has carved on it a face said to represent St Ciarán. They are clearly performing the customary ritual at this site, which is part of a sacred landscape which includes St Ciarán's Well close by.

Stockwell: Buckley 1995: 7. **Trinity Well:** Owen 1900: 126–8, 204–6. **St Bede's Well:** Hope 1893: 109. **Ireland:** Carroll 1999: 35–6, 47–8; Logan 1980: Ch.12.

Reverence

The local people who regularly visited the holy well in their parish all knew the customs, traditions and rituals of the well, what it could cure, and how it should be treated. They usually respected the well, indeed they showed due reverence towards it, and woe betide anyone who did not! There was an eye well (Ffynnon Fach – Little Well) at Llanfihangel-yng-Ngwynfa (St Michael in the Winds) (Powys) whose water was used by bathing the eyes in it – but not by drinking it. Anyone who drank the water was guilty of desecration and would immediately die. A tale was told of a man who took no notice, and drank the water, then fell down dead. A hole was dug at the roadside by the well and his body was buried there. When the Reverend Elias Owen visited the well at the end of the nineteenth century a ridge was pointed out as the grave, but on a later visit he was informed that the mound had been opened and no bones had been discovered.

The **rituals** performed at many holy wells often demonstrate reverence, as at St Patrick's Well, Clonfad (Monaghan), where the procedure involved frequent kneeling and bowing, as shown in this extract from a 1727 account by John Richardson:

> The pilgrims to this place first kneel at the north side of the well, salute St Patrick and say fifteen Paters, and one Credo. They rise up, bow to him, walk thrice round the well, and drink of the water every round at a place where they began. From thence they go to the heap of stones, bow to the cross, kiss the print of St Patrick's knee, and put one of their knees, always kissing the stone that hath the print of St Patrick's knee, when they come to it. They rise up and bow to it, and walk thrice round, bowing to the said stone when they come before it, and the last time kiss it. From the heap of stones they go to the alder tree. They begin at the west side

with bowing to it, they go thrice round and bow to it from East and West, and conclude their great superstition and idolatry with fifteen Paters and one Credo.

Sources: Ffynnon Fach: Owen 1898: 310. **St Patrick's Well:** Ó Mórdha 1975: 283–4.

Rituals

To effect a cure at a holy well, it was often not sufficient simply to go there, dab the water on the afflicted part and hope for the best. Often a precise ritual had to be followed if the cure was to be effective, such as at Skimmington Well (Curry Rivel) in Somerset, where the 'old witch' advised a man crippled by rheumatism that he should bathe in the well at sunrise for three mornings, 'and the use will come back to your limbs' – which it did. Sometimes the ritual was quite elaborate, as at Chibbyr Undin on the Isle of Man, where pilgrims seeking a cure had to take a mouthful of water from the well and hold it in their mouths until they had walked round the well 'sunways' twice. They then tore some cloth from a garment they were wearing, wetted it with well water (in one version, this should be the water held in the mouth) and hung it on the hawthorn that grew by the well. When the cloth had rotted, the cure was complete.

Toothache could be cured by the water from Fuaran Tràigh Theinis on the Isle of Lewis (Western Isles), but the correct ritual had to be followed. The sufferer should visit the well with an empty stomach early in the morning. Someone had to go with them, but nothing must be said, either on the way there or on the way back. The sufferer should take three mouthfuls of the water, and spurt the first two into the sea before drinking the third. Perhaps this symbolised throwing away the toothache? A similar ritual was performed at another toothache well on Lewis, Fuaran an Dèididh, where the first six mouthfuls had to be discarded on to a certain stone by the well, and the seventh drunk. Alternatively, according to a different source, three mouthfuls were taken and all three spurted on to the stone. These variations show that even the most precise rituals cannot have been essential to the success of the cure. At the toothache well Tobar Chuidhearaidh on North Uist (Western Isles) reciting a Gaelic verse was part of the ritual; the English translation is:

> I hereby leave the toothache
> Pain almost wasting my head
> In the well that will never dry,
> In the name of the Father, the Son and the Holy Ghost.

In Wales too the well ritual was sometimes preserved in folk poetry. One from Glamorgan in translation reads:

> Wash your eyes by the mill
> On the 1st of June;
> Drink of the well below Trapa Hill,
> And the King's Evil will leave you.

There was endless variety in the rituals to be performed: drink the water from the palm of the hand, or a limpet shell, or a special cup, or a skull (see **Skulls**); process around a chapel or a stone nearby (see **Circumambulation**); carry the water in the mouth and spit it in a certain place; sleep on a nearby standing stone or tombstone (see **Incubation**); make an offering into the well (see **Offerings; Pins; Votive offerings**); hang a rag on the bush or tree (see **Cloutie wells; Rags**) – the variety is almost endless. Not all the rituals performed at holy wells were done with cures in mind. People sometimes went to the wells for other reasons, most notably **divination**, but again it was usually believed to be very important that the correct ritual was performed or else an answer would not be forthcoming (see also **Love magic**).

The importance of ritual at holy wells was because carefully following the required procedure would help to put the pilgrim into the correct frame of mind and promote due **reverence**, which was necessary if the pilgrim was to obtain whatever end was desired. The performance of a ritual is akin to yoga technique, stilling body and mind and creating a receptive or passive state which enables the pilgrim to approach whatever it is (god/saint/spiritual being/one's own innermost self) that one expects to receive assistance from. It is not the ritual itself, but the precision with which one performs it, which is important.

Sources: Skimmington Well: Tongue 1965: 23. **Chibbyr Undin:** Paton 1941: 187. **Toothache wells:** MacLeod 2000: 21–2, 36, 53. **Glamorgan verse:** Jones 1954: 85.

Roman water shrines

Structures that have been identified as water shrines, usually associated with natural springs, have been discovered at some Roman sites, such as Chedworth Roman villa (Gloucester) and Blunsdon Ridge, Swindon (Wiltshire), and are suspected at others. The Roman site at Chedworth was at first thought to be a straightforward villa, but continuing examination has revealed that it may rather have been some kind of religious sanctuary similar to the Sulis Minerva shrine at **Bath**. There were two suites of baths, with the water supply coming from the water shrine located between them, and it seems very possible that Chedworth may have been a healing shrine similar to others in the area, namely Bath, Great Witcombe and Lydney. Part of an uninscribed altar was found buried within the shrine, and part of a column which probably stood at the entrance was also discovered, together with a slab on which the Christian chi-rho symbol was carved, possibly indicating that the shrine was Christianised towards the end of its life. Water still flows at the water shrine at Chedworth, which has been preserved and can be seen by visitors to the Roman villa and baths.

Following an archaeological investigation in the 1990s, the Blunsdon Ridge site in Wiltshire revealed itself as a probable early second to late fourth century sanctuary located at a group of natural springs – the ten-acre site contained a palatial villa, shrines, terraced gardens and pools built around the springs – and appears to be the largest known Roman religious complex in the western counties except for Bath. At

The water shrine at Chedworth Roman villa, Gloucestershire.

Frilford in Oxfordshire, recent (2001–2) excavation at the site of a Romano-British temple has uncovered a small circular stone-built structure which was at first thought to be an amphitheatre, but since this identification was problematical for various reasons, and the excavators hit water when they reached the base of the wall, they began to wonder if the structure might be a ritual pool. They also found possible votive deposits around the outside, including items of bronze, glass and bone.

Another possible rural religious sanctuary is the Roman site at Great Witcombe south of Gloucester, once thought to be a villa, where a spring feeds into a series of baths. The temple of Nodons at Lydney Park, again in Gloucestershire, is known to have been a healing centre with a large guest-house, baths, and cells where pilgrims would sleep in hopes of receiving a visit from a healing god (see **Incubation**). These Roman healing centres have been paralleled on the Continent, most notably at Fontes Sequanae (the springs of Sequana) in Burgundy, France, near the source of the River Seine where there was an important healing sanctuary from the first century BC. The recent archaeological discoveries at Roman sites in southern England are providing support for the belief that water shrines were far more common in Roman times than was once thought likely. Other noted sites where the Romans created religious sites based on water in Britain include **Coventina's Well** (Northumberland), the hot spring at Aquae Sulis (**Bath**, Somerset), a temple at Springhead (Kent) sited at eight natural springs, and the Roman bath at St Anne's Well, Buxton (Derby).

Once Christianity became dominant in Britain and the Roman pagan temples were being demolished, the pagan cult objects and statues of deities were not simply broken up but were despatched with intent, sometimes being dropped into wells, which may have symbolised their journey back to the demonic underworld so that they would pose no threat to the Christians. Other damaged statues and reliefs of deities were probably thrown into rivers – though it is of course not possible to determine whether such items as have been found in recent years were originally deposited as offerings or as rubbish. Some of the anatomical **votive offerings** found at post-Roman sites have been limbs and heads removed from former bronze and stone statues, suggesting that objects linked to an earlier religion were not universally considered to be dangerous but were capable of safe reuse.

Sources: Chedworth: Haigh 2001: 8–9; Goodburn 2003. **Blunsdon Ridge:** 'Swindon: Blunsdon Ridge', *Current Archaeology*, 163 (vol. XIV no. 7)(June 1999): 256–8.

Gloucestershire sites: Haigh 2001: 8–9. **Frilford:** Gosden & Lock 2003: 156–9. **Christian destruction:** Merrifield 1987: 96–106.

S

Saints and wells

Many holy wells were named for saints, usually the particular saint already associated with the local Christian church; but some wells were, according to folklore, actually created by saints.

When St Edmund, king and martyr, landed in Norfolk circa 855 at his accession as ruler of East Anglia, he knelt and prayed to God to bless his coming and make it profitable to the land and the people. As he mounted his horse, twelve springs gushed forth from the earth. According to Gaufridus de Fontibus, in his twelfth-century De Infantia sancti Edmundi *(Of the Childhood of St Edmund), 'These springs to this our own day excite the admiration of the beholder, flowing as they do with a continuous sweet and cheering murmur to the sea. Many sick wash in these fountains and are restored to their former health, and pilgrims carry the healing water to remote parts for the infirm and others to drink.' Gaufridus referred to twelve springs, while this illustration from John Lydgate's fifteenth-century verse* Life of St Edmund *shows five springs. The springs were believed to be located at Hunstanton, and were in the late nineteenth century known as the Seven Springs. They were not far from St Edmund's Chapel (now ruined), and a quarter-mile from St Mary's church in Old Hunstanton, and in earlier times were visited by many pilgrims. Photo: British Library*

The sea monster snarls in disgust as St Patrick escapes its clutches and safely reaches land on the Isle of Man. Artwork: Anthony Wallis

Often the reason for creating the spring was simply a basic need for a water supply – perhaps because of drought, or simply because the site was such that there was unlikely to be a natural spring, such as on a hilltop. St Cynog lived in a cell on top of a hill called Van near Brecon (Powys) and as there was no water supply he had to carry it from the river at the foot of the hill, until God gave him water close to his cell (see also **Saints' deaths**). Sometimes the saint prayed for water (as did St Elian, resulting in the appearance of Ffynnon Elian, Llanelian, Conwy), or else he smote the ground with his staff, thus causing water to appear (e.g. St Augustine's Well, Cerne Abbas, Dorset); or it burst forth where the saint's horse struck the rock with its hoof, as for example St Milburga's or Milborough's Well at Stoke St Milborough, Shropshire. However it was the saint herself who ordered her horse to strike the rock: she needed water to bathe her wounds after falling from her horse and striking her head while fleeing from her enemies.

On the Isle of Man St Patrick created a holy well by making the sign of the cross on the ground (Chibbyr Noo Pherick – St Patrick's Well – at Peel). An alternative version is that St Patrick was being chased by a sea monster as he came to the island, and he made his horse climb up a steep hill in order to escape from it. Once at the top, they rested, and a spring began to flow at their feet (or, it began to flow where he made the sign of the cross on the ground).

Also on the Isle of Man, St Maughold's Well (Chibbyr Vaghal) began to flow where St Maughold's horse's knee touched the ground as they crossed over from Ireland. St David's Well (Ffynnon Ddewi) at Brawdy (Pembroke) began to flow where the saint's tears had fallen; another Ffynnon Ddewi (inside a cottage in Llanddewibrefi parish, Ceredigion) flowed when the saint restored the cottager's son to life. On occasion, wells appeared when needed for the baptism of holy persons, for example at Porthclais (Pembroke) where a well sprang up to provide water for the baptism of the infant St David – and not only did the water baptise him, but it also cured the blindness of the child's godfather. Wells where saints had drunk the water became holy (e.g. Ffynnon Non, Llanon, Carmarthen); likewise wells where saints had bathed and been cured of some ailment (e.g. Ffynnon Enddwyn, Llanenddwyn, Harlech, Gwynedd), or had practised penance while standing in its waters (e.g. Ffynnon Ddyfnog, Llanrhaeadr, Denbigh) also became known as holy wells (see also **Immersion**).

Many of Ireland's holy wells were named for saints, and the whole range of legends is recorded there, plus some not found elsewhere, like the well in Co. Longford which flowed where St Brigid dropped a hot coal, and the well in Co. Roscommon which appeared where the virgin saint Caolainn pulled up two rushes. She did this because she had just torn out her eyes, in response to an admirer who told her how fine they were, whereupon she threw them on the ground in his direction. When she bathed the empty sockets in the water from the new well, her sight was restored. In another version of this story involving St Brigid, she used an existing well, St Brigid's Well in Killinagh parish (Cavan), to restore her sight. In Scotland, St Medana's Well at Glasserton (Dumfries & Galloway) was created by the saint to restore her sight after she too threw her eyes at the feet of a persistent suitor.

On one occasion a saint blessed a pagan holy well, thus reversing its qualities. The saint was Columba, and while in Scotland he came upon a well in the Pictish area of Scotland (no one knows exactly which well it was) which had dire results for anyone who drank the water or bathed in it, as they came away with leprosy, or were left blind or crippled. As a result, the heathens were treating the well as a god. St Columba called on the name of Christ and then blessed the well, drank from it, and washed his hands and feet, the well's pagan devotees eagerly anticipating his demise as he did so, since they were eager to get their revenge on him for having opposed them. But nothing happened to him, and the well was then used, at least during the saint's lifetime, as a source of healing for the local people.

Sources: St Edmund: J.B. Mackinlay 1893. **St Cynog:** Jones 1954: 36. **Chibbyr Noo Pherick:** Paton 1941: 189. **St David's Well:** Jones 1954: 35. **Porthclais:** Jones 1954: 34. **Ffynnon Non:** Jones 1954: 35. **Irish saints' wells:** Logan 1980: 53. **St Columba:** Reeves 1988; Adomnán of Iona 1995: 162–3.

Nineteenth-century repainting of the fresco by Pomerancio (1583) in the chapel of the Venerable English College in Rome, showing the martyrdom of St Winefride, with her head lying in the water of the spring which began to flow where her head fell.

Saints' deaths

According to legend, some holy wells came into existence as a result of a saint's violent death. The most famous instance of a saint's death resulting in the creation of a holy well concerns St Winefride who as a young girl was being pursued by an ardent suitor, Caradoc. She resisted his advances, and in his anger he cut off her head. Luckily her uncle, St Beuno, was at hand to place her head back on her neck and bring her back to life, the only trace of this event being a permanent line around her neck, often to be seen in depictions of St Winefride. A spring began to flow where her head fell to the ground, which in due course became one of the most famous, and still most active, holy wells in Britain, at **Holywell** in Flintshire.

St Eiliwedd (known sometimes as Lludd) was another Welsh female saint whose beheading resulted in the creation of a holy well where her head fell: Penginger Well at Pencefngaer (Powys). In England, St Sidwell was beheaded in the eighth century on the orders of her stepmother who wanted some land the saint had inherited. She ordered a servant to murder St Sidwell while she was at prayer, and he decapitated her using a scythe. A spring began to flow where her head fell – St Sidwell's Well at Exeter (Devon). St Osyth, a seventh-century abbess in Essex, was beheaded by 'some roving Danes', whereupon she picked up her head and carried it to the nearest church, where she died. A spring, later St Osyth's Well, flowed where her head had fallen, the place being also known as St Osyth.

Although she has been decapitated, St Sidwell still has her head, and is carrying a second head, in this early sixteenth-century painting of her on the screen in Hennock church, Devon. This form of depiction symbolises the nature of her martyrdom, by decapitation. Photo: Roy Fry

Male saints were also occasionally slain by decapitation, and springs began to flow at the places where their heads fell. St Justinian was beheaded on Ramsey Island, where a spring then flowed. He carried his head across to the mainland and was buried at St Justinian's Chapel, close to which is another well dedicated to him (at St Justinian near St Davids, Pembroke), which appeared so that he could wash his head after the decapitation. St Decuman was a Welsh saint who had crossed the River Severn on a raft made of reeds and had established a hermitage at Watchet in Somerset, where he was attacked and beheaded by a band of pagan robbers, St Decuman's Well appearing at the spot where the attack took place. He picked up his head and made his way back to Wales, St Decuman's Well at Rhoscrowther (Pembroke) marking the place where he returned to.

Sometimes there was no decapitation involved, the spring flowing at the site of the saint's murder. St Oswald, King of Northumbria, died in 642 following a battle with Penda, the pagan king of Mercia, at Winwick (Warrington), and where he died a spring began to flow – or it might have been at Oswestry in Shropshire, where another St Oswald's Well can also be found. The Oswestry tradition was that after his martyrdom, Penda had St Oswald's head and arms chopped off and nailed to

St Walstan's Well near Bawburgh church, Norfolk.

posts (the 'tree'), but an eagle stole one of the arms and flew off with it. Where it dropped the arm, the well sprang up.

A variation on the murder theme is that the spring starts to flow where the saint's body has lain soon after death, not necessarily where they died or were murdered. The body might have been taken somewhere for burial, and a spring flowed where it was laid en route; or it might have been buried at a certain place for some time before being moved elsewhere, a spring afterwards starting up in the empty grave. An English king whose death resulted in such a legend was St Edward the Martyr, who was murdered aged 17 in 979 at Corfe Gate in Dorset. He was at first buried where his body was found, but later the incorrupt body was discovered at a place where miraculous cures had been reported, and he was taken to Shaftesbury Abbey for reburial. A well near Wareham reputedly marks the place of his first burial.

Two springs arose at points where St Walstan's body had lain on its way to burial: he died in 1016 in Norfolk, having foreseen his own death. He requested that his body be placed on a cart and the two oxen which drew it should be allowed to go where they wished. They passed through Costessey Wood, and where they briefly stopped, St Walstan's Well arose. Another spring flowed at Bawburgh where they stopped again (still to be seen close to the church), and he was buried where the church now stands.

Three springs arose where St Cuthbert's coffin rested on its route north from Yorkshire to Durham in the seventh century. Further south, the child-king Kenelm of Mercia was murdered early in the ninth century in the Clent Hills (Worcestershire) and his body buried under a thorn tree. A miraculous message was taken to the Pope in Rome, in the form of a scroll carried by a white dove, and the message said:

> In Clent, at Cowbach, lieth under a thorn,
> His head off-shorn, Kenelm king-born.

Searchers went to the Clent Hills and found the body, with a blood-stained knife beside it, and when they removed it from the temporary grave, a spring, which became *St Kenelm's Well*, began to flow. (This well is still maintained today, at an atmospheric location beside Romsley church.) The body was taken away to

Gloucestershire for burial since his father King Kenulf had founded an abbey at Winchcombe, and on Sudeley Hill, where the body was briefly laid before burial, another spring began to flow.

The presence of St Ethelbert's body resulted in two wells in Herefordshire, after he was murdered by order of King Offa of Mercia, whose daughter he wished to marry. He was buried first of all at Marden, but when the body was removed to Hereford a spring began to flow in the empty grave (this well is now located inside Marden church – see **Wells inside and close to churches**). Later another spring flowed at the place in Hereford where the body briefly lay (the site can be seen in a wall near the entrance to Castle Green, not far from the cathedral). King Offa came to regret the murder, and had a shrine erected to Ethelbert's memory in 795, on the site of which now stands Hereford Cathedral, of which Ethelbert is the patron saint. In Norfolk the original location of St Withburga's grave can be seen in the churchyard at East Dereham. The body was stolen and taken to Ely in 974, a miraculous spring rising from the empty grave 'to compensate Dereham for the loss of its saint'. *St Withburga's Well* was described as 'a spring of the purest water, gifted with many healing virtues'.

On the other hand, the decapitation of St Cynog resulted in the disappearance of a well. According to the legend, he was beheaded while saying prayers at St Cynog's Well near the summit of a hill known as the Van and his head fell into the well, which dried up. He picked up his head and carried it down the hillside for several miles to the place now known as Merthyr Cynog (Powys), now an isolated hamlet whose name literally means the *martyrium* (i.e. shrine) of Cynog, and the place where he was buried. Cynog is likely to have been an abbot who founded a monastery at Merthyr Cynog, but in later life he withdrew to a hermitage on the Van. After his death, his body would have been brought back to his monastery, and his tomb there became a shrine, the legend of his decapitation at the well developing over time as pilgrims visited both sites.

Sources: St Winefride: Hole 1966: 95–9. **St Sidwell's Well:** Hope 1893: 65. **St Osyth's Well:** Hope 1893: 72–4. **St Justinian:** Jones 1954: 36. **St Decuman's Wells:** Horne 1923: 49–50; Jones 1954: 37. **St Oswald's Wells:** Hole 1966: 105–19. **St Edward the Martyr:** Hole 1966: 92–3. **St Kenelm's Wells:** Hole 1966: 88–90, 94–5. **St Ethelbert's Wells:** Hole 1966: 91–2. **St Withburga's Well:** Hope 1893: 93–5. **St Cynog's Well:** Jones 1954: 37.

Saints in the landscape

The saint's connection with his or her well was not merely that of a name – the local people who used the well did not doubt the continuing presence of the saint at that place. The author of *The Holy Wells of Ireland*, Patrick Logan, once asked a visitor to a holy well in Carna townland at Mullaghhorne, Co. Cavan, how he could be sure that St Patrick had visited the well, to which the man indignantly replied: 'Of course I am sure he came here. How else could he have left the track of his knees in that

The landscape of St Non, just outside St Davids (Pembroke): her ruined chapel is roughly in the centre of the photograph, with the well close by, where the two people are standing.

stone?' He was referring to the frequently found stones considered to be marked with a saint's **footprints**, or in this case knee-prints. Such physical traces play a part in the sanctification of the landscape around the holy well, even when no longer visible and only remembered through legend. The *well of St Non* at St Davids (Pembroke) was believed to be the place where she gave birth to St David. At the time of the birth she pressed her hand hard on to a stone close to the well, leaving the permanent impression of her hand. The *Lives* of St David state that for a long time this stone was kept in St Non's Chapel close by as a relic, but it is now lost. The ruins of the tiny chapel are part of the sacred landscape at this evocative cliff-top location, as too is a circle of standing stones (which, however, despite their formation, are unlikely to be prehistoric). In recent times a new chapel has been built close to the well, where fine stained-glass windows of Celtic saints can be seen, and where the atmosphere of the site has been perpetuated and enhanced.

Some wells had close to them a structure known as the saint's bed, or chair, which played a part in the healing **rituals** at the well. Usually the person seeking a cure would have to spend some time lying or sleeping on the bed or sitting on the chair (where it was believed the saint him- or herself had once sat) in order for the cure to be effective (see also **Incubation**). The 'bed' would have been a structure believed to be the saint's tomb, and so by sleeping there, the pilgrim would have believed that he had been lying in close contact with the saint's final resting place. Examples include St Patrick's Bed, cut out of a rock cliff above St Patrick's Well at the top of

St Patrick's Chair at Altadaven in Co. Tyrone is a chair-shaped stone block about two metres tall, located just above St Patrick's Well, which is a circular depression in a huge stone. On 'the Big Sunday of the Heather' in July, people would gather here, sitting on the chair to make a wish and leaving offerings of pins and pennies at the well. The well mysteriously refills itself with water within half an hour of being emptied, and the tradition explaining its existence is that it was created by St Patrick himself. He sat on the chair to preach, and then he ordered water to come from the rock when he needed water for baptisms. Photo: Anthony Weir

the pass of Mám Ean (Galway); St Patrick's Chair above his well at Altadaven (Tyrone); St Derivla's Bed near to St Derivla's Vat, a holy well on the Mullet Peninsula (Mayo); St Canna's Chair close to St Canna's Well at Llangan (Carmarthen) (illustrated in **Incubation**); St Madron's Bed at *Madron well* (Cornwall); and St Maughold's Chair close to St Maughold's Well on the Isle of Man, where barren women would sit in order to become fertile.

Sources: Saints' imprints: Logan 1980: 38; Bord *Footprints* 2004. **St Non:** Hole 1966: 85. **St Patrick's Bed:** Logan 1980: 65; Meehan 2002: 616. **St Patrick's Chair:** Meehan 2002: 143–4.

Shrines

In the Middle Ages shrines were developed at some popular holy wells: James Rattue lists thirty-three medieval well-shrines (excluding Ireland) in his book *The Living Stream*. These were places where a specific saint was revered, often focusing on a relic of the saint (a small piece of bone, perhaps) or a sacred image. Two familiar examples are *St Winefride's Well* at **Holywell** (Flint) and *St Mary's Well* at Fernyhalgh (Lancashire) – both these shrines were focused on holy wells. Some other

The pilgrim nearing the end of a long walk to Penrhys sees ahead the small stone building housing St Mary's Well, sited dramatically above the Rhondda Valley in South Wales.

shrines had wells as adjuncts of pilgrimages, such as **Walsingham** (Norfolk) and St Mary's Well, Penrhys (Rhondda). There are other surviving holy wells that a casual visitor today would not realise were important shrines in the Middle Ages, such as St Margaret's Well, Binsey (Oxford) and *St Kenelm's Well* in the Clent Hills (Worcester).

At saints' shrines in pilgrimage churches in the eleventh and twelfth centuries, healing was often practised by dipping saints' relics in water or wine and in this way transferring the saint's power to the pilgrim when he or she drank the liquid. For example, the hand of St James would be dipped in water at Reading Abbey, and the water placed into small phials and sent off to the sick. At Norwich Cathedral, the pilgrims would drink water that had cement from the tomb of St William mixed with it. The **blood** of the martyred St Thomas Becket was mixed with well water at his shrine at Canterbury Cathedral before being used for healing. But some healing liquids were less acceptable to the squeamish: a sick monk at the monastery of Mont-St.-Michel in northern France refused to drink wine that had been used to wash the skull of St Aubert, saying that he preferred 'to die than drink wine swilled in the head of a corpse'. People became increasingly sensitive about drinking such 'macabre beverages' and they went out of fashion after the twelfth century. (See also **Roman water shrines.**)

Sources: Medieval well-shrines: Rattue 1995: 80–2. **Macabre beverages:** Sumption 2002: 83.

This late-nineteenth century photograph shows a member of the Melchior family with St Teilo's skull.

Skulls

Skulls have been found deposited in Roman-period wells, though these were usually wells that had been used as a domestic water supply rather than being sacred wells. However the evidence suggests that these were not always accidental depositions: one well at Odell (Bedford) dating to the first century had had a skull with lower jaw placed behind the lining of the well when it was being constructed; and a complete decapitated head that had been placed into the third-century well at a Roman villa at Northwood (Hertford) was accompanied by a crude stone head. These appear to have been examples of ritual **deposition** rather than rubbish disposal, a conclusion strengthened by the finding of part of a human skull in **Coventina's Well**. Some depositions, such as the skull in the well lining, may have been foundation sacrifices; whereas on other occasions a skull may have been placed in a well to mark the end of its life in a termination ritual.

The most famous holy well associated with a human skull was St Teilo's Well (Ffynnon Deilo) at Llandeilo Llwydiarth near Maenclochog (Pembroke), where the water was renowned for its ability to cure whooping cough and other ailments, but only if drunk out of the remains of St Teilo's skull. (St Teilo was a sixth-century Welsh

Left: *St Teilo's skull in its reliquary, kept safely behind glass, in Llandaff Cathedral.*

Right: *The place in Llandaff Cathedral where St Teilo's skull is kept.*

monk and bishop; his tomb was said to be in Llandaff Cathedral, and when it was opened in 1850 the body found was accompanied by items which suggested it was that of a bishop.) The skull was kept by the Melchior family who lived at the nearby farm, and a member of that family born in the house had to lift the water from the well in the skull and hand it to the patient, if the ritual was to be effective.

There were stories telling how people had visited the well and drunk the water but had not been cured. On learning later that they should have drunk from the skull, they had returned and performed the ritual correctly, being cured as a result. During the First World War people would also go and drink the well water from the skull in the hope that the war would soon end. The skull was lost for many years during the twentieth century, but is now in the safe-keeping of Llandaff Cathedral.

St Teilo's Skull is the longest surviving Welsh skull used for healing purposes, though even that practice only began in the seventeenth century. Water was also drunk from a human skull at Ffynnon Llandyfaen (Carmarthen), but this procedure may have been simply copying the Ffynnon Deilo ritual. Skulls were also kept as relics in medieval Wales (as they have been wherever Christian relics have been revered), two ancient ones encased in silver being destroyed by Bishop Barlow at St Davids in the sixteenth century because of their 'popish' connections. A reliable record of a healing ritual involving a skull in Wales several hundred years earlier than the ritual involving St Teilo's Skull concerns the skull of St Winefride. In his *Vita secunda*

Wenefredae (circa 1138) Robert of Shrewsbury describes taking the saint's relics from Gwytherin (Conwy) to Shrewsbury (Shropshire), and during the journey he cured a man by taking a pinch of dust from St Winefride's skull, putting it in water, and getting the patient to drink it.

There are occasional references to the use of skulls even up to the present day. There is a skull hidden in a crevice in a ruined chapel in County Roscommon which is claimed to cure toothache if you touch it. On the island of Lewis (Western Isles) a skull was sometimes used as part of a cure for epilepsy. The ritual involved going to the graveyard at night, digging up a skull, taking it home to the patient, and getting them to drink water from a holy well out of the skull. Then it was taken back to the graveyard and reburied. Folklorist Anne Ross was told of a relatively recent example of this happening (mid-twentieth century) by the Rev William Matheson:

> An elder of the United Free Church in Ness had an epileptic daughter. He eventually decided to try to cure her of epilepsy in a traditional manner. Between sunset and sunrise and without speaking to a living thing, he walked five miles to the family burial-ground at Teampull Chrò Naoimh at North Galson. There he dug up the grave and removed the skull from it. He came back home with the skull, awakened the epileptic girl and made her drink from the skull. He then walked back to Teampull Chrò Naoimh to re-bury the skull. My informant did not know the name of the well from which the water was taken, but it is likely to have been a healing well and its name should still be ascertainable.

Anne Ross has also written about a well called Tobar a' Chinn (the Well of the Head) in a remote part of Wester Ross (Highland) which was specifically visited by epileptics, where they would drink the well water out of a skull which was kept permanently at the well. This was generally believed to be the skull of a woman who had committed suicide 200 or so years ago, and had been buried on the moor, outside the churchyard. Her skull appeared miraculously on the surface of the ground, and this was taken as a sign that it was to be used in the cure of epilepsy, for which purpose it was moved to the well higher up the hill and kept there in a small stone container. Ross saw the skull for herself, and had the ritual explained to her by its guardian. Any patient had to call on the guardian who would accompany them to the well and instruct them in the correct procedure, without which the cure would not occur. It included the patient walking three times sunwise round the well, and drinking three times from the skull which the guardian had dipped in the well.

Sources: Roman-period wells: Merrifield 1987: 45–6. **Foundation and termination:** Merrifield 1987: 48–9. **St Teilo's Skull:** The full story is told in Buckley 1994: 10–13. **First World War:** Jones 1954: 81. **Lewis:** Ross 1962: 36–7. **Tobar a' Chinn:** Ross 1976: 81–2.

Stones

Stones of various kinds, large and small, are included in **rituals** performed at well sites, especially in Ireland. Some bear the imprint of the saint's foot, or hand, or knee – even other parts of the anatomy such as the head or bottom. (See **Footprints**.) Stones called **bullauns** were sometimes regarded as holy wells, since they held water in the hollows in their surfaces. There are even special stones underwater at some holy wells, the most notable example being Maen Beuno (St Beuno's Stone) at *St Winefride's Well,* **Holywell** (Flint). It is located at the base of the steps leading down into the bathing pool, and said to be where St Beuno prayed when he indulged in ascetic **immersion** in the early days of the well when St Winefride was alive. Its holiness was gained as a result of St Beuno's use of it, and indeed is the only object at the well that St Winefride would recognise if she came back today. The importance of Maen Beuno has continued to the present day, in that people following the bathing ritual in the well still finish their prayers kneeling on the stone. (There is a photograph of someone kneeling on the stone to pray reproduced in the entry for **Reverence**.)

According to tradition, Maen Beuno once had the ability to float, and did so once a year. St Winefride would fashion a chasuble for St Beuno annually on the anniversary of her martyrdom, and she would place it on Maen Beuno. The stone would then float downstream to the coast and find its way through the sea to Clynnog Fawr, where St Beuno was then living. Having delivered the chasuble to him, it would return to St Winefride's Well. When the time came that the stone did not move after St Winefride had laid the chasuble upon it, she then knew that St Beuno was dead. In more recent times, a Norman noble became paralysed when he tried to move the stone, and in the nineteenth century the stone was cemented into place to stop anyone trying to remove it.

Cairns of stones along the course of a pilgrimage route were added to by pilgrims who would place a pebble when performing the required ritual at a well or other holy site, again usually in Ireland. These pebbles may have been used as a counting device, to help the pilgrim keep track of the prayers said during the pilgrimage. They may also have acted as a form of **votive offering**, being placed afterwards on the cairn as a symbol of the prayer; and so they may have played a dual role as both prayer counter and votive offering. At *St Winefride's Well,* **Holywell** (Flint), visiting Irish travellers often leave a 'decade' (chain of ten beads from a rosary) at the shrine at the end of their pilgrimages. These decades are clearly both prayer counters and votive offerings, and they appear to have replaced the older **offerings** of pebbles at some holy sites.

Pillar stones were sometimes revered as part of the ritual, such as the ten-foot Cloch Patrick located on a prehistoric burial mound near the old church of St Mary's Priory at Dungiven (Derry). Pilgrims would bow to the well, walk round it, pray, wash their hands and feet, leave a rag on a bush by the well, and then move to a large stone in the river and walk around that, before finally moving to the pillar stone and likewise processing around it whilst praying. At another pillar stone the sick would rub the afflicted body part against the stone. Some pillar stones have circular holes and are

This photograph of St Winefride's Well, Holywell, was taken when the bathing pool had been drained for cleaning. Maen Beuno can be seen on the left, beside the steps.

known as holed stones. Occasionally they are found near to holy wells, such as at Glen Columcille (Donegal) where pilgrims would, on completion of their pilgrimage, look through the hole towards the south-east and 'if they were spiritually in a pure state it was believed they would get a glimpse of heaven'.

(Possible links between prehistoric standing stones and sacred springs can be found in the entry for **Prehistory**.)

Sources: Irish stones: Logan 1980: Ch.8. **Cloch Patrick:** Logan 1980: 101–2. **Holed stones:** Logan 1980: 105–7.

T

Treasure

Wells were considered good places to hide treasure, according to the legends. The Fairy or Pewter or St Peter's Well on Churn Clough, Heyhouses (Lancashire) was believed to hold silver and pewter placed there by local inhabitants for safe-keeping during the Civil War. The witch Meg of Meldon hid 'a bull's hide full of gold' in a well to the south-east of Meldon Tower (Northumberland). The money hidden inside Ffynnon Digwg (Gwynedd) could only be found by a girl with red hair tending a

Cures and curses

A storm breaks out over the well when a treasure-hunter starts to dig there, while the sun is still shining on the workers haymaking not far away. Artwork: Anthony Wallis

flock of sheep. Money in wells was sometimes not meant to be retrieved. A man haymaking at Hafod y Porth (Nant Gwynant, Gwynedd) went to a well and started to remove the stones to get at the money he knew to be inside, but a storm arose and he abandoned his quest and went back to the fields where there was no rain and the sun was shining brightly. According to Giraldus Cambrensis, there was a well in Pembrokeshire where a golden torque was guarded by a viper, which would bite anyone whose hand strayed too close.

White lady ghosts, who often frequented wells, were sometimes believed to have come back to earth in order to reveal the location of hidden treasure. The female ghost who haunted a well near the ruins of Bryncethin (Bridgend) wore 'old-fashioned clothes' and told a servant girl where to find treasure. The white lady who haunted the Goblin Well near Mold (Flint) also led a human helper to a cache of treasure, but for a strange reason, revealed in **Ghosts**.

Sources: Pewter Well: Taylor 2004: 64. **Meg of Meldon:** Parsons 1933: 303. **Welsh treasure wells:** Jones 1954: 134. **White ladies:** Parsons 1933: 304. **Bryncethin:** Jones 1954: 127.

Trees

Holy wells and trees are closely associated, in that numerous holy wells have notable trees growing beside them. In the Irish language there is a special name for an important tree at a holy well site – *bile* – and this is incorporated in some place names, such as Toberavilla (Westmeath), meaning 'the well of the ancient tree'. According to Petra Skyvova such trees 'often marked tribal centres, inauguration sites or locations of sacred springs'.

Certain tree species occur more often than others. The trees most often found with wells are hawthorn, hazel, elder, rowan, holly, yew, ash and oak. Nine hazel trees grew over Connla's Well (Tipperary), the nuts from which fed the sacred salmon

Long Lonkin's unhappy death beside the well at Nafferton. Artwork: Anthony Wallis

Cures and curses

This hollow dead tree in Arboe churchyard, Co. Tyrone, was used as a holy well, and votive coins were hammered into its bark using the rock visible at its foot. Photo: Allen Kennedy

living in the well (see also **Fishes and frogs**). Whether any specific tree was planted on purpose as part of the holy well environment, or whether their presence at a well is purely coincidental, cannot be determined. Sometimes the tree at a well may have played a part in the **rituals** performed there, and they were often used as a receptacle for the **rags** and **clouties** which were left hanging in them. Pilgrims would sometimes carve their initials on trees that grew beside holy wells, as at Ffynnon y Gwaunydd (Gwynedd), in the same way that they left their initials, or even verses, carved on the walls of buildings at holy wells. In a few instances, votive coins were hammered into the trunks of trees above sacred wells. This happened at St Beuno's Well, Holywell (Flint), to the extent that the tree was poisoned, and eventually died. The stump was finally removed by the Council some time in the 1960s.

Some trees associated with wells have a supernatural origin, according to legend, a saint having stuck his staff into the ground thus causing a spring to flow – but the staff itself took root and became a tree. The alder tree which was close to St Patrick's Well at Clonfad (Monaghan) sprang up immediately at the spot where St Patrick blessed the ground. It formed one of the stations visited by pilgrims to the well, and they would circle it and bow to it (see **Reverence**). Sometimes a special tree was protected by a superstitious belief, for example it was believed that a storm would erupt if the old hawthorn close to Ffynnon Digwg at Clynnog Fawr (Gwynedd) was ever cut down. There are numerous instances on record of thunderstorms having broken out when prehistoric sites have been disturbed either by archaeologists or in search of **treasure**.

Some trees had a more sinister reputation. An oak tree growing by a well at Nafferton (Northumberland) was where Long Lonkin hanged himself, or was hanged by others, or fell and was killed. He had built Nafferton Tower for Lord Wearie but never received any payment and in revenge he murdered Lord Wearie's wife and child. The well water turned to blood on one day each year – perhaps the anniversary of Lonkin's death there.

There are even a few examples, mostly in Ireland, of wells being located inside tree stumps. These are not wells in the conventional sense, of course, but hollow stumps where water has gathered, interpreted as holy wells for individual reasons. An early twentieth-century account tells of such a well in Ballydeloughry parish (Cork) which appeared after the real well was filled up.

> An old man showed me the hollow stump of a sycamore here...
> He told me it held water in the driest summer, even when the
> neighbouring spring wells ran dry. It was full of water when I saw
> it at the end of September 1905. The people are inclined to
> believe that it is the holy well resuscitated, the one which was
> filled in a long time ago near the old church.

Sources: Trees at Irish wells: Mac Coitir 2003; Skyvova 2005: 25. **Species:** Shepherd 1995: 2–3; Skyvova 2005: 26. **Connla's Well:** Jones 1954: 18. **Ffynnon y Gwaunydd:** Jones 1954: 84. **St Patrick's Well:** Ó Mórdha 1975: 283. **Ffynnon Digwg:** Jones 1954: 19. **Retribution:** Bord 1976: Ch.8 'The fate of the desecrators'. **Nafferton:** Binnall & Dodds: 67. **Tree-stump wells:** Logan 1980: 68. **At Irish wells:** Logan 1980: Ch.7.

V

Visions

On rare occasions the location of a holy well is revealed in a vision, as happened to Nora Arthurs, the Seeress of Canvey Island (Essex). After its precise location was dowsed by a Yugoslavian Roman Catholic named Georgovitch, the well was then dug in her garden, beneath a tree, in 1994. Pilgrims would arrive at the house and Nora Arthurs would seem to go into a trance and the Virgin Mary would speak through her, giving messages such as 'Oh my children, it is I, Mary, Queen of Heaven! Oh, my children, I know you pray every day, but I have a message for you, that such prayer is not enough! Go home and pray with your families! Go home and pray with your families!' She would also tell Nora to give the pilgrims water from the well. For at least ten years prior to the digging of the well, the 'holy water' used by Nora Arthurs was tap water blessed by Christ.

St Edmund's Well in a meadow at Oxford began to flow at the place where St Edmund Rich, a future archbishop of Canterbury who was at that time studying at the university, had a vision of Christ. It became much frequented because of its

A spring began to flow at the place where St Edmund Rich had a vision of Christ. Artwork: Anthony Wallis

healing powers, until Oliver Sutton, Bishop of Lincoln, sent an edict to the Archdeacon of Oxford in 1291 threatening excommunication to anyone who visited the well: he did not approve of 'how strangely the people were besotted with a fond imagination of its vertues and holinesse, and that they did neglect to serve the true God by hankering after and worshipping this well'.

There are also a few instances where the locations of holy wells have been revealed in dreams. In the seventeenth century an Irish holy well came into being after a woman living at Kilmihil (Clare) had a dream in which the Archangel Michael appeared and instructed her to dig at a certain rushy spot near a local church. The parish priest and her son helped her to dig, and a well was duly uncovered, the water from which cured her long-standing gout, as well as helping other people. This was presumably a previously existing well which had become lost (as so many sadly have today). Similarly in the early nineteenth century a woman spending the night at Ballynoe (Cork) dreamed of the location of a hidden holy well and next day, with the help of some local people, it was uncovered and became the centre of a cult. In the late eighteenth century the parish priest of Marmalane (Cork) dreamed that a certain well (presumably at that point simply used as a water supply) would become miraculous; so he blessed it and dedicated it to Saints Peter and Paul whose feast-day it was. It soon became the centre of a cult. Although these last wells were not new

The Mount Melleray grotto as it appears today. Photo: Pat Kiely

ones, the same theme is apparent: that someone receives external guidance to a water source that has the necessary qualities to make it holy.

A modern example of a holy well being revealed by a vision of the Blessed Virgin Mary is at Mount Melleray (Waterford). In 1985 pilgrims began visiting the Lourdes Grotto that had been erected at a spring in the valley close to the Cistercian monastery, when there were reports that the statue of the Immaculate Conception had been seen to move. One night a glowing light lit up the stream from the spring. There were multiple visions of the Virgin Mary and she was heard to speak, one message being 'Tell the people the water is blessed.' Afterwards the spring came to be regarded and used as a holy well. An older example of this, and one never before published, comes from Wales. The story was told to a friend of mine, by an old lady who had for many years lived close to Ffynnon Fair (St Mary's Well) at Cefn Meiriadog (Denbigh), who said that it was a vision of Our Lady at the spring some time in the Middle Ages which had caused it to be regarded as a holy well.

Sources: Nora Arthurs: Kerridge 1998 (Summer): 25–6; Hulse 1998: 28–32. **St Edmund's Well:** Hope 1893: 120–2. **Irish dreams:** Carroll 1999: 103. **Mount Melleray:** Hulse 1998: 28; Meehan 2002: 508–9. **Ffynnon Fair:** personal communication to me by Judy Welford, who was told about the vision by Peggy Williams.

Two men visiting St Colman's Well, somewhere in Co. Clare, during the early years of the twentieth century; notice that the man close to the well has respectfully removed his hat. Photo: National Museum of Ireland

Visiting

Most wells could be visited at any time, but there were some wells which should only be visited at certain special times. Among the most important days were Beltane/May Day (1 May), and Christian festivals such as Easter, Ascension Day, Whit Sunday, Trinity Sunday. Favourite days were Sundays, Thursdays in May, and Fridays, and favourite times included midnight, dawn, and while the dew still lay on the grass. The well waters were believed to be at their most potent during spring and summer, and that is the time when many were regularly visited. The first water taken on New Year's Day was also important: see **Flower of the well**.

Some curative wells had to be visited, and the **rituals** performed, at a certain specified time – presumably the cure did not work if they were done at the wrong time. The Bairns' Well at Barnwell (Northampton) was thought to cure sickly infants, who were dipped in the water on the eve of St John the Baptist's Day, which was when everyone gathered at the well, and one source says that the boys and young men would wrestle and engage in other 'youthful sports'. Another well used to cure children was at Lee Hall, Bellingham (Northumberland). They had to be dipped on Whitsunday Eve, Midsummer Eve, or St Peter's Eve, before sunrise; and then dipped in the River Tyne after sunset. The prognosis was judged by taking off the child's shift and throwing it in the river: if it floated the child would live, but if it sank the child would die.

On the Isle of Man, among other wells St Maughold's Well was at its most curative if visited on the first Sunday of Harvest, at the time when the priest was saying Mass in the church. However this latter belief was not confined to holy wells for, as noted by Sir John Rhys, 'even sea-water was believed to have considerable virtues if you washed in it while the books were open in church, as I was told by a woman who had many years ago repeatedly taken her own sister to divers wells and to the sea during the service on Sunday, in order to have her eyes cured of their chronic weakness.' There was one well on the Isle of Man, at South Barrule, that could only be visited once by anyone seeking to benefit from its health-giving properties. Local lore says that one man left a stick at the well to mark the place, but when he went back he could find neither the well nor the stick – though the latter was found on the seashore three miles away some weeks later.

Sources: Dates: Jones 1954: 88–92. **Bairns' Well:** Thompson 1913 (December): 138–9. **Lee Hall:** Binnall & Dodds:20. **St Maughold's Well:** Rhys 1891: 306–8. **South Barrule:** Moore 1894: 225–6.

Votive offerings

'Votive' comes from *votivus*, Latin for 'vow' or 'vote', and in the purest sense of the procedure, the pilgrim promises to deposit the votive offering (also known as an ex-voto) in recognition of the successful attainment of the desired objective, that is, the offering is a form of contract with whatever supernatural force (god, goddess, saint) is believed to be in control. However it seems likely that in many instances the votive offering, be it a humble bent pin or as in prehistoric times a valuable weapon, in fact

Pilgrims offer models of the sick parts of their bodies to the Virgin and Child at an altar, in exchange for receiving healing; numerous examples hang above the altar as evidence of cures.

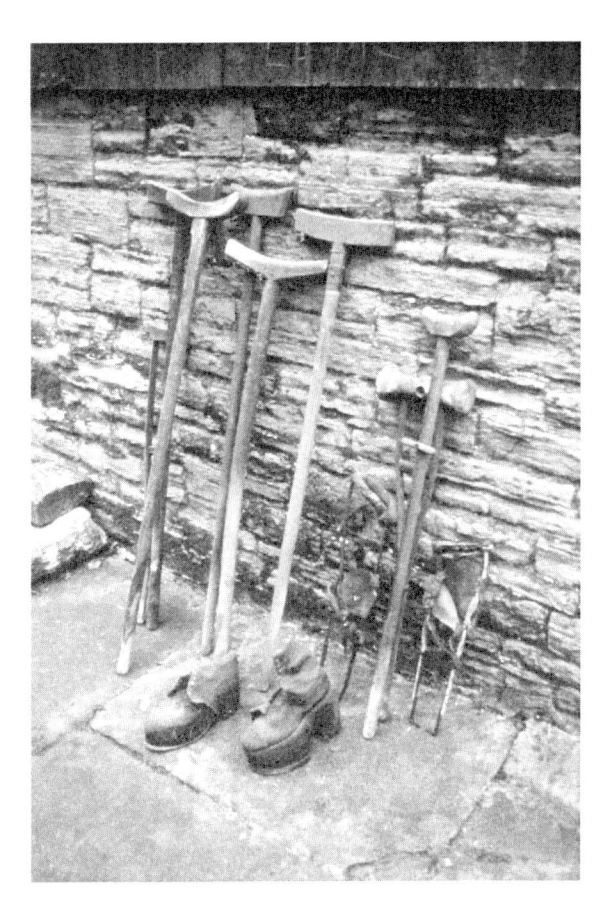

Some of the crutches and surgical boots discarded by people who had been cured at St Winefride's Well, Holywell.

signals the pilgrim's vow or wish or desire to make contact with the deity or saint, and on depositing the votive offering the pilgrim at the same time requests help in whatever their need may be, usually a search for **healing**.

As noted elsewhere, ex-votos or **offerings** can take many forms, including **pins** and **rags,** also coins, nails, fish-hooks, needles (see also **Cloutie wells**; **Deposition**). At the present time holy cards, pictures and rosaries are often left at holy wells in Catholic areas such as Ireland, and candles are now one of the commonest votive offerings at those holy wells where there are the facilities for them. At *St Winefride's Well,* **Holywell** (Flint), candles are the commonest form of votive, and have been for over a century. Today around 50,000 candles are burned there annually. When crutches and surgical boots were common, these were often left as ex-votos at healing wells by people who believed themselves cured.

Patrick Logan also notes some unusual votives at Irish wells, including locks of hair left at Tobar Keelagh (Mayo) and broken china left at St Luctigern's Well at Fenloe (Clare). At the holy well in Aghinagh parish (Cork) pilgrims would use a cup to take water and then add a little earth from the grave of Father John O'Callaghan. The

Votive offerings

Crutches and sticks were left by pilgrims at St Columba's Well near the Rock of Doon (also known as Doon Well), Kilmacrennan, Co. Donegal. Apparently they have then been used to hang rags from, perhaps because of a lack of suitable trees or bushes close to the well. Photo: National Museum of Ireland

earth and water mixture would be applied to external ailments or drunk if the complaint was internal, and the cup would be left on Fr O'Callaghan's grave as a votive offering.

In the Classical world, and at early Romano-Celtic healing shrines, the votive offerings would often take the form of models of the diseased parts of the pilgrims' bodies, offered to the god or goddess in hopes of receiving in exchange a healthy limb or organ. Some examples discovered in Britain include one ivory and one copper alloy breast offered to Sulis at **Bath** (Somerset); and model limbs offered at Springhead (Kent), Lydney (Gloucester) and Muntham Court (Sussex). More examples have been discovered at the sites of healing shrines elsewhere in Europe, and at Fontes Sequanae (the River Seine shrine in France) the evidence shows that models of eyes, breasts, heads, limbs and internal organs, made of oak, would be purchased at the shrine shop and then cast into the healing pool. Some of the models even show signs of the illness they represented, and from those discovered it is clear that eye diseases and breathing problems were prevalent.

Sources: Definitions: Carroll 1999: 33–5. **Ireland:** Logan 1980: 119–20. **Celtic shrines:** Green 1992: 132, 197–8. **Body-part models:** Merrifield 1987: 88–9. **Fontes Sequanae:** Green 1989: 156–63.

W

Walsingham

The village of Little Walsingham (in north Norfolk, just north of Fakenham) is unique, housing as it does two shrines dedicated to Our Lady, and being the centre of a vibrant **pilgrimage** tradition. Thousands of pilgrims are drawn here annually, many of them partaking of the virtues of the water of the holy well in the Anglican shrine, and some also paying a visit to the nearby wishing wells in the grounds of the ruined medieval Augustinian abbey, the original site of the shrine.

It all began in 1061, when the lady of the manor of Walsingham, Richeldis de Faverches, had three dreams or visions in which the Blessed Virgin Mary took her to the Holy House of Nazareth, and asked that a replica should be built at Walsingham. The original site for the small wooden structure was close to two holy wells, which were once believed to have healing powers, though they later declined into **wishing wells** after the Reformation. Richeldis chose the shrine's location after finding two dry patches of ground near the wells after a heavy dew-fall: she saw this as a sign from heaven. However her workmen encountered difficulties when they tried to erect it on one of the sites and gave up for the night: next morning it was found that angels had carried the building to the second site and set it firmly in place. The shrine grew in fame and stature in the succeeding centuries, with royalty among the pilgrims, but in the sixteenth century it was closed down as a result of the Reformation. Several hundred more years passed before, in the late nineteenth century, restoration began, and in the subsequent hundred years Walsingham's fame has grown so that it is now the main pilgrimage centre in England.

Today there are two focal points for pilgrims: the Anglican Shrine in the village of Little Walsingham, which consists of a replica Holy House enclosed in a large pilgrimage church, and the Roman Catholic Shrine at the medieval Slipper Chapel in the countryside a mile away. The Anglican Shrine was built in 1931, and at that time an ancient well was discovered which was found to have a direct link to the wishing wells not far away in the abbey grounds. The new-found well was incorporated into the structure of the Anglican Shrine and now plays an important role in its daily life, with 'Sprinkling at the Holy Well' being part of the daily liturgy during the pilgrimage season; and pilgrims also take bottles of the holy water home. The Shrine and well are open to the general public throughout the year, not only to people visiting on pilgrimage. The wishing wells can also be visited, the entrance to the abbey grounds being located in High Street.

Interestingly, in recent years the Roman Catholics have installed a holy water fountain in the courtyard behind the Slipper Chapel, and sell bottles so that pilgrims can take the water away with them – an example of a very new 'holy well'. (See also **Some Holy Wells to Visit**.)

Sources: Shrine history: Vail 2004: 177–91. **Visitor information:** www.walsingham.org.uk

A holy picture by Enid Chadwick showing one of Richeldis' visions of the Virgin Mary.

Warts

Warts, being a persistent and widespread, if not life-threatening, affliction, figure often in folklore as there have been so many country ways to get rid of them, each method more bizarre than the last. Here we will concern ourselves only with procedures involving holy wells, such as that told to Professor John Rhys when he was judging a competition on the folklore of North Wales at the London Eisteddfod in 1887.

> ... if you wished to get rid of warts, you should, on your way to the well, look for wool which the sheep had lost. When you had found enough wool you should prick each wart with a pin, and then rub the wart well with the wool. The next thing was to bend the pin and throw it into the well. Then you should place the wool on the first whitethorn you could find, and as the wind scattered the wool, the warts would disappear. There was a well of the kind, the writer went on to say, near his home; and he, with three or four other boys, went from school one day to the well to charm their warts away. For he had twenty-three on one of his

At Dungiven, Co. Derry, a bullaun is used as a wart well; note also the rags on the bushes. Photo: Allen Kennedy

hands; so that he always tried to hide it, as it was the belief that if one counted the warts they would double their number. He forgets what became of the other boys' warts, but his own disappeared soon afterwards; and his grandfather used to maintain that it was owing to the virtue of the well.

At the Wart Well on Almscliffe Crag, North Rigton (West Yorkshire), which was actually a natural stone bowl, the custom was to prick the offending wart with a pin, letting blood drip from it into the water in the bowl, and then dip the hand into the water. The Wart Well at Read (Lancashire) was also an unconventional 'well', it being in reality a six-inch deep hollow in a stone boulder that was thought to have been the socket-stone for the lost Simonstone Cross. Warts were bathed in the water that gathered in the cross base. In Ireland it was the custom at some wart wells to dip a pin into the well and bring out a little water, dropping this on to the wart and then placing the pin into the well: as it rusted, so the wart would vanish.

(See also **Cloutie wells; Pins**.)

Sources: Welsh ritual: Rhys 1901: 361–2. **Wart Well, West Yorkshire:** Bennett 2001: 50. **Wart Well, Lancashire:** Taylor 2004: 72. **Ireland:** Logan 1980: 119.

The simple yet evocative stone structure covering St Anne's Well at Whitstone (Cornwall).

Well buildings

Anyone who has visited a variety of holy wells will know that 'variety' is an appropriate word, for their appearance varies massively, from a small and apparently insignificant hole in the ground, to a large and impressive stone building covering the actual well. The nature and design of buildings that have been erected over some wells depend very much on the use to which the well has been put, and who has been involved in its development. The simplest buildings are small stone structures that were built to protect and cover the venerated water source; sometimes niches were provided into which statuettes of saints, and offerings, would have been placed. A good example is St Anne's Well in Whitstone churchyard, Cornwall.

If the well was used as a healing well, with pilgrims wishing to bathe, or at least immerse some part of their body, in it, a somewhat larger stone structure would often have been built. This would not necessarily be roofed, but it would usually encompass the well on three sides, with steps down into the water on the fourth side. Since **incubation** was sometimes a part of the healing procedure, an adjoining building may have been erected where pilgrims could spend the night as part of the cure.

Sometimes grander structures were erected over wells, as for example at *Dupath Well*, Callington, Cornwall, where the stone structure dating from around 1510 is the largest well building in Cornwall. It is in fact a proper well chapel, with a bath, and space for an altar, whereas most so-called 'well chapels' were never really such. A chapel, whether free-standing or part of a larger church, contains an altar, and most 'well chapels' are too small ever to have contained altars. The well chapel that now houses *Ffynnon Trillo* at Llandrillo-yn-Rhos (Conwy) also has an altar, with the well in the floor below it; but this building was not originally a well chapel. Originally

The exterior of the impressive building at St Winefride's Well, Holywell.

there was a well in an unroofed courtyard which was covered over some time after the Reformation. By the late nineteenth century, by which time it was ruinous, it had come to be considered as an early medieval chapel and it was then restored, with an altar being erected over the well. The position of the well clearly demonstrates that this structure could never have been intended as a chapel, as in the Middle Ages no altar would have been erected in such a position.

Undoubtedly the grandest well building is that at *St Winefride's Well,* **Holywell** (Flint), most probably built early in the sixteenth century. A vaulted well crypt surrounds the central well basin, which leads into a large exterior bathing pool, while above the crypt is a well chapel.

Almost as grand, though now a shadow of its former self, was St Triduana's Well at Restalrig, Edinburgh. The well was housed in a hexagonal building adjoining the parish church, but at the Reformation it was extensively damaged, and not restored until the early twentieth century. The well crypt is intact, though the upper chapel which probably housed the saint's shrine has gone, and the spring has dried up.

Architecturally this well shrine is, next to St Winefride's at Holywell, the most interesting well shrine in Britain.

Sources: Dupath Well: Quiller-Couch 1894: 63–5. **Ffynnon Trillo:** Hulse 1995: 31–42. **St Triduana's Well:** Morris 1982: 96.

Well cults

The cult of wells may have its origins in prehistoric times (see **Prehistory**), continuing to develop through Celtic practices in some parts of Europe (see **Celtic influence**), and eventually consolidating as Christianity took hold in Britain. However this apparently straightforward development may be some way from the reality of what really happened, and scholars are regularly finding new evidence which changes the picture. The earliest physical evidence for any form of Christian well cult in Britain is the Menas ampulla which cannot date from any later than the seventh century (see **Ampullae**), and the British finds of Menas ampullae that came from Egypt suggest that the cult of sacred wells was being absorbed into Britain as part of an already flourishing universal cult of saints. One logical conclusion from this might be that the well cult in Britain was not a survival from Celtic or Romano-Celtic pre-Christian religions at all. It is likely that the practices brought back to Britain by Christians visiting foreign shrines became established here, and possibly that traditional Romano-Celtic practices relating to water sources also became part of the overall well cult.

The well cult thrived throughout Britain in medieval times; but in the sixteenth century the whole cult of saints was devastated when the Reformation took hold. Until that time each church would have had several altars dedicated to different saints, which were lovingly maintained, often with candles and costly ornamentations, by the parishioners, and the local saints' wells were also part of this communal practice. An insight into religious life at the parochial level at this time, and how it all fell apart at the Reformation, can be found in Eamon Duffy's superb study of the parish of Morebath in Devon, *The Voices of Morebath*, while his earlier book *The Stripping of the Altars* contains information on pilgrimages including those to wells. Despite all the upheavals of the Reformation in the sixteenth century, the well cult survived through succeeding centuries, albeit with changes. However, the religious associations weakened, and wells were later being visited primarily for **healing** purposes – except in Ireland, and one or two British sites including *St Winefride's Well*, **Holywell** (Flint) and *St Mary's Well*, Fernyhalgh (Lancaster), where the older pilgrimage patterns survived.

In the eighteenth century some springs and wells (though these were generally not holy wells) were developed as commercial spas – there were once more than a hundred flourishing throughout Britain – the names of such places as Llandrindod Wells, Llanwrtyd Wells and Builth Wells (all in Powys) demonstrating the importance of the mineral waters to the prosperity of these small Welsh towns. The more enlightened attitudes of the nineteenth and twentieth centuries, not to mention

TREATISE
On the THREE
Medicinal MINERAL WATERS
AT
LLANDRINDOD,
IN
Radnorshire, SOUTH WALES
WITH SOME
REMARKS
ON
Mineral and Fossil Mixtures,
IN THEIR
Native VEINS and BEDS;
At least as far as respects
Their INFLUENCE on WATER.

By DIEDERICK WESSEL LINDEN, M.D.

Multùm diuque Desideratum.

LONDON:
Printed by J. EVERINGHAM and T. REYNOLDS,
for the AUTHOR:
And Sold by W. OWEN, at *Homer's Head*, Temple Bar. 1756.

Hail sacred Springs! of future Bards the Themes!
When known the Virtues of your healing Streams.

This 1756 publication on the merits of the mineral waters at Llandrindod Wells heralded the development of what was still, in the early eighteenth century, a small Welsh hamlet into an important Welsh spa town.

the development of modern medicine available to all, contributed to the decline of the holy well as a place of local importance, and a great many have fallen into disuse, and sometimes been destroyed, over the last 200 years. However the well cult has not entirely disappeared, as the continuing vitality of some wells demonstrates: St Winefride's Well is a case in point. Smaller more obscure wells have also managed to survive, and indeed many are now positively thriving again, being watched over and cared for by well devotees. There are even wells that, destroyed and closed at the Reformation, have reopened and again become the focus of pilgrimage and healing after 400 years, for example St Mary's Well at Willesden (London). **Pilgrimages** are organised to some wells; at others the quantity of **offerings** demonstrates a continuing flow of visitors. In the early twenty-first century the well cult is still very much alive.

Sources: Medieval and post-medieval Wales: Jones 1954: Chs 3 & 4. **Spas:** Denbigh 1981.

Tissington well-dressing: Reading psalms at the Coffin Well, photographed by Sir Benjamin Stone in the late nineteenth century.

Well-dressing

Derbyshire is now the best-known location of this traditional custom, with such villages as Tissington annually giving thanks for the village water supply by creating elaborate pictures from flowers and other natural materials and putting them on display at the wells.

Less well known are historical accounts of wells being dressed with flowers and greenery elsewhere in the country, such as a well at Colwell in Northumberland, where on or close to 4 July (Old Midsummer Day) a pilgrimage was made to the well which was decked with flowers and a festival held nearby. Wells which were the location for an annual fair or revel might also be decorated, such as the well at Rorrington (Shropshire) where 'green boughs, rushes, and flowers' were placed around it, and a maypole set up close by. Dancing and feasting took place; **pins** were thrown into the well for good luck and to protect the people from witchcraft. They also drank the water – and from a barrel of ale which was specially brewed for the event – and round buns marked with a cross were eaten with the ale. The festivities were discontinued in the 1830s at the death of the man who brewed the ale – showing where the priorities of the revellers lay! The dressing of St Richard's Well at

Droitwich (Worcester) with green boughs and flowers was discontinued during the Civil War, whereupon the well dried up, so the custom was revived and the water returned.

The impulse to decorate wells survives outside Derbyshire, and is likely to be spreading. In 1994 Gina Silverman decided to 'dress' the churchyard wells at *Gumfreston* (Pembroke) and to that end she held informal workshops where those interested could create their own 'dressings' using locally available plant material such as grasses, barley, holly, laurel, rosehips, ferns, ivy, fuchsia, etc. The first attempt at dressing the wells was so successful that the procedure was repeated in subsequent years. The *Seven Wells* at Bisley (Gloucester) are dressed annually, with a well-dressing ceremony taking place on Ascension Day to give thanks for the waters. A church service is held, and the children and a brass band then process to the wells carrying floral tributes which are laid on the wells, and a blessing ceremony conducted by the vicar.

Sources: Colwell: Binnall & Dodds: 26. **Rorrington**: Hope 1893: 147. **St Richard's Well:** Hope 1893: 170. **Gumfreston**: Silverman 1995: 21–2.

St Hilda's Well at Hinderwell (North Yorkshire) is a good example of a holy well close to a church. St Hilda was a local saint, who was Abbess of Whitby in the seventh century.

St Ethelbert's Well inside Marden church, Herefordshire.

Wells inside and close to churches

There are more churches with wells and springs beneath them than one might expect, and the question arises: Why place a building on top of a water source? If the church were being built at the site of an already sacred spring, you would expect the building to be erected close by so that the well or spring was within the churchyard, where it would be handy for collecting water for use in church baptisms. The answer probably is that the first church on the site was small and did originally stand beside the spring, but when the building was enlarged, it then enclosed the spring.

The following are some examples of wells within churches. In Leicestershire Whitwick church has a spring under the chancel, the water from which is piped into a nearby brook; and there is a cast-iron pump inside a cupboard at Melton Mowbray church; while it seems that St Margaret's church in Leicester may once have had more than one well. One was discovered under the north aisle in the 1950s or 1960s that has been dated as either Anglo-Saxon or twelfth century; and the eighteenth-century antiquarian John Nichols mentioned a deep well (now lost) under the tower. Whitwell church in Rutland has a stream flowing under the nave and chancel, and after heavy rain it can be heard beneath the chancel floor. In Cumbria, St Oswald's church at Kirkoswald stands beside a mound on which is the church bell-tower, and the well flows from under the mound, the water passing under the length of the nave and emerging outside the west wall, and into a well-house. In Marden church

(Herefordshire), the well at the west end marks the place where the murdered St Ethelbert, King of East Anglia until his death in 794, was buried. When his body was removed to Hereford, a well arose in the empty grave. Most probably, the grave was originally outside the first church, only being enclosed when the church was enlarged by extending the nave westward.

A high proportion of wells beneath religious buildings can be found under abbeys, minsters and cathedrals. Glastonbury Abbey (Somerset) has St Joseph's Well in the crypt of St Mary's Chapel, and Dunfermline Abbey (Fife) has a well in the nave for use in church services, while in Beverley Minster (East Yorkshire), during restoration of the choir in 1879, two old and worn steps were found which had been used as an approach to a well. Canterbury Cathedral's Well of St Thomas, formerly on the north side of the choir, no longer exists, nor does St Pandonia's Well at Ely Cathedral. In Carlisle Cathedral there is a well under one of the pillars: it is said to have been covered over at the request of a dean who believed that it was in some way adversely affecting the music. Ancient wells have also been found at St Patrick's Cathedral, Dublin, Winchester Cathedral, Wells Cathedral, Exeter Cathedral, and in the crypts of York Minster and Glasgow Cathedral. King Edwin was reputedly baptised in the York Minster well in 627, which was then covered only by a small wooden chapel – maybe the site of the future York Minster was determined by this event. The crypt of Glasgow Cathedral was built over the spot where the body of Fergus, an anchorite, was buried, brought there by Mungo (the same person as Kentigern), bishop of the kingdom of Strathclyde. St Mungo may have baptised his converts in the well now in the south-east corner of the crypt.

Interestingly, almost none of the above-mentioned wells in churches and cathedrals ever functioned as what we understand as 'holy wells'.

Sources: Leicestershire and Rutland: Trubshaw 2002: Whitwick; and in e-mail message to Wells-and-Spas online discussion group, 21 May 1999. **Cumbria:** Page 1990: 15. **Wells:** Rodwell 1981: 142–3.

Wishing wells

Nowadays the only wells that many people have heard of are wishing wells: you throw in a coin and make a wish. They are unaware that what they are actually doing is making a **votive offering** to the spirit of the well in exchange for their heart's desire. And it is not just at designated 'wishing wells' that the urge surfaces. It seems that the instinct to deposit **offerings** in water is so strong that other bodies of water also attract this behaviour, and coins are often seen in man-made pools wherever people congregate, such as shopping centres. Ralph Merrifield reported seeing 'votive coins' in the drinking bowl of the ravens at the Tower of London, and in a pool in the Museum of London which was intended to 'maintain the humidity necessary for the conservation of the Lord Mayor's coach' which was on display at the opening of the museum in 1976. Coins have also been spotted in the pools housing alligators and crocodiles at Chester Zoo, and in a fountain at Gatwick

St Oswald's Well, Oswestry, Shropshire – no longer accessible for use as a wishing well.

airport. Naturally a public pool or fountain where many coins have been thrown can act as a temptation to some people, and it would be interesting to know how often the coins are stolen. At the fountain in the garden of remembrance at Pentrebychan crematorium (Wrexham) a pair of swimming shorts was found in October 2005, left behind by the thief who had drained the water from the fountain before taking all the coins (totalling around £30) thrown into it by mourners.

In earlier days there was often a strictly defined procedure that had to be followed at wishing wells, such as at the **Walsingham** wishing wells (Norfolk) where the supplicant

> ... may expect to have one single wish granted if he will strictly observe the orthodox conditions. He must not speak after coming within a certain distance of the wells, he must kneel first at one well, then at the other in turn, as he drinks the water; above all, he must not let a soul know what his wish is.

St Catherine's Well at Fivehead (Somerset) was a wishing well, and there the procedure was to go round it three times at sunrise (presumably in a clockwise direction) when making your wish. If by chance you happened instead to crawl around it counter-clockwise, ill-luck would result. (See also **Circumambulation**.) You also had to walk three times round the Pin Well at Alnwick (Northumberland) – then jump across it, throw in a pin, and make your wish. On the Isle of Wight, anyone intending to make a wish at St Boniface's Well had to approach it walking backwards, before drinking some of the water while making a wish.

Among the most elaborate procedures at a wishing well must be those that were once in force at St Oswald's Well, Oswestry (Shropshire) where there were at least four separate **rituals**.

1. Go to the well at midnight, take some water in your hand, drink some of it and think your wish. Throw the rest of the water on to a certain stone at the back of the well where Oswald's head was believed to be buried and where there was once a stone head wearing a crown. (By the mid nineteenth century this had been damaged beyond recognition.) If you can throw the water on to that stone alone, not touching any other, your wish will be fulfilled.

2. Bathe your face in the water while making your wish.

3. Throw a stone on to a certain green spot at the bottom of the well, causing a jet of water; put your head under the jet and wish.

4. Find an empty beechnut husk among the beeches near the well that looks something like a human face, and throw it into the water with the face upwards. If it floats as you count to twenty, your wish will be fulfilled.

Why should the wishing ritual be so elaborate? Why is it not possible simply to drink some of the well water and make a wish? That seems far too casual. Perhaps all the specific actions which need to be performed are intended to focus the wisher's concentration so that his or her inner powers are brought to bear on the object of the wish and then by some supernatural power it will magically happen as wished for.

Sources: Modern practice: Merrifield 1987: 115; Sauer 2005: 21. **Theft:** *Daily Post*, 6 October 2005. **Little Walsingham:** Dutt 1909: 256. **St Catherine's Well:** Harte 'Somerset' 1985: 6. **Pin Well:** Balfour 1904: 1–2. **St Boniface's Well:** Hope 1893: 76. **St Oswald's Well:** Hope 1893: 145.

Witches

Some wells were believed to be the meeting places of witches, and there was one in the Quantock Hills of Somerset that was called the Witches' Well (at Pardlestone). It was considered to be a dangerous place because of its witch association, until a 'gifted man' took steps to deal with the problem. The well was 'down a dark lane, and folks were feared to death to go by it and to let their stock drink [presumably for fear that the animals would be bewitched]. So they got a gifted man, and he said the right words and threw salt in it and drove 'em all away.' In Wales, wells that incorporate *gwrach* or *wrach* in their names are witch wells.

An intriguing link between a witch (so-called) and a well was found in the writings of Richard Singleton, Vicar of Melmerby in Cumbria, who died in 1684. In writing about the parish wells, he included 'Margrett Hardies Well': 'It was so called from a woman who frequented it daily and lived to a great age: they report her to have been a witch.' Was this because of her habit of drinking the well water daily, or because

Some holy wells were believed to be the haunts of witches.
Artwork: Anthony Wallis

she was very old, or was there something else about her behaviour that caused the villagers to class her as a witch? One would like to know more!

Ffynnon Sarah at Caerwys (Flint) (also known as Ffynnon Deg) was locally said to have been named after a witch who claimed that the well water could only be used for healing through her mediation or intercession, in other words she had appointed herself guardian of the well. Whereas old women who behaved as well **guardians** may have been thought of as witches by some people, it is probable that they were simply poor people who welcomed the tips they might get by helping visitors to the well. Interpretations of these old women as pagan priestesses performing arcane rituals are mostly very far from the truth. However there are certainly examples of some old women claiming to be the only person able to interpret the signs when a visitor came to a well in search of answers rather than in search of healing, and their **divination** skills would be sought after, regardless of whether they really were able to make genuine predictions or were simply making it all up.

Witches were believed to be able to tie up winds in knots, which could be released when the wind was needed. This drawing shows a male witch preparing to release the knotted wind for sailors whose ship seems to be becalmed. From Olaus Magnus, Historia de Gentibus Septentrionalibus *(1555).*

On the Isle of Man, one use to which wells were put was 'raising the wind'. This was something that witches did – for various purposes including in order to sell it to sailors, by, according to a fourteenth-century record, putting the wind under three knots of thread which the sailors would then loosen one by one when they wished the wind to blow. In a record surviving from 1658, one Elizabeth Black was accused of emptying 'a springing well dry for to obtain a favourable winde'. In court several witnesses testified that the well had been emptied, though Black denied the allegations; still she was fined 'for such a folly tendinge to charminge, witchcraft, or scorcery'. There is also a well on the remote island of St Kilda which was used to control the wind, but by fishermen rather than by witches. If the wind was not favourable for fishing, each fisherman would go to the well and stand astride it for a moment, and the wind would then turn in their favour.

The notorious witches of Llanddona on Anglesey actually created a well, when they were in desperate need of water after sailing to the island with their husbands and receiving an unfriendly welcome from the Llanddona natives. They had been confined to the beach, and it was there they ordered a fresh-water supply to gush forth from the sand. They also cursed their enemies at Ffynnon Oer, and one of their curses reads in translation:

> You will roam for many ages;
> In every step you take, you will encounter a stile
> At every stile you will fall.

> At every fall you will break a bone –
> Not the largest or the smallest bone,
> But the bones of your neck every time.

No wonder country people were keen to avail themselves of any kind of protection against the harm witches were thought capable of inflicting. Holy well water drawn after midnight at Beltane (1 May) in Ireland was known as 'the purity of the well' and was kept throughout the year, as it was considered a powerful protection against witchcraft. (See also **Flower of the well**.) A church **baptism** was also believed to protect against witchcraft.

Sources: The Witches' Well, Pardlestone: Tongue 1965: 23. **Margrett Hardies Well:** McIntire 1944: 12. **Ffynnon Sarah:** Davies 1959: 62. **Priestesses:** Jones 1954: 127–8. **Raising the wind:** Higden's *Polychronicon* (c.1350) quoted in Roud 2003: 522; *Liber Scaccarii* quoted in Moore 1894: 219. **St Kilda:** MacLeod 2000: 79. **Llanddona witches/Ffynnon Oer:** Jones 1954: 129–30. **Purity of the well:** Jones 1954: 92.

Some holy wells to visit

Twenty-five favourite wells in England and Wales

I have personally visited all these wells and so know that they are all accessible, and all worth seeing. I am currently compiling a much more comprehensive guidebook to surviving holy wells in the British Isles.

England

Cornwall

This is the English county with the highest surviving number of holy wells, and there are many others well worth seeing in addition to the following four.

St Cleer holy well: A fifteenth-century stone building covers the well, and there is a stone cross beside it. Both are easily accessible beside a road in the small village of St Cleer 2 miles north of Liskeard. (SX 249683) (See **Bowssening** and **Desecration and destruction**)

Twenty-five favourite wells in England and Wales

Above: **St Clether's Well:** This well and accompanying chapel were restored from a ruinous state in the late nineteenth century. They are in a peaceful rural setting half a mile north-west of St Clether church, 8 miles west of Launceston. (SX 202846)

Right: **Dupath Well, Callington:** The early sixteenth-century well chapel is the largest and most impressive well building in Cornwall. Close to a farm a mile east of Callington, between Launceston and Saltash. (SX 375692) (See **Well buildings**)

Cures and curses

Madron Well: A mysterious site deep in woodland, the well itself is the most basic kind, a hole in the ground, with rags tied to the bushes; not far away is a ruined chapel. North-west of Madron village, itself a short distance north-west of Penzance; reached by footpath off a lane leading towards Boswarthen. (SW 445327) (See **Healing; Love magic; Pilgrimage**)

Gloucestershire

Seven Wells, Bisley: The water gushing from seven springs is an impressive sight in wet weather. The stone structure from which they flow was built in 1863, and can be found beside a lane literally below the church. Bisley is an attractive, and steep, village 4 miles east of Stroud. (SO 903059) (See **Well-dressing**)

Twenty-five favourite wells in England and Wales

Lancashire

Lady Well (St Mary's Well), Fernyhalgh: This pretty well in the garden of the Catholic shrine of Our Lady of Fernyhalgh is a haven of peace close to the M6 motorway, and still a functioning place of pilgrimage. It can be found beside a lane running south-east from Haighton Top, 2 miles west of Grimsargh and just north of Preston. (SD 555340) (See **Pilgrimage; Shrines**)

Norfolk

St Withburga's Well, East Dereham: Located in the churchyard, this well marks the place where the saint's body was buried before being taken away to Ely in 974. (TF 986134)

Above: **Wells at Little Walsingham:** There is a holy well in the Anglican Shrine, visited by thousands of pilgrims annually; and there are wishing wells (above) which seem to have functioned as the holy wells of the medieval shrine of Our Lady of Walsingham. These are in the abbey grounds, reached through the High Street entrance. (See **Ampullae; Walsingham; Wishing wells**)

North Yorkshire

Opposite top: **The Dropping Well, Knaresborough:** This famous petrifying well, and the nearby wishing well, are also close to Mother Shipton's Cave where the famous prophetess was born. All are reached by a pleasant walk beside the River Nidd, but an entrance fee is payable. (SE 348565) (See **Petrifying wells; Prophecy**)

Northumberland

Opposite bottom: **Lady's Well, Holystone:** The 'well' is a large pool, with a Celtic cross in the middle and a statue of St Paulinus who used the well as a baptistery. Reached by footpath from the village of Holystone, 7 miles west of Rothbury. (NT 953029)

Twenty-five favourite wells in England and Wales

159

Oxfordshire

Above: **Fair Rosamond's Well, Blenheim Park, Woodstock:** The name comes from the legend of Rosamond Clifford, King Henry II's lover, who was found dead in her bower, supposedly killed by the jealous Queen Eleanor. The water flows into a large pool located by the north shore of the lake (which is visible in the distance) and the well is accessible by footpath. (SP 436164)

Shropshire

Opposite top: **St Winifred's Well, Woolston:** The half-timbered building above this well was originally a pilgrimage chapel. Later used as a court-house, it is now a small cottage owned by the Landmark Trust and available for holiday lets. A footpath runs past the well. (SJ 322244)

Worcestershire

Opposite bottom: **St Kenelm's Well, Clent Hills:** This well, marking the place where the body of the murdered Mercian king was said to have lain in the ninth century, is close to St Kenelm's Church, Romsley (a mile north-west of the village), and reached through the churchyard. Rags now adorn the bushes all around the hidden well. (SO 945808) (See **Creation of wells; Saints' deaths; Shrines**)

Twenty-five favourite wells in England and Wales

Wales

Anglesey

Below: **St Gwenfaen's Well, Rhoscolyn:** Steps lead down into the stone chamber of this exposed well on a remote headland, reached by an often windy but always exhilarating walk from Rhoscolyn church, south of Holyhead. (SH 259754)

Left: **St Seiriol's Well, Penmon:** Although the holy well itself is old, the well-house is relatively recent. The well only became known as St Seiriol's in the twentieth century. Before that it was briefly known as St Mary's Well, and also as a wishing well. Easily found, being close to Penmon Priory on the eastern tip of Anglesey. (SH 631808) (See **Pins**)

Twenty-five favourite wells in England and Wales

Conwy

Right: **St Trillo's Well, Rhos-on-Sea:** The well is in the floor of the tiny stone chapel, Capel Trillo, on the seafront below the promenade, close to the public toilets. (SH 842812) (See **Well buildings**)

Denbighshire

Below: **St Beuno's Well, Tremeirchion:** South of the village, on the road to Bodfari, the well is in the front garden of the house Ffynnon Beuno. Through the gateway is a large bathing pool enclosed in stone walls, and the water flows out through the head of a stone figure low down in the wall facing the road. (SJ 083723) (See **Heads**)

Flintshire

St Winefride's Well, Holywell: If you can only visit one well, it should be this one. With its atmospheric gushing spring, open-air bathing pool and impressive stone well chapel, it provides the genuine holy-well experience. There is also a museum and exhibition. Sited below the town church, and signposted in the town. The photograph shows the actual well inside the well building; the outdoor bathing pool is to the left. (Photo: Roger Brown) (SJ 185763) (See **Ampullae; Blood; Eye wells; Healing; Holywell; Mosses and other plants; Pilgrimage; Saints' deaths; Shrines; Votive offerings; Well buildings**)

Gwynedd

Opposite top: **St Cybi's Well, Llangybi:** The ruined stone buildings round this well are in a valley setting, approached by footpath through the churchyard at Llangybi, 5 miles north-east of Pwllheli. (SH 427413) (See **Guardians**)

Monmouthshire

Opposite bottom: **Virtuous Well (St Anne's Well), Trellech:** The well set in a stone surround is in a field by a lane to the south-east of the village, while not far away are the impressive Harold's Stones, also worth a visit. (SO 503051) (See **Fairies**)

Twenty-five favourite wells in England and Wales

Cures and curses

Pembrokeshire

Above: **St Govan's Well, Bosherston:** Sadly the well itself is now dry, but the location is so spectacular that it is still worth visiting. At the cliffs a mile south of Bosherston (south of Pembroke) a long flight of steps leads down to the tiny chapel of St Govan, and below it among the rocks can be seen the little stone building over the former well. The chapel is behind the photographer; the well can be seen in the right foreground, blending in among all the huge boulders on the shore. (SR 967929)

Opposite top: **Gumfreston Church Wells:** No less than three wells are still flowing among the foliage in the churchyard at Gumfreston, not far from Tenby. (SN 109010) (See **Well-dressing**)

Opposite bottom: **St Non's Well, St Davids:** St Non is said to have given birth to St David close to this well, which is in a wonderful coastal location beside a lane leading south from the town to St Non's Bay. St Non is depicted in a window of the small modern chapel close by. (SM 751243) (See **Saints in the landscape**)

Twenty-five favourite wells in England and Wales

Cures and curses

Powys

Above: **St Issui's (Ishow's) Well, Partrishow (Patricio):** Hidden away in the Black Mountains to the north of Abergavenny, both the simple well, and the medieval church on the hillside above it, are worth visiting. Steps lead down from the lane to St Issui's Well, tucked down beside the stone wall at the right of the photograph. (SO 278223)

Left: **St Myllin's Well, Llanfyllin:** This well sited on a hill above the town is well maintained; reached by a dead-end lane (walk, don't drive, as there is nowhere to park or turn) just outside the town to the west; signposted. (SJ 138195)

Bibliography

Addis, William E., & Thomas Arnold, *A Catholic Dictionary* (London: Routledge & Kegan Paul, 17th edition revised, 1960)

Adomnán of Iona, *Life of St Columba* (translated by Richard Sharpe)(London: Penguin Books, 1995)

Allason-Jones, Lindsay, and Bruce McKay, *Coventina's Well: A Shrine on Hadrian's Wall* (Northumberland: The Trustees of the Clayton Collection, Chesters Museum, 1985)

Baker, Rowland G.M., 'Holy Wells and Magical Waters of Surrey', *Source* 1 (1985)

Balfour, M.C. (collected by) & Northcote W. Thomas (edited by), *County Folk-Lore Vol.IV – Printed Extracts No.6 – Examples of Printed Folk-Lore Concerning Northumberland* (London: published for the Folk-Lore Society by David Nutt, 1904; facsimile reprint by Llanerch Publishers, 1994)

Bates, A.W., 'Healing Waters: Holy Wells and Spas of Warwickshire', *Warwickshire History*, vol.IX no.2 (Winter 1993–4)

Bayley, Michael, 'The Ladywell at Speen', *Source* New Series 3 (Spring 1995)

— 'Rebecca's Well at Crazies Hill', *Strange Berkshire* (High Wycombe: Strange Publications, 1986)

Paul Bennett, *The Old Stones of Elmet* (Milverton: Capall Bann Publishing, 2001)

Billingsley, John, *Stony Gaze: Investigating Celtic and Other Stone Heads* (Chieveley: Capall Bann Publishing, 1998)

Binnall, Peter B.G., 'Collectanea: Some Theories Regarding Eye-Wells', *Folklore*, vol.56 (London: The Folklore Society, 1945)

Binnall, The Revd P.B.G. and Miss M. Hope Dodds, 'Holy Wells in Northumberland and Durham', *Proceedings of the Society of Antiquaries*, vols IX–XI

Bord, Janet, *Footprints in Stone* (Wymeswold: Heart of Albion Press, 2004)

— *The Traveller's Guide to Fairy Sites* (Glastonbury: Gothic Image Publications, 2004)

Bord, Janet and Colin, *The Secret Country: An Interpretation of the Folklore of Ancient Sites in the British Isles* (London: Elek Books, 1976)

— *Sacred Waters: Holy Wells and Water Lore in Britain and Ireland* (London: Granada Publishing, 1985)

— *The Enchanted Land* (London: Thorsons, 1995; Wymeswold: Heart of Albion Press, 2006)

Bowen, Dewi, 'The Holy Wells of Glamorgan', *Source* 8 (1988)

Bradley, Richard, *An Archaeology of Natural Places* (London and New York: Routledge, 2000)

Bradshaw, Jane, 'St Arilda of Oldbury on Severn, Gloucestershire', *Source* New Series 5 (Spring 1998)

Brenneman, Walter L., Jr., and Mary G. Brenneman, *Crossing the Circle at the Holy Wells of Ireland* (Charlottesville and London: University Press of Virginia, 1995)

Broadhurst, Paul, *Secret Shrines: In Search of the Old Holy Wells of Cornwall* (Launceston: Paul Broadhurst, 1988)
Brown, Theo, 'Holy and Notable Wells of Devon', *Transactions of the Devonshire Association for the Advancement of Science, Literature and Art,* vol.89 (1957)
Buckley, Kemmis, MBE, DL, MA, 'The Well and the Skull', *Source* New Series 2 (Winter 1994)
— 'Some Holy Wells of South Carmarthenshire', *Source* New Series 3 (Spring 1995)
Burl, Aubrey, *The Stone Circles of the British Isles* (New Haven and London: Yale University Press, 1976)
— *From Carnac to Callanish: The Prehistoric Stone Rows and Avenues of Britain, Ireland and Brittany* (New Haven and London: Yale University Press, 1993)
Carroll, Michael P., *Irish Pilgrimage: Holy Wells and Popular Catholic Devotion* (Baltimore and London: The Johns Hopkins University Press, 1999)
Caulfield, John, *Portraits, Memoirs and Characters of Remarkable Persons from the Reign of Edward III to the Revolution* (London: 1813)
Cleaver, Alan, 'Holy Wells: Wormholes in Reality? Part I – An Examination of Dragons and Their Fascination with Holy Wells', *Source* 3 (1985)
Cleaver, Alan, and Lesley Park, 'Strange Buckinghamshire', www.cleaverproperty.co.uk/strange/bucks/wells2.html
Crawshaw, John, letter in *Source* New Series 3 (Spring 1995)
Cunliffe, Barry, *English Heritage Book of Roman Bath* (London: B.T. Batsford/English Heritage, 1995)
Darwen, Norman, 'Some Holy Wells In and Around Preston', *Source* 8 (1988)
Davies, Ellis, *Flintshire Place Names* (Cardiff: University of Wales Press, 1959)
Davis, Paul, *Sacred Springs: In Search of the Holy Wells and Spas of Wales* (Abergavenny: Blorenge Books, 2003)
Denbigh, Kathleen, *A Hundred British Spas: A Pictorial History* (London: Spa Publications, 1981)
Doble, G.H., *Lives of the Welsh Saints* (Cardiff: University of Wales Press, 1971)
Doughty, Audrey, *Spas and Springs in Wales* (Llanrwst: Gwasg Carreg Gwalch, 2001)
Duffy, Eamon, *The Stripping of the Altars: Traditional Religion in England c.1400–c.1580* (New Haven and London: Yale University Press, 1992)
— *The Voices of Morebath: Reformation and Rebellion in an English Village* (New Haven and London: Yale University Press, 2001)
Durham, M.E., Correspondence in *Folklore,* vol.43 (1932)
Dutt, W.A., *The Norfolk and Suffolk Coast* (London: T. Fisher Unwin, 1909)
Ekwall, Eilert, *The Concise Oxford Dictionary of English Place-Names* (Oxford: Oxford University Press, 4th edition 1960)
Faull, Terry, *Secrets of the Hidden Source: In Search of Devon's Ancient and Holy Wells* (Tiverton: Halsgrove, 2004)
Finucane, Ronald C., *Miracles and Pilgrims: Popular Beliefs in Medieval England* (London: J.M. Dent & Sons, 1977)

Bibliography

Forbes, Alexander Robert, *Place-Names of Skye and Adjacent Islands With Lore, Mythical, Traditional and Historical* (Paisley: Alexander Gardner, Ltd, 1923)

Gillett, H.M., *Shrines of Our Lady in England and Wales* (London: Samuel Walker, Ltd, 1957)

Goodburn, Roger, *Chedworth Roman Villa* (London: The National Trust, 2003 reprint)

Gosden, Chris, and Gary Lock, 'Frilford: A Romano-British ritual pool in Oxfordshire?', *Current Archaeology* 184 (February 2003)

Gougaud, Dom Louis, *Devotional and Ascetic Practices in the Middle Ages* (London: Burns Oates & Washbourne, 1927)

Green, Miranda, *Symbol and Image in Celtic Religious Art* (London: Routledge, 1989)
— *Dictionary of Celtic Myth and Legend* (London: Thames and Hudson, 1992)
— 'The Religious Symbolism of Llyn Cerrig Bach and Other Early Sacred Water Sites', *Source* New Series 1 (Autumn 1994)
— *Celtic Goddesses: Warriors, Virgins and Mothers* (London: British Museum Press, 1995)

Green, Miranda Aldhouse, *Dying for the Gods: Human Sacrifice in Iron Age & Roman Europe* (Stroud: Tempus Publishing, 2001)

Greenwood, Dave, 'Island Athletes Draw on Divine Inspiration', *Daily Post*, 30 May 2003

Gregor, W., 'Guardian Spirits of Wells and Lochs', *Folklore,* vol.3 (1892)

Gruffydd, Eirlys, *Ffynhonnau Cymru: Cyfrol 1: Ffynhonnau Brycheiniog, Ceredigion, Maldwyn, Maesyfed a Meirion* (Llanrwst: Gwasg Carreg Gwalch, 1997)

Gruffydd, Eirlys a Ken Lloyd, *Ffynhonnau Cymru: Cyfrol 2: Ffynhonnau Caernarfon, Dinbych, Y Fflint a Môn* (Llanrwst: Gwasg Carreg Gwalch, 1999)

Haigh, Mike, 'Mike Haigh's Archaeology Round-up: Chedworth', *Northern Earth* 85 (Spring 2001)

Hamilton, Mary, *Incubation or the Cure of Disease in Pagan Temples and Christian Churches* (London: 1906)

Hamlin, Ann and Chris Lynn (editors), *Pieces of the Past: Archaeological Excavations by the Department of the Environment for Northern Ireland 1970–1986* (Belfast: H.M.S.O., 1988)

Hardy, Philip Dixon, *The Holy Wells of Ireland* (Dublin: Hardy & Walker; London: R. Groombridge; Edinburgh: Fraser & Co., 1840)

Harte, J.M., 'Dorset Holy Wells', *Source* 1 (1985)
— 'The Holy Wells of Somerset', *Source* 2 (1985)
— 'Holy Wells and Other Holy Places', *Living Spring* issue 1 (May 2000) www.bath.ac.uk/lispring/journal/issue1/research/jharhpl1.htm

Hartland, E. Sidney, 'Pin-Wells and Rag-Bushes', *Folklore,* vol.4 (1893)

Healy, Elizabeth, *In Search of Ireland's Holy Wells* (Dublin: Wolfhound Press, 2001)

Herity, Michael, 'The Chi-Rho and other early cross-forms in Ireland', in Michael Herity, *Studies in the Layout, Buildings and Art in Stone of Early Irish Monasteries* (London: The Pindar Press, 1995)

Hilton, J.A., 'Return to Peggy's Spout', *Northern Earth* 70 (Summer 1997)

Hole, Christina, *English Shrines and Sanctuaries* (London: B.T. Batsford, 1954)
— *Saints in Folklore* (London: G. Bell and Sons, 1966)
Holland, Richard, *Haunted Wales: A Survey of Welsh Ghostlore* (Ashbourne: Landmark Publishing, 2005)
Hope, Robert Charles, *The Legendary Lore of the Holy Wells of England* (London: Elliot Stock, 1893; Detroit: Singing Tree Press, 1968)
Horne, Dom. Ethelbert, *Somerset Holy Wells and Other Named Wells* (London: Somerset Folk Press, 1923)
Hough, C., 'The Place-Name Fritwell', *Journal of the English Place-Name Society* 29 (1996–7)
Howse, W.H., *Disserth, Radnorshire: Its Church and its History and Folk-Lore* (Disserth church booklet, 1991 edition)
Hughes, E. Rothwell, 'Rural Archaeology', *British Archaeology* 25 (June 1997)
Hulse, Tristan Gray, 'The Whistlebitch Well, Utkinton, Cheshire', *Source* New Series 1 (Autumn 1994)
— 'St Teilo and the Head Cult', *Source* New Series 2 (Winter 1994)
— 'Pilgrims' Ampullae and the Well of St Menas', *Source* New Series 4 (Summer 1995)
— 'A Modern Votive Deposit at a North Welsh Holy Well', *Folklore,* vol.106 (1995)
— 'New Wells for Old?', *Source* New Series 6 (Summer 1998)
— (ed.), *Father Ryan's Diary: 25 Years of Cures at St Winefride's Well, Holywell* (in preparation)
Hunt, Laurence, 'The Holy Wells of West Penwith, Cornwall', *Source* 3 (1985)
— 'Ancient, Healing and Holy Wells of County Durham', *Source* 7 (1987)
— 'Some Ancient and Holy Wells of Devon', *Source* 9 (undated, c.1988)
Hunt, Robert, *The Drolls, Traditions, and Superstitions of Old Cornwall (Popular Romances of the West of England), Second Series* (3rd edition published 1881; facsimile reprint by Llanerch Publishers, 1993)
Irwin, John C., 'The Stupa and the Cosmic Axis: The Archaeological Evidence', *South Asian Archaeology 1977* (papers from the Fourth International Conference of South Asian Archaeologists in Western Europe: Naples, 1979)
Jenkins, Simon, *England's Thousand Best Churches* (London: Penguin Books, 2000)
Jones, Francis, *The Holy Wells of Wales* (Cardiff: University of Wales Press, 1954; facsimile reissue 1992)
Jones, David, 'Old Well at Llanfihangel, near Cowbridge', *Archaeologia Cambrensis,* vol.45 (1890)
Jordan, Katherine M., 'Seven Wiltshire Wells and Their Folklore', *Source* New Series 6 (Summer 1998)
Kerridge, Roy, 'At St Winifred's Well', *Source* New Series 5 (Spring 1998)
— 'On Canvey Island', *Source* New Series 6 (Summer 1998)
Kift, Mary, *Life in Old Caversham* (Published in collaboration with John and Lindsey Mullaney of the Caversham Bookshop; 2nd edition 2004)
Lane-Davies, The Rev. A., *Holy Wells of Cornwall: A Guide* (Federation of Old Cornwall Societies, 1970)

Leach, Maria (ed.) and Jerome Fried (Associate Editor), *Funk & Wagnalls Standard Dictionary of Folklore, Mythology and Legend* (New York: Harper & Row, 1984 – paperback edition)
Leclerq, Henri, 'Ampoules. – I. Ampoules à eulogies', *Dictionnaire d'archéologie chrétienne et de liturgie*, vol.I (Paris, 1924), cols 1722–1747
— 'Ménas (Saint)', *Dictionnaire d'archéologie chrétienne et de liturgie*, vol.II (Paris, 1933), cols. 324–397
Leggat, P.O. and D.V., *The Healing Wells, Cornish Cults and Customs* (Redruth: Dyllansow Truran Publishers, 1987)
Logan, Patrick, *The Holy Wells of Ireland* (Gerrards Cross: Colin Smythe Ltd, 1980)
Lynch, Frances, *Prehistoric Anglesey* (Llangefni: The Anglesey Antiquarian Society, 1970)
Mac Coitir, Niall, *Irish Trees: Myths, Legends and Folklore* (Doughcloyne: The Collins Press, 2003)
MacDonald, A., 'Sacred Wells', *Folklore,* vol.19 (1908)
MacGregor, Alasdair Alpin, *Somewhere in Scotland* (London: Robert Hale Ltd, 1935 & 1948)
McIntire, W.T., 'The Holy Wells of Cumberland', *Transactions of the Cumberland and Westmorland Antiquarian And Archaeological Society,* vol.44 (1944)
M'Kenzie, Dan, M.D., 'Children and Wells', *Folklore,* vol.18 (1907)
Mackinlay, J.B., OSB, *Saint Edmund, King and Martyr: A History of His Life and Times* (London and Leamington: Art and Book Company, 1893)
Mackinlay, James M., *Folklore of Scottish Lochs and Springs* (Glasgow: William Hodge & Co., 1893; Felinfach: Llanerch Publishers, 1993)
MacLeod, Finlay, *The Healing Wells of the Western Isles* (Stornoway: Acair Ltd, 2000)
Mann, Nicholas R., and Philippa Glasson, *Avalon's Red and White Springs: A Guide to the Healing Waters at Glastonbury* (Sutton Mallet: Green Magic, 2005)
Martin, Valerie, 'Some Holy Wells in Kent', *Source* 2 (July 1985)
Meehan, Cary, *The Traveller's Guide to Sacred Ireland* (Glastonbury: Gothic Image Publications, 2002)
Merrifield, Ralph, *The Archaeology of Ritual and Magic* (London: B.T. Batsford Ltd, 1987)
Meyrick, J., *A Pilgrim's Guide to the Holy Wells of Cornwall* (Cornwall: J. Meyrick, 1982)
Miller, Joyce, *Myth and Magic: Scotland's Ancient Beliefs and Sacred Places* (Musselburgh: Goblinshead, 2000)
— *Magic and Witchcraft in Scotland* (Musselburgh: Goblinshead, 2004)
Moore, A.W., 'Water and Well-Worship in Man', *Folklore,* vol.5 (1894)
Morrell, R.W., *Nottinghamshire Holy Wells and Springs* (Nottingham: APRA Press, 1988)
— 'Correspondence', *Source* New Series 6 (Summer 1998)
Morris, Ruth and Frank, *Scottish Healing Wells: Healing, Holy, Wishing and Fairy Wells of the Mainland of Scotland* (Sandy: The Alethea Press, 1982)
Nelson, Carole L., 'Peg o'Nell's Well', *Source* New Series 6 (Summer 1998)

Nicholson, John, *Folk Lore of East Yorkshire* (London: 1890; Wakefield: EP Publishing, 1973)

Ó Cadhla, Stiofán, *The Holy Well Tradition: The Pattern of St Declan, Ardmore, County Waterford, 1800–2000* (Maynooth Studies in Local History: Number 45)(Dublin: Four Courts Press, 2002)

Ó Dubhthaigh, Bearnárd, 'Tobar Aibheog, Lismullyduff: Its Traditions and Associations', *Donegal Annual,* vol.VII no.3 (1968)

Ó Mórdha, Pilip, 'Saint Patrick's Well, Clonfad', *Clogher Record,* vol.VIII no.3 (1975)

Osborne, Bruce, 'The Springs and Wells of the South Downs', *Source* New Series 2 (Winter 1994)

— 'The Springs and Wells of the South Downs', *Source* New Series 3 (Spring 1995)

— 'The Springs and Wells of the South Downs – Part Three', *Source* New Series 6 (Summer 1998)

Osborne, Bruce, and Cora Weaver, *Aquae Britannia, Rediscovering 17th Century Springs and Spas* (Malvern: 1996)

— *The Springs, Spouts, Fountains and Holy Wells of the Malverns* (Malvern: Cora Weaver, 1997)

Otter, Laurens, 'Notes Towards a Survey of Shropshire Holy Wells', *Source* 3 (1985)

— 'Notes Towards a Survey of Shropshire Holy Wells – 2', *Source* 4 (1986)

— 'Notes Towards a Survey of Shropshire Holy Wells – 3', *Source* 6 (1987)

— 'Notes Towards a Survey of Shropshire Holy Wells – 4', *Source* 7 (1987)

— 'Notes Towards a Survey of Shropshire Holy Wells – 5', *Source* 8 (1988)

Owen, Revd Elias, 'Folk-Lore, Superstitions, or What-Not, in Montgomeryshire', *Collections Historical & Archaeological Relating to Montgomeryshire,* vol.15 (Welshpool: Powysland Club, 1882)

— 'Montgomeryshire Folk-Lore: Holy wells in the parish of Llanfihangel Ynghwnfa, Montgomeryshire', *Collections Historical & Archaeological Relating to Montgomeryshire,* vol.30 (Welshpool: Powysland Club, 1898)

— 'Montgomeryshire Folk-Lore: Trinity Well, Golfa, in the Parish of Buttington, near Welshpool', *Collections Historical & Archaeological Relating to Montgomeryshire,* vol.31 (Welshpool: Powysland Club, 1900)

Page, Jim Taylor, *Cumbrian Holy Wells* (Wigan: North West Catholic History Society, 1990)

Parish, R.B., 'The Holy Well, or St Cloud's Well, at Longthorpe Park near Peterborough', *Living Spring* issue 2 (November 2002) www.bath.ac.uk/lispring/journal/issue2

Park, Lesley, 'Cumbrian Well Waking', *Source* 6 (1987)

Parry, Bryn R., 'Ffynnon Elian', *Trans. Denbigh Historical Society* 14 (1965)

Parsons, Coleman O., 'Association of the White Lady with Wells', *Folklore,* vol.44 (1933)

Patchell, P.M. & E.M., 'The Wells of Old Warwickshire', *Source* 6 (1987)

Paton, Cyril I., 'Manx Calendar Customs: Wells', *Folklore,* vol.52 (1941)

Pennant, Thomas, *A Tour in Wales,* vol. 1 (London: Benjamin White, 1784)

— *The History of the Parishes of Whiteford and Holywell* (London: B. and J. White, 1796)

Pennick, Nigel, 'Cambridgeshire Wells', *Source* 1 (1985)
Portman, C.G., *The Sacred Stones, Sacred Trees and Holy Wells of Hay and the Neighbourhood and Their Connection with Paganism and Christianity* (1907) (the section on holy wells was reprinted, slightly edited, as 'The Holy Wells of Hay-on-Wye', *Wood & Water* 8)
Potter, Chesca, 'The River of Wells', *Source* 1 (1985)
Potter, Clive, 'The Holy Wells of Leicestershire and Rutland', *Source* 1 (1985)
Pryor, Francis, *Britain BC* (London: HarperCollins, 2003; Harper Perennial, 2004)
Quiller-Couch, M. and L., *Ancient and Holy Wells of Cornwall* (London: Chas J. Clark, 1894)
Quinn, Phil, *The Holy Wells of Bath and Bristol Region* (Almeley: Logaston Press, 1999)
Rattue, James, 'Some Wells in the South and West', *Source* 5 (1986)
— 'Some Wells in the South and West – 2', *Source* 6 (1987)
— 'Some Wells in the South and West – 3', *Source* 7 (1987)
— 'Some Wells in the South and West – 4', *Source* 8 (1988)
— 'Some Wells in the South and West – 5', *Source* 9 (undated c.1988)
— 'An Inventory of Ancient and Holy Wells in Oxfordshire', *Oxoniensia,* vol.LV (1990)
— *The Living Stream: Holy Wells in Historical Context* (Woodbridge: The Boydell Press, 1995)
— *The Holy Wells of Buckinghamshire* (High Wycombe: Umbra Press, 2003)
— *The Holy Wells of Kent* (High Wycombe: Umbra Press, 2003)
Reeves, William, *Life of St Columba* (Felinfach: Llanerch, 1988)
Rhys, Sir John, 'Manx Folklore and Superstitions', *Folk-Lore,* vol.2 (1891)
— 'Sacred Wells in Wales', *Folklore,* vol.4 (1893)
— Chapter VI: 'Folklore of the Wells' in *Celtic Folklore Welsh and Manx* (Oxford: Clarendon Press, 1901)
Rodwell, Warwick, *The Archaeology of the English Church* (London: B.T. Batsford, 1981)
Ross, Anne, 'Severed Heads in Wells: An Aspect of Well Cult', *Scottish Studies* (1962)
— *The Folklore of the Scottish Highlands* (London: B.T. Batsford, 1976)
Roud, Steve, *The Penguin Guide to the Superstitions of Britain and Ireland* (London: Penguin Books, 2003)
Sant, Jonathan, *Healing Wells of Herefordshire* (Bodenham: Moondial, 1994)
Sauer, Eberhard, 'Secrets of a Sacred Spring', *Current World Archaeology* 13 (October/November 2005)
Shepherd, Val, *Historic Wells In and Around Bradford* (Wymeswold: Heart of Albion Press, 1994)
— 'Wells and Trees', *Source* New Series 4 (Summer 1995)
— *Holy Wells of West Yorkshire and the Dales* (Bradford: Lepus Press, 2002)
Sikes, Wirt, *British Goblins: Welsh Folk-Lore, Fairy Mythology, Legends and Traditions* (London: Sampson Low, 1880; East Ardsley: EP Publishing, 1973)
Silverman, Gina, 'Gumfreston Wells', *Source* New Series 3 (Spring 1995)
Simpson, Jacqueline, *British Dragons* (London: B.T. Batsford, 1980)

Simpson, Jacqueline and Steve Roud, *A Dictionary of English Folklore* (Oxford: Oxford University Press, 2000)
Skyvova, Petra, *Fingallian Holy Wells* (Ireland: Fingal County Libraries, 2005)
Smith, Revd W., *The Ancient Springs and Streams of the East Riding of Yorkshire* (London: A. Brown & Son, 1923)
Smith, D.J., 'The Shrine of the Nymphs and the Genius Loci at Carrawburgh', *Archaeologia Aeliana*, 4th series, vol. 40 (1962)
Spencer, B.W., 'A Scallop-Shell Ampulla from Caistor and Comparable Pilgrim Souvenirs', *Lincolnshire History and Archaeology,* vol.1 no.6 (1971)
Spencer, Brian, *Medieval Pilgrim Badges from Norfolk* (Norfolk Museums Service, 1980)
Stewart, Bob, *The Waters of the Gap: The Mythology of Aquae Sulis* (Bath: Bath City Council, 1981)
Straffon, Cheryl, 'The Three Wells Walk', *Source* New Series 4 (Summer 1995)
— *Fentynyow Kernow: In Search of Cornwall's Holy Wells* (St Just: Meyn Mamvro Publications, 1998; 2nd revised edition, 2005)
Sumption, Jonathan, *Pilgrimage: An Image of Mediaeval Religion* (London: Faber and Faber, 1975, 2002)
Taylor, Henry, *The Ancient Crosses and Holy Wells of Lancashire: A Condensed Version* (Wigan: North West Catholic History Society, 1993)
— *The Ancient Crosses and Holy Wells of Lancashire: Volume I Lonsdale Hundred* (Wigan: North West Catholic History Society, revised version 1999)
— *The Ancient Crosses and Holy Wells of Lancashire: Volume II Amounderness Hundred* (Wigan: North West Catholic History Society, revised version 2002)
— *The Ancient Crosses and Holy Wells of Lancashire: Volume III Blackburn Hundred* (Wigan: North West Catholic History Society, revised version 2004)
— *The Ancient Crosses and Holy Wells of Lancashire: Volume IV Salford Hundred* (Wigan: North West Catholic History Society, revised version 2005)
— *The Ancient Crosses and Holy Wells of Lancashire: Volume V West Derby* (Wigan: North West Catholic History Society, revised version 2006)
— *The Ancient Crosses and Holy Wells of Lancashire: Volume VI Leyland* (Wigan: North West Catholic History Society, revised edition planned for 2007)
Thomas, Chris J., *Sacred Welsh Waters* (Milverton: Capall Bann Publishing, 2004)
Thompson, Beeby, 'Peculiarities of Waters and Wells', *Journal of the Northamptonshire Natural History Society and Field Club,* vol.16 no.128 (1911) – vol.18 no.142 (1915)
Thompson, Ian, *Lincolnshire Springs and Wells: A Descriptive Catalogue* (Scunthorpe: Bluestone Books, 1999)
Thompson, Ian and Frances, *The Water of Life: Springs and Wells of Mainland Britain* (Cribyn: Llanerch Press, 2004)
Tomlin, R.S.O., *Tabellae Sulis: Roman Inscribed Tablets of Tin and Lead From the Sacred Spring at Bath* – Part 4 (The curse tablets) of Barry Cunliffe (ed.), *The*

Temple of Sulis Minerva at Bath, II: Finds from the Sacred Spring (Oxford: Oxford University Committee for Archaeology: Fascicule 1 of Monograph No.16, 1988)

Tongue, R.L., *Somerset Folklore* (London: The Folk-Lore Society, 1965)

Trier, Julie, 'The Sacred Springs and Holy Wells of the St Davids Peninsula', *Source* New Series 4 (Summer 1995)

Trubshaw, Bob, *Holy Wells and Springs of Leicestershire and Rutland* (Wymeswold: Leicestershire and Rutland Earth Mysteries series part 2: Heart of Albion Press, 1990)

— *Interactive Little-known Leicestershire and Rutland* (CD-ROM) (Wymeswold: Heart of Albion Press, 2002)

Vail, Anne, *Shrines of Our Lady in England* (Leominster: Gracewing, 2004)

Valentine, Mark, 'Buckinghamshire Wells', *Source* 2 (1985)

Varner, Gary R., *Sacred Wells: A Study in the History, Meaning, and Mythology of Holy Wells and Waters* (Baltimore: PublishAmerica, 2002)

Vaux, J. Edward, *Church Folk Lore* (London: Skeffington & Son, 1902)

Verrill, A. Hyatt, *Secret Treasure: Hidden Riches of the British Isles* (New York & London: D. Appleton and Company, 1931)

Wade-Evans, A.W. (ed.), *Vitae Sanctorum Britanniae et Genealogiae* (Cardiff: 1944)

Walters, Cuming, *Holy Wells* (Wymeswold: Hark Back Editions No.3: Heart of Albion Press, 1991) (first published 1898 as a chapter of William Andrews, *The Church Treasury*)

Walters, R.C. Skyring, *The Ancient Wells, Springs, and Holy Wells of Gloucestershire: Their Legends, History, and Topography* (Bristol: The St Stephen's Press, 1928)

Weaver, Cora and Bruce Osborne, *Aquae Malvernensis: A History and Topography of the Springs, Spouts, Fountains and Wells of the Malverns and the Development of a Public Water Supply* (Malvern: Cora Weaver Press, 1994)

Webster, Jane, 'Sanctuaries and Sacred Places', ch.24 in Miranda J. Green (ed.), *The Celtic World* (London and New York: Routledge, 1995)

Weir, Anthony, *Early Ireland: A Field Guide* (Belfast: Blackstaff Press, 1980)

Whelan, Edna, 'Yorkshire's Holy Wells and the Severed Head', *Source* New Series 5 (Spring 1998)

— *The Magic and Mystery of Holy Wells* (Chieveley: Capall Bann Publishing, 2001)

Whelan, Edna, and Ian Taylor, *Yorkshire Holy Wells and Sacred Springs* (York: Northern Lights, 1989)

Wilson, Rob, *Holy Wells and Spas of South Yorkshire* (1991)

Index

Aberdeenshire 46, 47, 50, 52, 61
Abererch 9
Abu Mina 6
Acton Burnell 48
Adam of Usk 62
Aghinagh 136
Agnes, St 79
Allesley 100
Almscliffe Crag 140
Alnwick 149
Alsia Well 80
Altadaven 121
Altar of Cursing 31
Altarnun 15
Amlwch 47
ampulla 5–7, 14, 33–4, 66, 143
Anglesey 28, 30, 32–3, 47, 76–9, 80, 83, 152, 162
Angus 38
animals 8, 34, 68–9
Annat 47
Anne, St 56–8
Antrim, Co. 96
Aquae Sulis 10–12; see also Bath
Arboe churchyard 130
Argyll & Bute 52, 53
Armagh, Co. 32, 96
Arthur's Quoit 98, 99
Arthurs, Nora 131
Ashill 100
Ashmore 53
Atherstone 100
Atwick holy well 55
Aubert, St 122
Augustine, St 26, 114
Avon, River 96, 97

Bairns' Well 134
Bala Lake 91
Ballyboy 27
Ballydeloughry 131
Ballyhaunis 48
Ballynoe 132

Ballyvourney 93
Bann, River 32
baptism 3, 8–10, 16, 25, 71, 74, 153
Barlow, Bishop 124
Barnwell 134
Barra 52, 62
Barry, St 38
Barry, Gerald 40
Bath 10–12, 18, 27, 30, 58, 59, 111, 112, 137
Bawburgh 118
Beauclerk, Fr 7
Becket, St Thomas 5, 14, 122
Beckhampton avenue 97
Bede, St 66
Bede's Well 66
Bedfordshire 123
Bell Well 12–13
Bellingham 134
bells 12–14, 16, 23, 101
Ben Newe 61
bent objects 95–6
Berkshire 83
Beuno, St 26, 72, 73, 116, 126
Beuno Stone 108, 126, 127
Bevercotes, Sir Everard 62
Beverley Minster 148
Biddestone 87
Big Cold Well 61
Bingfield 46, 50
Binsey 122
Birtley 49
Bishop's Castle 32
Bishop's Lydeard 28
Bisley 146, 156
Blenheim Park 160
blood 5, 14, 85, 122, 131
Blunsdon Ridge 111
Bodfari 19, 75
Boilton Spa 63
Book of British Ballads, The (Hall) 45
Book of Leinster 43
Borewell 46
Bosherston 166; church 13
Bottle Shaking Sunday 105
bowssening 9, 15–16, 75
Boyle, Francis 67

Boyne, River 43, 91, 97
Bradford 46, 87
Brahan Seer 99
Bratton 50
Brawdy 38, 115
Breach Well 67
Brecon 114, 119
Breviary of Britayne, The (Lhuyd) 40
Briddle Springs 50
Bride, St 50, 115
Bride's Well 46
Bridewell Springs 50
Bridgend 128
Bridget, St 50, 115
Brigid, St 50, 115
Brill 57
Brinsop 38
Britain BC (Pryor) 97
Britannia (Camden) 40
British Goblins (Sikes) 44
British Piety Display'd 26
Brittany 25
Bromfield 105
Broomend of Crichie 96
Bryncethin 128
Bryncroes 21
Buckinghamshire 26, 57, 69
bullauns 3, 16–18, 126, 140
burial chambers 98; *see also* stones
Burke, Thomas 108
Burl, Aubrey 96–7
Buxton 112
Bwci's Wave 75

Cadog, St 66
Cae'r Ladi 90
Caernarfon 25
Caerwent 57, 58
Caerwys 151
Callanish 96
Callington 141, 155
Cambria Depicta (Pugh) 29
Camden, William 40
Canterbury Cathedral 5, 14, 95, 122, 148
Canvey Island 131
Caolainn, St 115

Caradoc 72, 116
Carbury Hill 91
Cardiff 13, 55
Cardigan Bay 91
Carew, Richard 15–16
Carlisle Cathedral 148
Carmarthenshire 42, 43, 91, 106, 115, 121, 124
Carn Euny Well 94
Carna 119
Carnguwch 71
Carrawburgh 23, 25
Carreg Cennen Castle 42
Castlekeeran 47
Cattle Well 54
Cavan, Co. 91, 115, 119
Cefn Meiriadog 85, 133
Celts 9, 18–19, 32, 33, 56–8, 61, 62, 74, 78, 143
Ceredigion 12, 76, 115
Cerne Abbas 26, 114
Cerrig Bach, Llyn 32–3, 76–9
Chadwell 50
Chalice Well 69
Chancellor, Matthew 69
Chapel Hole 50, 51
chapels 141–2, 163
Charlcombe 40
Charles I, King 14
Chattle Hole 50, 51
Checkley 52
Chedworth Roman villa 111, 112
Cheshire 6, 86–7, 148
Chew, River 96
Chibbyr Baltane 69
Chibbyr Beltain 101
Chibbyr Lansh 19
Chibbyr Noo Pherick 114
Chibbyr Undin 19, 110
Chibbyr Uney 88
Chibbyr Vaghal 115
Chibbyr yu Argid 88
Chich 61
Chinkwell Wood 57
Christ 131–2
Christ's Well 101
christening 10

churches, wells close to 147–8
Churn Clough 127
Cilcain 40
Cilmeri 62
circumambulation 19–20, 75, 91, 92–3, 125, 149
Clare, Co. 107, 132, 134, 136
Clegyr Boia 41
Clent Hills 26, 118, 122, 160
Clifford, Rosamond 160
Clitheroe 87
Cloch Patrick 126
Clonfad 52, 70, 109, 130
Clonmacnoise 18, 109
Cloutie Well 21
clouties 21, 88, 101, 110
Clungunford 32
Clynnog Fawr 76, 126, 130
Clyro 81
Coetan Arthur 98, 99
Coffin Well 145
coins 11, 12, 22, 23, 32, 88, 130, 148–9
Colan 36
Cole, Herbert 37
Collen, St 14
Collie Well 80
Colonsay 52
Columba, St 53, 115
Colwell 145
Comrie 52
Coney Island 96
Connla's Well 129
Conwy 28, 31, 56, 83, 95, 101, 114, 125, 141, 163
Corfe Gate 118
Corgarff 46, 47, 61
Cork, Co. 93, 131, 132, 136
Cormac mac Cuilennáin 57
Cormac, St 27
Corn Spring 100
Cornwall 9, 10, 15–16, 25, 26, 34, 35, 36, 40, 43, 47, 49, 60, 64, 66, 70, 74, 75, 80, 81, 82, 86, 92, 94, 121, 141, 154–6
Corwen 13
Costessey Wood 118

Cothelstone 79
Coventina 23, 58
Coventina's Well 23–5, 58, 112, 123
Coventry 100
Crantock 64
creation of wells 25–7, 66
Croagh Patrick 93
Crochan Llanddwyn 47, 80
crop of the well 50
Crowfoot Well 49
Cuby, St 9
cults 143–4
Cumbria 8, 34, 43, 44, 45, 105, 147, 148, 150
Curry Rivel 110
cursing 12, 17–18, 27–31
Cuthbert, St 103, 118
Cynog, St 114, 119

Dartmoor 82
David, St 12, 98, 115, 120, 166
De Infantia sancti Edmundi (Gaufridus) 113
decapitation 14, 25, 26, 61–2, 116–17
Decuman, St 117
Deer Stone 17, 18
Denbighshire 13, 14, 19, 62, 74, 75, 77, 85, 95, 115, 123, 133, 163
deposition 32–4, 76–8, 123
Derbyshire 112, 145
Derg, Lough 74, 93
Derry, Co. 126, 140
desecration 34–6
Detchant 54
Devil 12, 19, 48, 50, 51
Devil's Whispering Well 28
Devon 82, 116, 117, 143, 148
Diana's Well 62
Dineley, Thomas 42
Disserth 50
divination 36–7, 69, 79–80, 151
Don, River 96
Donegal, Co. 34, 66, 67, 89, 93, 102, 137
Doon Well 66, 102, 137
Dorset 14, 26, 53, 114, 118
Dorstone 48

Doulting 68
Dragon's Well 38
Dragonby 92
dragons 37–8, 47
Drayton, Michael 40
dreams, wells revealed in 132, 138
Droitwich 146
Dropping Well 100, 101, 158
Druids 33, 78, 79
Drumhill Spring 40
drumming wells 39–40
Drumming Well (Harpham) 39, 40
Drumming Well (Oundle) 39
Dublin, Co. 35, 148
Dublin: St Patrick's Cathedral 148
Dudley's Spring 100
Duffy, Eamon 143
Duloe 9
Dumfries & Galloway 115
Dunfermline Abbey 148
Dunfillan 52
Dungiven 126, 140
Dupath Well 141, 155
Durham 37, 47, 118
Durrington Walls 97
Durris 50
Dyfnog, St 74

East Dereham 119, 157
ebbing and flowing wells 40–1
Edenhall 44, 45
Edinburgh 142
Edmund, St 113
Edmund Rich, St 131–2
Edward the Martyr, St 118
Edwin, King 148
eels in wells 37, 47
Egypt 6, 75, 143
Eiliwedd, St 116
Elian, St 28–9, 114
Ely Cathedral 148
Eòrapaidh 16
Eoropie 16
Eshton 63
Essex 61, 116, 131
Ethelbert, St 119, 147, 148
Exeter 116; Cathedral 148

Eye Well 41
eyes 41–3, 109, 115

Fair Rosamond's Well 160
fairies 10, 43–6, 63, 87
Fairy Well (near Abergavenny) 43
Fairy Well (Aikton) 43
Fairy Well (Churn Clough) 127
Fairy Well (Laugharne) 43
Fairyland 43, 44
Fanad holy well 89
Fatfield 37
Fawr, Llyn 33
Fenloe 136
Fernyhalgh 121, 143, 157
fertility 46
Ffynnon Arthur 66
Ffynnon Bedrog 36
Ffynnon Beris 47
Ffynnon Beuno 62, 63, 76, 163
Ffynnon Cefn Lleithfan 21
Ffynnon Celynin 76
Ffynnon Ddeier 19, 75
Ffynnon Ddewi 115
Ffynnon Ddôl Erw Llyw 56
Ffynnon Ddyfnog 74, 115
Ffynnon Deg 151
Ffynnon Degla 75
Ffynnon Deilo 59, 60, 123–4
Ffynnon Digwg 127, 130
Ffynnon Dydecho 53, 63
Ffynnon Eilian 28, 30
Ffynnon Elaeth 47
Ffynnon Elian 28–31, 101, 114
Ffynnon Enddwyn 115
Ffynnon Fach 109
Ffynnon Faglan 95
Ffynnon Fair (Cefn) 85, 133
Ffynnon Fair (Llanfair) 53
Ffynnon Fair (Llanfairfechan) 31
Ffynnon Fair (Lleyn) 53
Ffynnon Gadfarch 9
Ffynnon Gloch 12–13
Ffynnon Gollen 14
Ffynnon Grassi 90–1
Ffynnon Gwynwy 95
Ffynnon Gybi (Ceredigion) 76

Ffynnon Gybi (Holyhead) 80
Ffynnon Gybi (Llangybi) 28, 47, 59, 60, 76
Ffynnon Gynhafal 95
Ffynnon Gywer 91
Ffynnon Leinw 40
Ffynnon Llandyfaen 124
Ffynnon Lygad 41
Ffynnon Non 115
Ffynnon Oer 152
Ffynnon Penarthur 98
Ffynnon Sarah 151
Ffynnon Stockwell 106
Ffynnon Trillo 141, 163
Ffynnon y Gaer 28
Ffynnon y Gloch Felen 13
Ffynnon y Gwaunydd 130
Ffynnon-y-Flameiddan 67
Fife 148
fishes in wells 37, 47–8, 49
Fitz, John 82
Fitz's Well 83
Fivehead 149
Flag Fen 32
Flintshire 7, 14, 22, 26, 40, 42, 43, 54, 66, 67, 68, 69, 71–3, 74, 85, 86, 94, 104, 108, 116, 121, 126, 127, 128, 130, 136, 142, 143, 151, 164
flower of the well 49–50, 83, 134, 152
Foel 63
folklore 50–2
font 9, 27
Fontes Sequanae 112, 137
footprints 52–3, 109, 119–20, 126
fortune-telling 53
France 18, 25, 112, 122, 137
Freni-fawr 43, 44
Fretwell 36
Frilford 112
Fritham 68
Fritwell 36
Frog Well 48
frogs in wells 48
From Carnac to Callanish (Burl) 96–7
Fuaran an Dèididh 110
Fuaran Tràigh Theinis 110

Galway, Co. 20, 89, 121
Gamhna, Loch 91
Garendon 102
Garthbeibio 63
Garton 46
Gaufridus de Fontibus 113
Gent, Thomas 26
George, St 38
Gerddi Bach Trewilym 56
ghosts 10, 53–6, 87, 90, 128
Giggleswick 8, 40, 41
Gilsland Spa 34
Giraldus Cambrensis 40, 128
Glamorgan 55, 56, 66, 67, 80, 110
Glasfryn, Llyn 90–1
Glasgow Cathedral 148
Glasserton 115
Glastonbury 69–70; Abbey 148
Glen Elg 47, 85
Glendalough 17, 18
Glossary (Cormac) 57
Gloucestershire 18, 26, 27, 85, 92, 111, 112, 119, 137, 146, 156
Goblin Well, 54 128
goddesses 23, 56–9
Golden Well 48
Golfa Hill 107
Goulceby 92
Gower 98, 99
Grace's Well 90–1
Great Witcombe 111, 112
Green, M.A. 32, 78, 96
Gregor, W. 61
Greystock 105
Griffith, Moses 86
Griffydam 38
Grimsargh 63
Grinston Well 38
guardians 43, 56, 59–61, 125, 151
Gulval Well 36, 60
Gumfreston church wells 146, 166–7
Guy, Earl of Warwick 37
Gwinear church 25
Gwinear, St 25
Gwynedd 9, 21, 28, 36, 47, 53, 59, 60, 71, 76, 90, 91, 95, 115, 127, 128, 130, 164

Gwytherin 72, 125

Hadrian's Wall 23, 25, 58
Hampshire 68
Harlech 115
Harlestone 87
Harlyn Bay 66
Harmonik Ireland 84
Harpham 39, 40
Harris 34, 65
Hartley 80, 103
Haverfordwest 80
Hay-on-Wye 14, 81
hazel 129
head cult 61, 62
Head Well 69
heads 14, 23, 59, 61–4, 116–17, 123, 150, 163
healing 6, 9, 13, 14, 18, 21, 31, 41–3, 64–70, 75–6, 103, 122, 137, 141, 143
Hell's Cauldron 50
Hennock church 117
Hereford 119, 148
Herefordshire 38, 48, 119, 147, 148
Herity, Michael 17
Hertfordshire 123
Heyhouses 127
Highland 16, 21, 47, 62, 85, 125
Hilda, St 146
Hill of Craigour 50
Hinderwell 106, 146
Hindon 100
Historia de Gentibus Septentrionalibus (Magnus) 152
History of Britain (Speed) 62
hobgoblin 44, 46
Holderness 44
holed stones 127
Holy Well Haw 102, 103
holy well: definition of 3
Holy Wells of Ireland, The (Logan) 119
Holyhead 80
Holystone 158
Holywell 7, 14, 22, 26, 42, 43, 66, 67, 68, 69, 71–3, 74, 85, 86, 93, 94, 104, 108, 116, 121, 126, 127, 130, 136, 142, 143, 164

Holywell Bay 92
horses 56, 68–9
Horsham 8
Hunstanton 113
Hutton 40

Ilkley 46, 63
immersion 9, 74–5, 126
incubation 18, 68, 75–6, 77, 98, 112, 120, 141
Inishmurray 31
inundations 90–1
Irwin, J.C. 19
Islay 52
Italy 19
Itinerary (Giraldus Cambrensis) 40

James, St 122
Jarrow 107
Jervaulx Abbey 63
Jones, David 57
Jones, Francis 69, 98, 101
Jordan, River 64, 66
Justinian, St 117

Keil 53
Kells 47
Kelpie 14, 56
Kemsing 95
Kenelm, St 26, 118
Kennet avenue 96
Kent 5, 14, 46, 95, 112, 122, 137
Kenulf, King 119
Kettle Stone 61
Kevin, St 18
Kidwelly 106
Kilcormack 27
Kildare, Co. 43, 91
Killinagh 115
Killybegs 34
Kilmacrennan 137
Kilmanaheem 107
Kilmihil 132
King's Stables 32
Kintyre 53
Kirkoswald church 147
Knaresborough 92, 93, 100, 101, 158

Knockfergan 52

Lady Well (Fernyhalgh) 94, 157
Lady's Well (Holystone) 158–9
Ladywell (Speen) 83
Lady Well (Whitton Lea) 54
Lagan, Lough 38
Lambton Worm 37, 38
Lancashire 63, 83, 87, 94, 106, 121, 127, 140, 143, 157
Laugharne 43
Lee Hall 134
Leicester: St Margaret's church 147
Leicestershire 38, 102, 147
Lepers' Well 68
Letter to Coroticus (St Patrick) 9
Lewis, Isle of 16, 36, 99, 110, 125
Lhuyd, Edward 13, 29
Lhuyd, Humphrey 40
Lichfield 66
Life of St Edmund (Lydgate) 113
Lifris 66
Lincolnshire 92
Lismullyduff 66, 67
Little People 43–6, 87
Little Walsingham; *see* Walsingham
Living Stream, The (Rattue) 121
Llanarth church 12
Llanarthney 91
Llanbadarn Fawr church 12
Llanbedrog 36
Llanberis 47
Llanblethian 80
Llancarfan 66, 67
Llandaff Cathedral 13, 124
Llanddewibrefi 115
Llanddona 152
Llandegla 75, 77
Llandeilo Llwydiarth 123
Llandrillo-yn-Rhos 141, 163
Llandrindod Wells 144
Llandudno 83–4
Llanelian-yn-Rhos 28, 114
Llanenddwyn 115
Llanfaglan 95
Llanfair 53
Llanfihangel-yng-Ngwynfa 66, 109

Llanfyllin 168
Llangan 76, 121
Llangelynin 76, 95
Llangollen 14
Llangower 91
Llangybi 47, 59, 60, 76, 90, 164
Llangynhafal 95
Llanidan old church 71
Llanishen 55
Llanllawer 28
Llanllwchaiarn 56
Llanmihangel 56–7
Llanon 115
Llanreithan 43
Llanrhaeadr 74, 115
Llanrhos 83
Llantarnam 94
Llanymawddwy 53
Llech Gybi 76
Llech Owen, Llyn 91
Llewellyn ap Griffith 62
Lleyn Peninsula 53
Llygad Llychwr 42
Logan, Patrick 119, 136
London 5, 96, 144, 148
Long Lonkin 129, 131
Longford, Co. 91, 115
Longthorpe holy well 51
Longwitton wells 37–8
Loughor River 42
Louth, Co. 35
love magic 79–82
Lower Well 83
Luck of Edenhall 44, 45
Ludgvan 10
Ludwell 40
Lusk 35
Lydgate, John 113
Lydney Park, Roman temple at 18, 111, 137

MacGregor, A.A. 52
MacKenzie, K. 99
McPhillips, J. 70
MacRae, A. 47
Machar, St 47
madness 15–16, 69, 75

Madron holy well 70, 75, 80, 94, 121, 156
Maen Beuno 108, 126, 127
Maen Ceti 98, 99
Maenclochog 123
Magherinagaw 96
Magnus, Olaus 152
Maguire, Fr Bernard 70
Mám Ean 121
Man, Isle of, 19, 68, 86, 88, 101, 104–5, 110, 114, 115, 121, 135, 152
Marcross well 55
Marden 119, 147
Maree, Loch 16
Margaret of Antioch, St 87
Margrett Hardies Well 150
Marmalane 132
Matheson, Revd William 125
Maughold, St 105, 115
Mayo, Co. 48, 93, 121, 136
Meath, Co. 47
Medana, St 115
Meg of Meldon 127
Melchior family 123, 124
Meldon Tower 127
Mellifont 35
Melmerby 150
Melton Mowbray church 147
Menas, St 6, 143
Menteith 101
Meols 6
Merrifield, Ralph 148
Merthyr Cynog 119
Michael, St 132
Midsomer Norton 34
Milburga, St 114
Minerva 58; *and see* Sulis Minerva
Mitchell, Arthur 16
Mithraeum 25
Mithras, Temple of 23
Mold 54, 128
Monaghan, Co. 52, 70, 109, 130
Monenna, St 74
Monk's Well 102, 103
Monknewton 'ritual pond' 97
Monkton 66
Monmouthshire 14, 43, 55, 57, 58, 164

Mont-St-Michel 122
Moore, Thomas 68–9
More Hall 37, 38
Morebath 143
Morwenna, St 26
Morwenstow 26, 27
moss 85
Mother Red Cap 87
Mother Shipton 100, 101, 158
Mount Melleray grotto 133
Mullaghhorne 119
Mullet Peninsula 121
Mungo, St 148
Munlochy 21
Muntham Court 18, 137
Mynydd Mawr 91

Nafferton 129, 131
Nant Gwynant 128
Naw Ffynnon 98
Nechtan, King 91
Neot, St 47, 49, 74
Ness 125
New Year's Day 49–50
Newark 62
Newborough 47, 80
New-Found Well 86–7
Newgrange 97
Nichols, John 147
Nidd, River 158
Nine Maidens' Well 38
Nine Wells 98
Non, St 120, 166
Norfolk 5, 7, 33, 95, 113, 118, 119, 122, 138, 149, 157–8
Normandy Well 8
North Galson 125
North Marston 26
North Rigton 140
North Uist 110
Northamptonshire 14, 39, 44, 87, 103, 112, 127, 134
Northumberland 23, 37–8, 43, 46, 49, 50, 51, 54, 58, 80, 83, 87, 131, 134, 145, 149, 158–9
Northwood 123
Norwich Cathedral 122
Nottinghamshire 36, 62

Nymphaeum 25

Ó Dubhthaigh, Bearnárd 67
Odell 123
Offa, King 119
Offaly, Co. 18, 27
offerings 11, 12, 18, 21, 22, 43, 75, 83, 88–9, 95–6, 112, 126, 135–7, 148
Oich, Loch 62
Old Hunstanton 113
Old Peter Dodd's Well 83
Old Woman's Spring 57
Oldbury on Severn 85
Oll Phiast 38
Omey Island 89
Oran 52
Oswald, St 63, 117
Oswestry 63, 117, 149, 150
Osyth, St 61, 116
Otterburn 51
Oudoceus, St 13
Oundle 39
Our Lady of Nance holy well 36
Our Lady's Well (Llanfair) 53
Our Lady's Well (Stow) 53
overflowing 36, 90–1
Owen, Rev Elias 30, 66, 107, 109
Oxford 131–2
Oxfordshire 36, 112, 122, 131–2, 160
Oxwich 56

Pardlestone 150
Parochialia (Lhuyd) 13, 29
Partrishow 168
paterae 11
Patricio 168
Patrick, St 9, 52–3, 109, 114, 119, 121, 130
Patterdale 8
Paulinus, St 158
pebble pool 83–4
pebbles 88, 89, 126
Peel 114
Peg o' Nell's Well 87
Peg/Peggy 87
Peggy Well 87

Peggy's Spout 87
Pelynt 34, 35, 43
Pembrokeshire 13, 28, 38, 41, 43, 44, 50, 56, 59, 60, 69, 76, 80, 98, 115, 117, 120, 123, 124, 128, 146, 166–7
Pencefngaer 116
Penda 63, 117
Penginger Well 116
Penmon 83, 162
Pennant, Thomas 29, 43, 76, 85
Penrhys 94, 122
Penrith 105
Pentrebychan crematorium 149
Penylan Well 55
Perth & Kinross 52
Perthshire 87
Peterborough 32; Cathedral 51–2
Peterchurch church 48
Petrifying Springs 92
petrifying wells 92, 93, 100, 101, 158
Pewter Well 127
Pilgrim's Way 95
pilgrimage 5, 6, 11, 14, 17, 52–3, 72, 73, 74, 92–5, 104, 122, 126, 138, 143, 144, 157, 158, 160
pillar stones 126
Pin Well (Alnwick) 149
Pin Well (Coney Island) 96
Pin Well (Wooler) 43
pins 22, 23, 28, 31, 43, 77, 82, 88, 95–6, 140, 145
Piskies' Well 43
Pittempton 38
Pizien Well 46
plants 85–6
Polyolbion (Drayton) 40
Pomerancio 116
Porthclais 115
Portman, C.G. 81
Poulaphuca Lakes 3
Powerstock 14
Powys 30, 50, 56, 62, 63, 66, 75, 81, 107, 109, 114, 116, 119, 143, 144, 168
prediction 39–40
prehistoric sites 96–8

Preseli hills 43
Priest's Well 14
prophecy 39–40, 99–101
Pryor, Francis 32, 97
Puck Well (Aynho) 44
Puckwell (West Knoyle) 44

Quantock Hills 36, 150
quartz 88
Quiller-Couch, T. 92
Quinn, Phil 12, 40

rags 21, 88, 101, 102, 137, 140, 156, 160–1
Ramsey Island 117
Rattue, James 121
Read 140
Reading Abbey 122
Red Well 14
Redbeard's Well 50
Red Cap, Mother 87
Redcap 87
rejuvenation 102
relics 5, 6, 85, 94, 103–5, 121, 122, 124
Restalrig 142
revels 105–8
reverence 20, 108, 109–10, 130
Rhaeadr 75
Rhigyfarch 12
Rhondda 94, 122
Rhoscolyn 162
Rhos-on-Sea 163
Rhys, Sir John 135, 139
Richardson, John 109
Richeldis de Faverches 138, 139
rituals 19, 109, 110–11, 124, 125, 126, 134, 149–50
Riverside Well 83
Roag, Loch 96
Robert of Shrewsbury 125
Roberts, Aled 83
Robin Round-Cap Well 44
Rochdale 106
Roche Rock 16, 40
Romans 10–12, 18, 19, 22, 23, 27–8, 29, 33, 58, 75, 111–12

Romsley 118, 160
Rorrington 145
Rosaveel 20
Roscommon, Co. 38, 52, 115, 125
Ross, Anne 125
rounding 19–20, 92–3; *see also* circumambulation
Rushton Spencer 99
Rutland 147

sacrifice 32
saints: *see individual saints' names*
St Agnes Eve 79, 80
St Agnes Fountain 68
St Agnes Well 79
St Aldhelm's Well 68
St Alphege's Well 40
St Ambrew's Well 64
St Ambrusca's Well 64
St Andrew's Well 36
St Anne's Well (Buxton) 112
St Anne's Well (Llanmihangel) 56–7
St Anne's Well (Trellech) 164–5
St Anne's Well (Whitstone) 141
St Arilda's Well 85
St Augustine's Well 26, 114
St Baglan's Well 95
St Bede's Well 107
St Beuno's Stone 126, 127
St Beuno's Well 130, 163
St Boniface's Well 21, 149
St Bridget's Well (Kilmanaheem) 107
St Brigid's Well (Killinagh) 115
St Buryan 80
St Cadoc's Well 66
St Canna's Chair 76, 98, 121
St Canna's Well 76, 98, 121
St Caradog's Well 80, 81
St Catharine's Well (Newark) 62
St Catherine's Well (Fivehead) 149
St Catherine's Well (Killybegs) 34
St Catherine's Well (Staffordstown) 35
St Chad's Well 66
St Ciaran's Well 47, 109
St Cleer holy well 16, 34, 154
St Clether's Well 155
St Colman's Well 134

St Columba's Well 137
St Columcille's Well 20
St Cubert's Well 92
St Cuby's Well 9
St Cuthbert's Well (Bromfield) 105–6
St Cuthbert's Well (Holywell Bay) 92
St Cybi's Well 164–5
St Cynog's Well 119
St David's Well (Brawdy) 115
St Davids 41, 98, 117, 120, 124, 166
St Decuman's Well (Rhoscrowther) 117
St Decuman's Well (Watchet) 117
St Denis's Well 55
St Derivla's Bed 121
St Derivla's Vat 121
St Edith's Well 95
St Edmund's Well 131–2
St Edrin church 38, 69
St Ethelbert's Well 147
St Fechín's Well 89
St Fergus well 52
St Fillan's Bell 13
St Fillan's Pool 13, 16
St Fillan's Spring 52
St Fintan's Well 35
St Govan's Well 166
St Gundred's Well 16. 40
St Gwenfaen's Well 162
St Helen's Well (Eshton) 63
St Helen's Well (Rushton Spencer) 99
St Hilda's Well 106, 146
St Ishow's Well 168
St Issui's Well 168
St John's Well (Kilkenny) 108
St Joseph's Well 148
St Julian's Well 54
St Justinian 117
St Justinian's Chapel 117
St Kenelm's Chapel 26
St Kenelm's Well 26, 118, 122, 160–1
St Keyne Well 82
St Kilda 102, 152
St Luctigern's Well 136
St Machar's Well 47
St Madron's Bed 75, 121
St Madron's Chapel 75
St Maelrubha's Well 16

St Margaret's Well (Binsey) 122
St Mary's Chapel, Glastonbury 148
St Mary's Priory 126
St Mary's Well (Fernyhalgh) 94, 121, 143, 157
St Mary's Well (Penmon) 162
St Mary's Well (Penrhys) 94, 122
St Mary's Well (Willesden) 144
St Maughold's Chair 121
St Maughold's church 105
St Maughold's Well 115, 121, 135
St Medana's Well 115
St Milburga's Well 114
St Myllin's Well 168
St Neot church 49, 74
St Neot's Well 47, 49
St Non's Chapel 120
St Non's Well (St Davids) 120, 166–7
St Nonna's Well (Altarnun) 15–16
St Nun's Well (Pelynt) 34, 35, 43
St Oswald's Well (Oswestry) 63, 117, 149, 150
St Oswald's Well (Winwick) 117
St Osyth 61, 116
St Osyth's Well 116
St Pandonia's Well 148
St Patrick's Bed 120
St Patrick's Chair 121
St Patrick's Well (Ballyhaunis) 48
St Patrick's Well (Clonfad) 52, 70, 109–10, 130
St Patrick's Well (Mam Ean) 121
St Patrick's Well (Oran) 52
St Patrick's Well (Patterdale) 8
St Patrick's Well (Peel) 114
St Peter's Well (Churn Clough) 127
St Richard's Well 145–6
St Runy's Well 88
St Sativola's Well 98
St Seiriol's Well 83, 162
St Sidwell's Well 116
St Stephen's Well 86–7
St Teilo's Skull 59, 60, 123–4
St Teilo's Well 123–4
St Thomas's Blood 5
St Thomas's Well 5, 14, 148
St Triduana's Well 142–3

St Trillo's Well 163
St Tydecho's Well 53
St Walstan's Well 118
St Winefride's Well 7, 14, 22, 26, 42, 43, 66, 67, 68, 69, 71–3, 74, 85, 86, 94, 104, 108, 116, 121, 126, 127, 136, 142, 143, 160–1, 164
St Winifred's Hair 85, 86
St Withburga's Well 119, 157
salmon 47–8
Sancreed Well 94
Schorne, Sir John 26
Scottish Borders 53
Seine, River 112, 137
Seven Springs 113
Seven Wells 146, 156
Severn, River 117
Shaftesbury Abbey 118
Shaking Bottle Sunday 105
Shannon, River 32
Shrewsbury 72, 125
shrines 121–2; Roman water 111–12
Shropshire 32, 36, 48, 63, 114, 117, 125, 145, 149, 150, 160
Sidwell, St 116, 117
Silbury Hill 97, 98
Silver Nut Well 51
Silver Well 80
Silverman, Gina 146
Simonstone Cross 140
Singleton, Richard 150
Sir John Schorne's Well 26
Skimmington Well 110
skulls 23, 32, 59, 60, 61, 123–5
Skye 14, 47, 99
Skyvova, Petra 129
Slieve Badhan 38
Slieve Sneacht 36
Sligo, Co. 31, 40, 53
Somerset 18, 27, 28, 32, 34, 36, 40, 41, 43, 54, 58, 59, 68, 69, 79, 92, 98, 100, 110, 112, 117, 137, 148, 149, 150
South Barrule 135
South Tyneside 66, 107
South Uist 69
Southey, Robert 81

Spanish Water Day 106
spas 143–4
Spaw Well 106
Speed, John 62
Speen 83
Spo Well 106
Springhead 18, 112, 137
Staffordshire 52, 66, 100
Stanton Drew avenues 96
Starwell 87
Stirling 13, 16, 101
Stoke St Milborough 114
Stone Circles of the British Isles, The (Burl) 96
Stone of Ceti 98, 99
Stonehenge 96, 97
stones 96–8, 120, 126–7
stoup 71
Stow 53
Stowe Missal 9
Stowe 66
Stowey 92
Stowey-Sutton 40
Strathdon 61
Strathfillan 16
Stripping of the Altars, The (Duffy) 143
Strokestown 38
Sudeley Hill 119
Sugar Water Sunday 105
Sulis Minerva 11, 12, 18, 58, 59
Surrey 100
Sussex 137; West 8
Sutton, Oliver 132
Swansea 56, 98, 99
Sweet Track 32
Swindon 111

Taff's Well 55
Teampull Chrò Naoimh 125
Tees, River 87
Teilo, St 13, 59, 60, 123–4
Tetbury 92
Thames, River 32, 96
Thomas Becket, St 5, 14, 122
Thomas, T.H. 44
Thompson, Beeby 39, 51
Three Wells Walk 94

Tipperary, Co. 129
Tissington 145
Tobar Bhan 85
Tobar a' Chinn 125
Tobar Aibheog 66, 67
Tobar an Teampaill 16
Tobar an t-Solais 35
Tobar Anndrais 36
Tobar Barry 38
Tobar Bhan 47
Tobar Chuidhearaidh 110
Tobar-Fuar-Mòr 61
Tobar Keelagh 136
Tobar Mhàraig 65
Tobar na Fala 14
Tobar-na-Glas a Coille 61
Tobar na h-Annait 47
Tobar na Suil 36
Tobar nan Ceann 62
Tobar Rònain 16
Tobar Tath 99
Tobar Thiobartain 69
Tobar Vacher 47
Toberavilla 129
Tobernalt Well 53
toothache 110
Top Lock 87
Torfaen 56
Tour in Wales (Pennant) 76, 85
Tray 32
treasure 54, 61, 127–8
trees: at wells 129–31; wells in 96, 130, 131
Trelille, John 70
Trellech 43, 164
Tremeirchion 62, 163
Trent, River 32
Trevethin 56
Trinity Well (Golfa Hill) 106, 107
Trinity Well (Kildare) 43
trout 47, 48
Tullaghan Well 40
Tydecho, St 53, 63
Tyne, River 134
Tyneside, South 66, 107
Tyrone, Co. 121, 130

Uley 27
underground passages 51–2
Utkinton 86

Vale of Glamorgan 55, 56, 66, 67, 80
Van 114, 119
Vilbia curse 29
Virgin Mary 133, 138, 139, 157
Virtuous Well 43, 164–5
visions 131–3, 138, 139
Vita secunda Wenefredae (Robert of Shrewsbury) 125
Voices of Morebath, The (Duffy) 143
votive offerings 18, 23, 95–6, 112, 126, 135–7, 148

Walsingham 5, 7, 33, 93, 94, 122, 138–9, 149, 158
Walstan, St 118
Wantley Dragon 37, 38
Wareham 118
Wark on Tyne 49
Warlingham 100
Warrington 117
Wart Well (Almscliffe Crag) 140
Wart Well (Read) 140
warts 18, 21, 95, 139–40
Warwickshire 100, 101
Washers Pit 53
Watchet 117
Water of St Thomas 14
water, holy 3, 8–10, 70–1
Waterford, Co. 133
Wateringbury 46
Wear, River 37
Wearie, Lord 131
Weir, Anthony 16–17
Well in the Grey Wood 61
Well in the Wall 52
Well of Blood 14
Well of Light 35
Well of the Annat 47
Well of the Head 125
Well of the Heads 62
Well of the Yellow Bell 13
Well of Youth 102
well-dressing 145–6

Wellingborough 14
Wellow 54
Wells Cathedral 148
Welshpool 107
West Knoyle 44
Western Isles 16, 34, 36, 52, 62, 65, 69, 99, 110, 125
Westhoughton 83
Westmeath, Co. 129
Weston-super-Mare 41
Whistlebitch Well 86–7
Whitchurch 69
White Wells 46, 63
Whitstone 141
Whitton 92
Whitton Lea 54
Whitwell church 147
Whitwick church 147
Wick 98
Wicklow, Co. 3, 17, 18
widdershins 19
Wight, Isle of 149
Willesden 144
William, St 122
Williams, Alun 22
Williams, William 80
Wiltshire 44, 50, 87, 96–8, 100, 111
Winchcombe 26, 119

Winchester Cathedral 148
wind, raising the 152
Winefride (Winifred), St 7, 26, 66, 72–3, 104, 116, 124–5, 126
Winwick 117
wishing wells 22, 63, 83, 138, 148–50, 158, 162
Witch Hole Spring 92
witches and witchcraft 10, 68, 127, 145, 150–3
Witches' Well 150
Witham, River 32
Withburga, St 119
Witton Fell 62
Woodhenge 97
Woodstock 160
Wooler 43
Woolston 160–1
Wor Well 92
Worcestershire 26, 118, 122, 146, 160
Worm Well 37, 47
Wrexham 149

York Minster 148
Yorkshire 36, 118; East 39, 40, 44, 55, 148; North 8, 40, 41, 62, 63, 92, 93, 100, 101, 106, 146, 148, 158; South 37, 38; West 63, 140

Also from Heart of Albion Press

The Enchanted Land

Myths and Legends of Britain's Landscape

Revised, fully illustrated edition

Janet and Colin Bord

Britain's landscape is overlain by a magic carpet of folklore and folktales, myths and legends. Enchantment and legend still lurk in places as diverse as hills and mountains, rivers and streams, caves and hollows, springs and wells, cliffs and coasts, pools and lakes, and rocks and stones.

The dramatic stories woven around these places tell of sleeping knights, beheaded saints, giants, dragons and monsters, ghosts, King Arthur, mermaids, witches, hidden treasure, drowned towns, giant missiles, mysterious footprints, visits to Fairyland, underground passages, human sacrifices, and much more.

The 'Places to Visit' section locates and describes in detail more than 50 sites.

This revised edition is fully illustrated, with around 130 photographs and illustrations.

Janet and Colin Bord live in North Wales, where they run the Fortean Picture Library. They have written more than 20 books since their first successful joint venture, *Mysterious Britain* in 1972.

> **From reviews of the first edition:**
>
> 'Janet's own enthusiasm for a number of the sites is conveyed vividly and lends credibility to the notion that Britain is still an enchanted land.'
> *Mercian Mysteries*

ISBN 1 872883 91 5. March 2006. 245 x 175 mm, over 200 illustrations, paperback
£16.95

Also from Heart of Albion Press

Footprints in Stone

The significance of foot- and hand-prints and other imprints left by early men, giants, heroes, devils, saints, animals, ghosts, witches, fairies and monsters

Janet Bord

'A delightful exploration of a truly mysterious subject. 9 out of 10'
Bob Rickard *Fortean Times*

'Fascinating stuff and highly recommended.' Mike Howard *The Cauldron*

'... a good and wide-ranging first step into investigating the significance of the foot imprint.' John Billingsley *Northern Earth*

From the earliest humans to the present day, there has always been a compulsion to 'leave one's mark': early cave art includes thousands of hand outlines, while many churches in Britain have foot outlines inscribed in lead and stone. These two extremes span almost 30,000 years during which time all kinds of persons, real and legendary, have left visible traces of themselves. But 30,000 years ago seems almost recent, when compared with the finding of some (admittedly controversial) fossilized human footprints in rocks apparently contemporary with dinosaur footprints that are tens of millions of years old.

Most of the footprints – and hand-prints, knee-prints, and impressions of other body parts – are clearly not real, having allegedly been impressed into rocks around the world by such high-profile figures as the Buddha, Vishnu, Jesus Christ, and the Virgin Mary, as well as a vast panoply of saints, whose footprint traces and associated stories occupy two chapters. Their horses also left hoof-prints, and other animals are represented too. Not surprisingly, the ubiquitous Devil has a whole chapter to himself – but giants, villains and heroes, such as King Arthur, also feature strongly. Witches, fairies, ghosts and assorted spirits have made their mark: there are many modern instances of phantom hand- and foot-prints, the latter often bloodstained and indelible.

Hundreds of imprints are described in this book, which concludes with location details for more than 100 imprint sites all around the world.

ISBN 1 872883 73 7. 2004. 245 x 175 mm, 263 + x pages, 112 b&w photos, 26 line drawings, paperback. **£14.95**

Also from Heart of Albion Press

Taliesin's Travels

A demi-god at large

Michael Dames

Taliesin's Travels brings fresh significance to one of Britain's best-loved tales.

For over a thousand years the impish Taliesin has enthralled and enlightened people. As a farmer's son, he is grounded in the land. Yet, because his mother is the goddess Nature, he can travel, free as a demi-god, throughout time and space.

Thanks to his intimate contact with spirits of place, sun and underworld, Taliesin reveals and portrays the interconnecting, ever-transforming essence of life. His often painful and sometimes ludicrous adventures engage with creation in its entirety. Transcending history, he invites us to see our own millennium as a cyclical, mythic journey so that, like him, each individual comes to identify with the whole of creation.

With a keen sense of enjoyment, Michael Dames provides a deep and imaginative account of the tales and poetry associated with Taliesin. Prehistoric, Romano-British and Christian aspects of Taliesin's persona are brought together in a magical synthesis.

Michael Dames is well-known for his pioneering studies of the myths and legends of the British Isles. His previous books include *The Silbury Treasure, The Avebury Cycle, Mythic Ireland* and *Merlin and Wales*.

> *Taliesin's Travels* offers 'a mind-gripping itinerary, full of tales and stories, wonderful folk and demi-folk, strange events and scenery we can still merge ourselves into. All very evocative.'
> **Francis Cameron** *Pentacle*

EAN 978 1872 883 892. ISBN 1 872883 89 3. February 2006. 245 x 175 mm, over 200 illustrations, paperback £16.95

Also from Heart of Albion

Sacred Places
Prehistory and popular imagination
Bob Trubshaw

Sacred Places asks why certain types of prehistoric places are thought of as sacred, and explores how the physical presence of such sacred sites is less important than what these places signify. So this is not another guide book to sacred places but instead provides a unique and thought-provoking guide to the mental worlds – the mindscapes – in which we have created the idea of prehistoric sacred places.

Recurring throughout this book is the idea that we continually create and re-create our ideas about the past, about landscapes, and the places within those landscapes that we regard as sacred. For example, although such concepts as 'nature', 'landscape', 'countryside', 'rural' and the contrast between profane and sacred are all part of our everyday thinking, in this book Bob Trubshaw shows they are all modern cultural constructions which act as the 'unseen' foundations on which we construct more complex myths about places.

Key chapters look at how earth mysteries, modern paganism and other alternative approaches to sacred places developed in recent decades, and also outline the recent dramatic changes within academic archaeology. Is there now a 'middle way' between academic and alternative approaches which recognises that what we know about the past is far less significant than what we believe about the past?

Bob Trubshaw has been actively involved with academic and alternative approaches to archaeology for most of the last twenty years. In 1996 he founded *At the Edge* magazine to popularise new interpretations of past and place.

> '*Sacred Places*... is a very valuable addition to the small body of thoughtful work on the spiritual landscapes of Great Britain and therefore recommended reading.' Nigel Pennick *Silver Wheel*
>
> 'One of the best books in the field I have ever read.'
> D J Tyrer *Monomyth Supplement*

ISBN 1 872883 67 2. 2005. 245 x 175 mm, 203 + xiv pages, 43 b&w illustrations and 7 line drawings, paperback. **£16.95**

Also from Heart of Albion Press

Stonehenge:
Celebration and Subversion

Andy Worthington

This innovative social history looks in detail at how the summer solstice celebrations at Stonehenge have brought together different aspects of British counter-culture to make the monument a 'living temple' and an icon of alternative Britain. The history of the celebrants and counter-cultural leaders is interwoven with the viewpoints of the land-owners, custodians and archaeologists who have generally attempted to impose order on the shifting patterns of these modern-day mythologies.

The story of the Stonehenge summer solstice celebrations begins with the Druid revival of the 18th century and the earliest public gatherings of the 19th and early 20th centuries. In the social upheavals of the 1960s and early 70s, these trailblazers were superseded by the Stonehenge Free Festival. This evolved from a small gathering to an anarchic free state the size of a small city, before its brutal suppression at the Battle of the Beanfield in 1985.

In the aftermath of the Beanfield, the author examines how the political and spiritual aspirations of the free festivals evolved into both the rave scene and the road protest movement, and how the prevailing trends in the counter-culture provided a fertile breeding ground for the development of new Druid groups, the growth of paganism in general, and the adoption of other sacred sites, in particular Stonehenge's gargantuan neighbour at Avebury.

The account is brought up to date with the reopening of Stonehenge on the summer solstice in 2000, the unprecedented crowds drawn by the new access arrangements, and the latest source of conflict, centred on a bitterly-contested road improvement scheme.

> '*Stonehenge Celebration and Subversion* contains an extraordinary story. Anyone who imagines Stonehenge to be nothing but an old fossil should read this and worry. [This book is] ... the most complete, well-illustrated analysis of Stonehenge's mysterious world of Druids, travellers, pagans and party-goers'. Mike Pitts *History Today*

ISBN 1 872883 76 1. 2004. Perfect bound, 245 x 175 mm, 281 + xviii pages, 147 b&w photos, **£14.95**

Also from Heart of Albion Press

Winner of the Folklore Society Katharine Briggs Award 2005

Explore Fairy Traditions

Jeremy Harte

We are not alone. In the shadows of our countryside there lives a fairy race, older than humans, and not necessarily friendly to them. For hundreds of years, men and women have told stories about the strange people, beautiful as starlight, fierce as wolves, and heartless as ice. These are not tales for children. They reveal the fairies as a passionate, proud, brutal people.

Explore Fairy Traditions draws on legends, ballads and testimony from throughout Britain and Ireland to reveal what the fairies were really like. It looks at changelings, brownies, demon lovers, the fairy host, and abduction into the Otherworld. Stories and motifs are followed down the centuries to reveal the changing nature of fairy lore, as it was told to famous figures like W.B. Yeats and Sir Walter Scott. All the research is based on primary sources and many errors about fairy tradition are laid to rest.

Jeremy Harte combines folklore scholarship with a lively style to show what the presence of fairies meant to people's lives. Like their human counterparts, the secret people could kill as well as heal. They knew marriage, seduction, rape and divorce; they adored some children and rejected others. If we are frightened of the fairies, it may be because their world offers an uncomfortable mirror of our own.

> '... this is the best and most insightful book on fairies generally available... ' John Billingsley *Northern Earth*

> '*Explore Fairy Traditions* is an excellent introduction to the folklore of fairies, and I would highly recommend it.' Paul Mason *Silver Wheel*

ISBN 1 872883 61 3. Published 2004. Demy 8vo (215 x 138 mm), 171 + vi pages, 6 line drawings, paperback. **£9.95**

Also from Heart of Albion Press

Explore Dragons

Richard Freeman

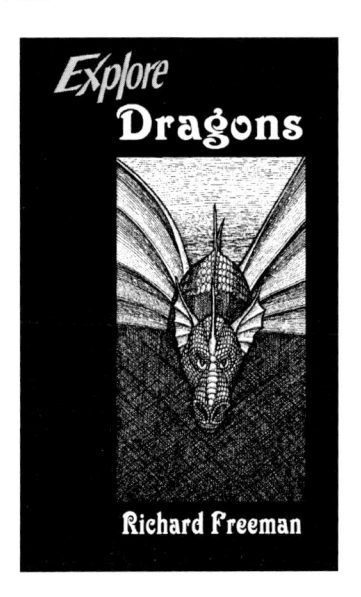

The dragon is the most ancient and widespread of all monsters. Dragon legends are told in every culture and in every continent on Earth. Its breath condenses and forms rain in China. It slithers across the heavens in Mexico as Quetzalcoatl. In Scandinavian lore its coils encircled the whole earth. No other monster is so universal in its occurrence or so varied.

But the Britain Isles are the homeland of the dragon. Although a small country, it is seething with dragon legends. *Explore Dragons* puts British dragon stories into their international context and attempts to fathom out what really lurks behind these fanciful tales. Could dragons once have been real creatures? Are such creatures still alive?

Richard Freeman is a former zookeeper and has a degree in zoology. He is the zoological director of the Centre for Fortean Zoology in Exeter. A full-time cryptozoologist, he has searched for monsters and mystery animals in Indo-China, Sumatra, and Mongolia as well as in the UK.

ISBN 1 872883 93 1. Published 2006. Demy 8vo (215 x 138 mm), 187 + viii pages, 7 b&w photographs, 13 line drawings, paperback. **£12.95**

Also from Heart of Albion Press

'Highly recommended'
Folklore Society Katharine Briggs
Award 2003

Explore Folklore

Bob Trubshaw

'A howling success, which plugs
a big and obvious gap'
Professor Ronald Hutton

There have been fascinating developments in the study of folklore in the last twenty-or-so years, but few books about British folklore and folk customs reflect these exciting new approaches. As a result there is a huge gap between scholarly approaches to folklore studies and 'popular beliefs' about the character and history of British folklore. *Explore Folklore* is the first book to bridge that gap, and to show how much 'folklore' there is in modern day Britain.

Explore Folklore shows there is much more to folklore than morris dancing and fifty-something folksingers! The rituals of 'what we do on our holidays', funerals, stag nights and 'lingerie parties' are all full of 'unselfconscious' folk customs. Indeed, folklore is something that is integral to all our lives – it is so intrinsic we do not think of it as being 'folklore'.

The implicit ideas underlying folk lore and customs are also explored. There might appear to be little in common between people who touch wood for luck (a 'tradition' invented in the last 200 years) and legends about people who believe they have been abducted and subjected to intimate body examinations by aliens. Yet, in their varying ways, these and other 'folk beliefs' reflect the wide spectrum of belief and disbelief in what is easily dismissed as 'superstition'.

Explore Folklore provides a lively introduction to the study of most genres of British folklore, presenting the more contentious and profound ideas in a readily accessible manner.

ISBN 1 872883 60 5. Published 2002. Demy 8vo (215x138 mm), 200 pages, illustrated, paperback **£9.95**

Heart of Albion

Publishing folklore, mythology and
local history since 1989

Further details of all Heart of Albion titles online at
www.hoap.co.uk

All titles available direct from Heart of Albion Press.

Heart of Albion Press
2 Cross Hill Close, Wymeswold
Loughborough, LE12 6UJ

email: albion@indigogroup.co.uk
Web site: www.hoap.co.uk